THE AA GUIDE TO
Norfolk
& Suffolk
WITH CAMBRIDGE

About the author

A BBC-trained journalist, author and member of the British Guild of Travel Writers, Carole French travels the world in search of inspirational lifestyles, but always loves to come home to her beloved East Anglia. Carole was born in the region and remembers an idyllic childhood spent horseriding in the countryside and taking trips to towns likes Lavenham in Suffolk and the castle in Norwich at weekends.

Carole was first bitten by the travel bug as a child; one of her favourite activities was packing for family beach holidays in Caister-on-Sea and Great Yarmouth, weeks in advance. During her career, Carole has worked with some of the largest media names in East Anglia: Archant Life, for which she was editor of the prestigious *Cambridgeshire Life* magazine; the *East Anglian Daily Times* in Suffolk; and the *Eastern Daily Press* in Norfolk. Her work has taken her to all corners of the region.

Published by AA Publishing (a trading name of AA Media Limited, whose registered office is Fanum House, Basing View, Basingstoke, Hampshire RG21 4EA; registered number 06112600)

© AA Media Limited 2016
First published 2014
Second edition 2016. Reprinted 2017
Third edition 2018

Maps contain data from openstreetmap.org
© OpenStreetMap contributors Ordnance Survey data © Crown copyright and database right 2018.

A CIP catalogue record for this book is available from the British Library.

ISBN: 978-0-7495-7944-9

Cartography provided by the Mapping Services Department of AA Publishing.
Printed and bound in Italy by Printer Trento Srl.

Every effort has been made to trace the copyright holders, and we apologise in advance for any accidental errors. We would be happy to apply the corrections in the following edition of this publication.

The contents of this book are believed correct at the time of printing. Nevertheless, the publishers cannot be held responsible for any errors or omissions or for changes in the details given in this book or for the consequences of any reliance on the information it provides. This does not affect your statutory rights. We have tried to ensure accuracy in this book, but things do change and we would be grateful if readers would advise us of any inaccuracies they may encounter by emailing us at travelguides@theaa.com.

A05591

THE AA GUIDE TO

Norfolk & Suffolk

WITH CAMBRIDGE

YOUR TRUSTED GUIDE

CONTENTS

USING THIS GUIDE

Introduction – has plenty of fascinating background reading, including articles on the landscape and local mythology.

Top attractions – picks out the very best places to visit in the area. You'll spot these later in the A–Z by the flashes of yellow.

Before you go – tells you the things to read, watch, know and pack to get the most from your trip.

Campsites – recommends a number of caravan sites and campsites, which carry the AA's Pennant rating, with the very best receiving the coveted gold Pennant award. Visit theAA.com/self-catering-and-campsites, theAA.com/hotels and theAA.com/bed-and-breakfasts for more places to stay.

A–Z of Norfolk & Suffolk – lists all the best of the region, with recommended attractions, activities and places to eat or drink. Places Nearby lists more to see and do.

Eat and drink – contains restaurants that carry an AA Rosette rating, which acknowledges the very best in cooking. Pubs have been selected for their great atmosphere and good food. Visit theAA.com/restaurants and theAA.com/pubs for more food and drink suggestions.

Index – gives you the option to search by theme, grouping the same type of place together, or alphabetically.

Atlas – helps you find your way around, as every main location has a map reference, as will the town plans throughout the book.

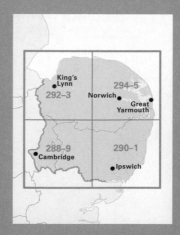

INTRODUCTION

With landscapes that stretch as far as the eye can see, the counties of Norfolk and Suffolk, and the countryside around Cambridge, are some of the most enchanting places to visit anywhere in England. They have fabulous sweeping skies and sunsets, and countryside dotted with impossibly pretty villages, full to bursting with centuries-old timber-framed cottages and medieval churches; there are vast country estates, ancient archaeological sites, cathedrals, castles and fortresses; and a coastline both tranquil and treacherous.

Add to all this vibrant cities that will bowl you over – such as Cambridge, where for centuries academics have pioneered world-changing advances in medicine, astronomy and science, and the county towns of Norwich and Ipswich – and you have a region just waiting to be explored. It's an area full of possibilities for great days out, but you could spend weeks here without running out of things to see and do.

Each of the counties has its own character. Norfolk is characterised by marshland with reedbeds, dykes and creeks, dense wetland woodlands and a landscape dotted with

flint-and-brick villages and pumps, not unlike windmills, that keep water levels safe. Its coast, once a bustling place of tiny quayside streets lined with merchants' houses and fishermen's cottages, and harbours full of fishing boats unloading their catches to the cries of seagulls and the hammering of boat builders, is famous for its biodiversity and wildlife.

Norfolk is now a magnet for holidaymakers too, from exuberant Great Yarmouth, with its legendary end-of-pier seaside fun, to the more genteel Cromer and Lowestoft. Norwich is its administrative, financial and cultural hub.

Suffolk, meanwhile, is full to bursting with pretty villages, such as Kersey and Somerleyton, and quiet fishing and seaside towns, such as Aldeburgh and Southwold. It has rolling rural countryside, lots of market towns and magnificent medieval wool towns, such as Lavenham: strolling around the streets of England's most complete medieval town is like stepping into an extremely pleasant timewarp.

In contrast, you have Felixstowe, a seriously busy place where container ships load their cargo for trips to Europe, Asia and beyond, and the elegant Bury St Edmunds and Ipswich, both of which have a plethora of shops, restaurants, sports centres and art galleries.

Cambridge, the capital of Cambridgeshire, is a dazzling place of jaw-droppingly gorgeous Gothic colleges, elegant homes, vast open spaces and the Backs, a delicious area dominated by the meandering River Cam where students and visitors punt on the river or party on the greens near King's College and the world-famous King's College Chapel. This is fen country; and one of Britain's most magical sights is nearby Ely Cathedral rising like a massive cruise liner from the flat misty landscape.

Norfolk, Suffolk and the countryside around Cambridge may inspire you to enjoy all manner of outdoor activities too. Here, you can while away some time boating on the inland waterways, cycling, painting, walking or even riding on horseback. Stables offering hacks to experienced riders can be found in most of the larger towns or, if your passion leans more to watching horses being ridden, then there are racecourses at Fakenham, Great Yarmouth and, of course, Newmarket, where racing has been a constant since the time of James I. Over the centuries, trainers and jockeys have come to East Anglia to perfect their skills, including Sir Henry Cecil, Sir Michael Stoute and Saeed bin Suroor, and jockey Frankie Dettori, and the region has even provided inspiration for novels written by former steeplechase jockey turned crime writer, Dick Francis.

East Anglia has been an inspiration for centuries. You only have to sit awhile on the grassy riverbank looking across the rippling water to Flatford Mill to understand what so moved John Constable to immortalise the Dedham Vale on canvas, or stand on windswept Aldeburgh's shingle beach to know exactly how poet George Crabbe and composer Benjamin Britten felt when they penned their great works. East Anglia will be an inspiration to you too.

TOP ATTRACTIONS

▲ Southwold Pier

For a proper British seaside experience, head to Southwold Pier (see page 246) and its quirky range of attractions – best being the Under the Pier Show, where you can 'Whack a Banker' in a modern take on the penny arcade, before or after taking to the beach.

◄ Fitzwilliam Museum

See works by Rembrandt, Constable, Rubens and Picasso alongside antiquities from the ancient world and a collection of medieval and renaissance illustrated manuscripts at Cambridge's Fitzwilliam Museum (see page 93).

◂ Norwich Castle & Cathedral

Go back in time in Norwich; the magnificent Norman Norwich Castle (see page 215) was built for William the Conqueror, while Norwich Cathedral (see page 216) has the second highest spire and the largest monastic cloister in England.

▸ Imperial War Museum Duxford

If planes are your passion, visit the country's largest aviation and war museum, the Imperial War Museum Duxford. You can see 200 or more planes, naval and military vehicles in original listed wartime hangars (see page 124). Look out for air shows on event days.

◂ BeWILDerwood

One for the kids – and big kids – BeWILDerwood (see page 161) is an adventure park based on a children's story book. Spend a day climbing in treehouses, taking boat trips and meeting the imaginative resident creatures. Fun for the kids too...

◂ Pleasurewood Hills

'Pleasurewood Hills' (see page 191) might sound more like a location from an American sitcom, but this theme park on the Suffolk coast is actually vaguely pirate themed. There's a good mix of adult and kids' rides.

▸ Africa Alive!

If staycationing gets tiring and you'd prefer to pretend you're on safari, this African-themed zoo (see page 63) will be a big help – though you might still have to imagine the good weather.

◂ Sutton Hoo

No one should come to Norfolk and Suffolk without visiting Sutton Hoo (see page 36 and page 262), site of the discovery of an Anglo-Saxon burial ship that lay hidden here for over 1,300 years. It's considered to be one of the most important archaeological finds in British history.

▲ Cambridge

Explore the old university city, taking in famous colleges like King's College (above) and the historic marketplace. A morning walk along the college Backs through the thin mist that often blankets the area is particularly atmospheric (see page 88).

▶ Holkham Hall

A palatial stately home surrounded by parklands. The nature reserve is part of the estate as well, as is Holkham beach and the church of St Withburga (see page 154).

◀ Sandringham

One of Britain's several royal residences, there's plenty to see at Sandringham (see page 236): the state rooms, a museum including a collection of royal cars, and lots of parkland and gardens.

HISTORY OF NORFOLK & SUFFOLK

East Anglia has been inhabited for a very long time; certainly, there's plenty of evidence pointing to neolithic people living here, followed by the Iceni tribes who developed the region from around the first century BC and the Romans who established settlements on sites such as that occupied by present-day Ipswich in Suffolk.

This gloriously flat region, with its shores lashed by the North Sea, is also famously the land of the Anglo-Saxons who arrived here after the Romans had upped sticks and moved on. You can still sense the Anglo-Saxon legacy as you stand on the cliffs at Dunwich – once a prosperous and important Saxon port city now swallowed by the sea – or at Sutton Hoo – where it is widely believed that the first King of the East Angles, King Raedwald, was buried with his ship.

Originally, the Anglo-Saxon Kingdom of the East Angles, or East Anglia as we know it today, comprised just Norfolk and Suffolk. It was formed around AD 520 and quickly became one of the most powerful kingdoms in England. King Raedwald (c.580–c.624), who ruled the kingdom from around 599 until his death, was one of its legendary rulers. Although few documents detailing his reign

survive today – most having been destroyed when the Vikings invaded East Anglia in the 9th century and targeted the monasteries where important documents were kept – what is known of King Raedwald is that he was regarded as a great leader. In fact, at one time he was the most powerful king in the south of England.

The kingdom grew in size when Ethelthryth, the daughter of the then King of East Anglia, King Anna, married in AD 652 and was presented with the Isle of Ely as a gift. Ethelthryth – who was later canonised as St Etheldreda or Audrey – adored the Isle of Ely, today part of Cambridgeshire, and founded a monastery here.

Over the next few decades, East Anglia was targeted by the Mercians, an Anglo-Saxon tribe from the region that is today known as the Midlands. Mercian kings ruled the kingdom until they were defeated in c.825 and the East Angles once again became independent. In 869, the Vikings invaded and, having killed King Edmund, who ruled the kingdom from 855 to 869, assumed control. They destroyed the kingdom's monasteries, including the one so lovingly founded by Ethelthryth in Ely.

East Angles, which now covered an area from the coast of Norfolk and Suffolk inland to the fenlands around Ely, was renamed East Anglia by the Vikings. In the early 900s, the

Anglo-Saxons sought to regain the kingdom and defeated the Vikings in battle, only to lose it temporarily to the Danes. Harold II (c.1022–66) was the last Anglo-Saxon king of England. He died at the Battle of Hastings fighting the Norman invasion led by William the Conqueror.

In 1066, William arrived in East Anglia. He too loved the region and decided that Norwich, which by then had grown through Roman and Anglo-Saxon habitation to become the largest city in England after London, was the ideal place in which to build a new royal palace.

William had some fanciful ideas. He had plans drawn up for the grandest palace the country had yet seen; in fact, architecturally it was so ambitious that it must have been the most talked about building of the period. The result was Norwich Castle, a fabulous structure that became the king's favourite palace. You can visit the castle today – its museum is one of the best in the region.

From the Middle Ages to around the time King Charles I ascended the throne in 1625, East Anglia became enormously wealthy as a result of its wool and cloth trade. Wool was exported to far-flung destinations such as Africa and Asia, and to many European countries. In fact, Norwich and towns such as Lavenham and Hadleigh in Suffolk, and Diss in Norfolk, were being transformed as more and more churches and large country houses were built by merchants and clothiers who had vast sums of money to spend.

The region's ports were thriving, too. The quaysides at places such as Cley-next-the-Sea and Dunwich were bustling with boats,

▼ Norwich Castle

laden to the gunwales with wool and cloth, preparing for their often perilous voyages. Larger ports, such as those at Great Yarmouth and Lowestoft in Norfolk, and Southwold and Aldeburgh in Suffolk, were also becoming increasingly prosperous through their fishing and shipbuilding industries.

Over time, the region's wool, fishing and shipbuilding industries all but disappeared. The Industrial Revolution in the late 1700s and early 1800s saw manufacturing move to the Midlands and north of England, signalling the decline of the East Anglian wool industry, while the region's fishing and shipbuilding industries gradually diminished due to silting that made it impossible for large sea-going fishing boats to navigate the region's waters and reach its ports. It wasn't until Victorian times and the coming of the railways that the coastal towns were able to reinvent themselves as seaside resorts, while the wool towns sought wealth through independent enterprise.

Meanwhile, in Ely, an abbey built to replace the monastery founded by the Anglo-Saxon Ethelthryth and destroyed by the Vikings, had become an important place of worship. The isle county became a bishopric, governed by the Bishop of Ely. In 1837, an Act was passed, known as the Liberty of Ely, which saw the county become part of Cambridgeshire. Its county town was Cambridge.

By this time, Cambridge was a thriving place, famous for its colleges and scholars' achievements. The first students arrived as far back as 1209. They had been studying at Oxford University, but fled when the townspeople turned hostile, enraged by stories of two students who were found guilty of murder. Oxford University

▼ Ely Cathedral

▲ Front Court, Emmanuel College

consequently closed. It reopened some time later, of course, but by this time many of its students had settled in Cambridge and had been joined by others. Numbers grew and so a second major place of learning gradually evolved. The two universities have been rivals ever since.

Peterhouse was Cambridge's first college. Founded in 1284 by Hugo de Balsham, the then Bishop of Ely, during the reign of the Plantagenet Edward I, it is one of the city's smallest colleges. Nevertheless, it has produced a number of famous Petreans. Charles Babbage, who brought us the forerunner of modern-day computers, was a Petrean in the 19th century. Others include newsreader Richard Baker, poet Richard Crashaw, the Duke of Grafton, Augustus Fitzroy, who was Prime Minister from 1768 to 1770, film star James Mason and film director Sam Mendes.

The following century saw the colleges Pembroke, Clare, Trinity Hall, Gonville and Caius, and Corpus Christi opening, as well as 'lost' colleges King's Hall and Michaelhouse. Henry VI drew up plans for the magnificent King's College and King's College Chapel himself, and laid the first stone on 25 July 1446. The project took 70 years to complete.

King's College was joined by many other colleges in the 15th century, most notably Queens' in 1448, St Catherine's in 1473 and

Jesus College in 1496. John Flamsteed, the first Astronomer Royal, studied at Jesus in 1670, as did astronaut Dr Michael Foale, Archbishops of Canterbury Thomas Herring and Matthew Hutton, broadcaster Alistair Cooke, playwright David Hare and HRH Prince Edward, who read history here from 1983 to 1986.

In 1546 Trinity College was founded through the amalgamation of several smaller colleges and became a centre for science, largely due to the extraordinary work of one of its students, Sir Isaac Newton. In fact, Cambridge's colleges have long been pioneering institutions. Girton became the first women's college in Cambridge in 1869, although female students were not awarded degrees until 1947. Today, almost half of all students admitted to the university are women.

In the 20th century, East Anglia was at the forefront of wartime activity. Here, numerous Royal Air Force bases became central to England's war effort during World War II, including RAF Duxford near Cambridge, which is now one of the homes of the Imperial War Museum. On the coast at Orford, the isolated Orford Ness spit was a secret Ministry of Defence testing centre, where radar pioneer Sir Robert Watson-Watt (1892–1973) and a small team of scientists took the first steps in the development of the air defence system.

BACK TO NATURE

East Anglia is a gloriously flat region, made up almost entirely of marshland with swaying reedbeds, wetland woodlands and a coastline deeply indented by rivers, creeks and dykes. Only a ridge of gently undulating hills in north Norfolk punctuates this idyllic landscape. The varied habitats created over millennia in Norfolk's Broadland and Breckland regions, along Suffolk's Heritage Coast and in Cambridgeshire's fenlands provide a home to a spectacular variety of plants and wildlife.

The Norfolk Broads landscape is incised by the rivers Bure, Waveney and Yare, and dotted with flint-and-brick villages and windpumps that keep water levels safe. The region is resplendent with fish and amphibians, birds, animals and plants, especially in the Broads National Park, which covers nearly 120 sq miles of countryside in Norfolk and north Suffolk and is Britain's largest nationally protected wetland. The habitats found here can be divided into four main types: the open broads and rivers, the Fens, the grazing marshes and wet, or carr, woodland.

The waters support a wide variety of plants, providing abundant shelter and food for fish, amphibians, birds and animals. You can

▲ Cley Marshes   ▲ Blue heron

see water plants such as water lily, hornwort and bladderwort, and birds, including the great crested grebe, heron, shoveler, tufted and mallard ducks, and the kingfisher.

The grazing marshes, such as those at Halvergate, form the heartland of the Broads. This flat area between the rivers Bure and Yare once formed part of the estuary emptying into the sea, but now lies largely below sea level and the rivers have high embankments to avoid the risk of flooding.

The area is threaded by drainage ditches, known locally as dykes, which were first cut in the 14th century, and these are important for plants, such as water violet, frogbit, arrowhead and the carnivorous bladderwort. If you are lucky you may see damselflies and dragonflies flitting delicately over the channels in summer, and lapwings, redshanks, snipe and wagtails nesting between the grassy tussocks in the wetter, boggier meadows. Herons are often seen standing motionless by the water's edge.

Another important wildlife habitat on the Broads is the carr woodland, which has been described as the closest thing Britain has to a tropical rainforest. It is characterised by wetland-loving trees such as alder, sallow and, in drier areas, silver birch. Inside, these woodlands are dense and swampy, and it is practically impossible to walk through them in any degree of comfort. Birdlife here includes woodpeckers, redpolls, siskins and blackcaps. To the west of the park is Cambridgeshire's supremely flat fenland region, which supports an astonishing number of different plant and wildlife species. In the Wicken Fen National Nature Reserve alone, which is Britain's oldest wetlands park, more than 8,500 species of plants and wildlife have been recorded.

The reserve is dominated by tall stands of reeds and sedge. It is probably the most important area of the region for wildlife. In fact, the Fens are of international importance for the wide range of plants, insects and birds they support. The rare Norfolk hawker dragonfly and the spectacular swallowtail butterfly frequent these areas.

Overhead, you may be lucky enough to see the ghostly shape of the rare marsh harrier. Another extremely rare bird found deep in the reedbeds is the highly secretive bittern. Its low, booming, foghorn-like call is one of the great sounds of the Fens.

To the south of the Norfolk Broads National Park is Suffolk. Here, the landscape has deep indentations created by the estuaries of the rivers Deben, Orwell and Stour, the Blyth and Alde, and their

▼ Hunstanton cliffs

creeks. When the water of these yacht-strewn rivers flows out to sea, mudflats are created and quickly teem with wading birds.

The coastal region of Suffolk, known as the Suffolk Heritage Coast, is designated as an Area of Outstanding Natural Beauty, a protection that is vital since it suffers badly from silting, crumbling low sea cliffs and tidal shingle spits. Here, you may catch sight of the spoonbill, a long-legged wading bird, the exotic purple heron, or the rare black-and-white avocet – returned some years ago, it is one of the RSPB's greatest success stories. These birds now form one of the country's biggest breeding colonies at the Minsmere RSPB Reserve in Suffolk, which can be found a few miles south of Southwold.

Inland, ancient heathlands of heather and bracken are home to birds and wildlife too, including the rare nightjar, Dartford warbler and woodlark, and Britain's only venomous snake, the adder. Thousands of roosting starlings can be seen flying over the countryside here in the autumn evenings – it's a dramatic and unforgettable sight.

▼ Wicken Fen windmill

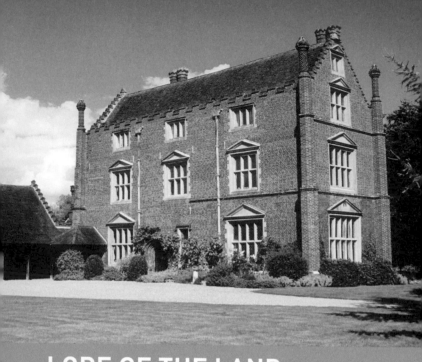

LORE OF THE LAND

Across East Anglia, a creature as black as the peaty fenland soil stalks the land. Black Shuck, the devil-dog, leaves his lair at nightfall, finding his way with eyes the size of saucers lit with flames of green or red fire. In Norfolk it's said that anyone setting eyes on Black Shuck is doomed to die, while in Suffolk – where he makes his presence known by the brush of his shaggy coat as he passes by – he's regarded as harmless as long as he isn't approached, but if attacked he will strike a deathly blow. On the plus side, however, he's reputed to care for lonely travellers. At Clopton Hall (where he helpfully guards a hoard of golden treasure) he takes on a particularly odd form, having the head of a monk. Around the coast, for example at Sheringham, he's even said to emerge from the sea.

More bizarre yet is the Dragon of Wissington, in the south of Suffolk, whose image remains painted above the north doorway of the village church. He appeared in nearby Bures in 1405 and was said by a monk to be 'vast in body with a crested head,

◄ Roos Hall, Beccles

saw-like teeth and a tail of enormous length' and clothed in arrow-proof armour. Having turned on and devoured the villagers, the beast dived into the River Stour and swam to Wormingford Mere, where it still churns the waters.

Coastal mysteries

Around the coast tales of mystery abound. On the bleak shore at Happisburgh in Norfolk, a hideous legless smuggler, head hanging backwards between his shoulderblades, sweeps silently in from the sea, a sack slung over his shoulder. He glides inland until he comes to a well, into which he drops the sack. This story has a basis in reality: the torso of a smuggler, murdered in a quarrel by his accomplices, was indeed found in a local well.

Just as weird is the Wild Man of Orford. One day, fishermen caught what they thought was a massive fish but was in fact a naked man covered in hair with a long straggly beard; he could talk only in grunts. The astonished fishermen tied him up and took him to the castle where he was kept in the dungeon. His favourite food was raw fish which he would squeeze until the water ran out of it into his hands and then he would drink it. When one day his gaolers took him to the river estuary for a swim, the wild man dived deep, swam under the nets erected to enclose him, and escaped into the open sea, leaping elatedly up and down in the water.

As midnight strikes, the Long Coastguardsman makes his way along the coast of Norfolk between Bacton and Mundesley. The nights this phantom likes best – when he's most likely to be seen – are those when it's cloudy and windy. If you listen carefully as a gale abates, you can hear him laughing; at other times you can hear him calling for help.

Norfolk fisherman have always been especially aware of voices apparently coming from the sea. A voice rising from the deep was usually a signal to head for home quickly before a deadly storm struck. Even more ominous is the yell of the Shrieking Woman, the spirit of an underwater hag who is heard only when bad times are imminent.

▶ Wild man carving, Orford

In pursuit of witches

East Anglia is witch country and famous as the centre of
17th-century witch hunts. The self-styled Witchfinder General,
Matthew Hopkins, a Puritan, arrested hundreds of 'suspects'
between 1645 and 1647. It's estimated that around 100 were
executed, most of them single women, but among them was an
80-year-old clergyman, John Lowes, accused of using magic to
sink a ship. In Bury St Edmunds in 1645, a single trial resulted in
18 executions.

Even before Hopkins' time, women thought to be witches were
persecuted. The region's best-known witch, Margaret Read, was
burned alive in Kings Lynn's Tuesday Marketplace in 1590. Legend
relates that as the fire swept through her body her heart burst out
and hit the wall of the house opposite, leaving a permanent scar on
the brickwork. Stranger still, her heart then bounced into the River
Ouse, where it created a sulphurous, cauldron-like bubbling.

After Hopkins' death the witch hunts continued – in fact, the
laws against witchcraft were not repealed until 1735. Two
Lowestoft widows, Rose Cullender and Amy Duny, accused of
bewitching seven children by infesting them with lice and bringing
on fits, as well as overturning farm carts and making chimneys
collapse, were brought to trial at Bury St Edmunds in 1662.
Furthermore, the children were said to be paralysed, to spit nails
and to have had their skin tainted with 'witches' marks'. Despite
their protests of innocence the pair were hanged.

Haunted houses

Explore East Anglia and you'll soon find yourself a ghost or
three. Roos Hall at Beccles in Suffolk is reputed to be among
England's most haunted, with ghosts in the guest room and
garden. A phantom coachman drives up to the door each
Christmas Eve and the footprint of the devil can be seen on one
of the walls. At Oulton High House in the same county, a white-
robed woman and a ghostly huntsman, complete with pack of
hounds, inhabited the site. The woman may have been a poisoned
wife or one who stood by as her husband thrust a sword into the
heart of her lover.

Fairies

And there are fairy stories aplenty too. This one is a version of
Rumpelstiltskin. At Stowmarket, a girl was once promised that
she would be saved from execution by a king who commanded
her to spin five skeins of flax a day. As she sat weeping at the
impossibility of the task, a Brownie with a ghastly visage appeared
and promised to help her if she could guess his name within a
month. Every day she guessed wrongly, until the last possible day

when she heard him singing, 'Nimmie-nimmie-not, my name is Tom Tit Tot.' Once properly named, the spirit vanished. Not only was she saved from execution, she married the king.

Griston in Norfolk's claim to fame is as the place where the tale of the Babes in the Wood originates. One day in the 1700s, Arthur Truelove, who was dying, passed his small son and daughter into the safekeeping and care of an uncle. In an attempt to make off with their inheritance, the uncle hired two men to kill them. Having a heart, one villain could not complete the task and instead killed his compatriot and left the children to starve. A robin who found their bodies covered them with dead leaves and their ghosts, so the story goes, still wander around the woodland as a reminder of those dreadful deeds.

College legends, city tales

Cambridge, home of the 'light blue' university, boasts many a spooky college tale. At Corpus Christi College, the ghost of Dr Butts, Master from 1626 to 1632, and praised for his bravery as the university's Chancellor in the dreaded plague year of 1630, is still believed to haunt the upper rooms of Old Court. Brought to a desperate low in spirits by the devastating losses that the plague induced, he hanged himself by his garters on Easter Sunday of 1632. In the early 1900s, some students tried to exorcise his ghost but only succeeded in 'ordering up' a mist, which slowly coalesced into a human figure. Also stalking the college is the ghost of a student who, in the 17th century, fell in love with the Master's daughter. They were interrupted during a tryst so she hid him in a kitchen cupboard where he suffocated. Heartbroken, she threw herself from the roof of Old Court.

Over at St John's, Dr Wood, Master until 1839, still climbs Staircase O, transmogrified into the impoverished student of his youth. A stranger being stalks Merton Hall (part of the same college) – a large, furry creature shaped like a penguin. Rumour has it that the beast wandered in from Abbey House in Newmarket Road, which itself is haunted by the Grey Lady, the ghost of a nun who reputedly still makes frequent appearances.

To the north, at Ely, a healing tradition goes right back to St Etheldreda, who attributed her death from a tumour of the neck to her youthful vanity and love of necklaces. Today, the saint is still invoked for healing throat complaints, and at the Church of St Etheldreda, in London's Ely Place, a Blessing the Throats service takes place each year on 3 February.

On misty evenings on Ely's River Ouse, a phantom barge bearing the body of St Withburga drifts along the water, a reminder that her body was stolen from East Dereham and brought to Ely in 974 by an abbot hoping to attract wealthy pilgrims.

EAST ANGLIAN WATERWAYS

Before the proliferation of the canal system in the late 18th and 19th centuries, the movement of freight across large distances had been a practical impossibility, effectively limited to something like 12 miles by both the cost and the poor state of the roads. The only exceptions were those areas lucky enough to be on one of the larger rivers such as the Great Ouse, which flows from central England through parts of Cambridgeshire and Norfolk to the North Sea.

Attempts to find a way of improving river navigation date back to the days of the Romans, perhaps even earlier, with the construction of artificial waterways near Lincoln and Cambridge. From the 12th century onwards the idea was resurrected and small-scale navigation allowed the passage of narrow barges.

The first pound locks in Britain were introduced in 1566, having already been in existence in Holland for 200 years. The domestication of rivers became much easier and their continued development and use increased throughout the 17th century.

The Great Ouse was first made navigable from the sea upstream to Bedford in the 17th century, when the surrounding land was

▲ Horsey windpump

drained by the Dutchman Cornelius Vermuyden (1595–1677) who worked extensively on Cambridgeshire's Fens, creating new waterways in and out of East Anglia. But the river's commercial usefulness had vanished by the late 19th century, and by the turn of the 20th century much of it lay derelict. Mills along its length had long been established, including Houghton Mill, further into Cambridgeshire, which is still a working mill today.

These projects were not generally government financed but were instead investments made by wealthy merchants, who were driven by the expectation of being able to make even greater profits. Large-scale construction was nevertheless surprisingly slow to get off the ground considering that most of the technical problems had already been overcome in projects undertaken in the 17th century.

It was really only with the construction of the Bridgewater Canal in northwest England in the 18th century that canals began to be built. Their success encouraged the formation of joint stock companies to build others throughout the country. However, this flurry of activity created its own problems. The companies built their canals as they saw fit and according to local conditions. This lack of coordination meant that some canals were open to just about any size of craft, while others were restricted to narrowboats only. Nevertheless, it became clear that canals were useful and construction continued until the 1830s, at which point nearly every town of any importance was within distance of a stretch of navigable water.

East Anglia and central England were the two areas where waterways were particularly important. The Midlands were at the heart of the Industrial Revolution and there are still 130 miles of navigable canal in Birmingham and the Black Country alone. In its heyday, canal transport carried eight million tonnes a year, and even as late as the 1950s a million tonnes a year were still being transported on the waterways.

Ironically, the canal system, with its network linking large industrial sites, was to become instrumental in its own downfall. Waterways were used to transport the coal that powered the steam locomotives on the railways, which were new, much faster and more efficient. Canals were gradually abandoned, and in some cases drained in order to become rail beds.

With one or two major exceptions, commercial traffic has all but died out and the canals have assumed a new role as leisure amenities. And not only on the water – the old towpaths are ideal for walking and cycling, and many tourist offices produce routes and trails to follow. In Norfolk and Cambridgeshire, the enthusiastic Great Ouse Restoration Society was responsible for the reopening of navigation on the greatest river in the area.

▼ The River Ouse at Ely

HORSERACING
AT NEWMARKET

Surrounding Cambridge and Ely is a vast landscape
that captivated the monarchy. James I, as well as
Charles I and Charles II, adored the region. They were
all passionate about horses, and James created a
summer court at Newmarket. Even the Celtic Queen
Boudicca is said to have raced her horses across
Newmarket Heath. Today, horseracing and this part
of East Anglia go hand in hand.

The Suffolk market town of Newmarket, with its elegant red-brick
Georgian houses surrounded by flat greens and countryside, is
utterly devoted to the sport. The day starts early with the horses
being exercised and trained on the various turf gallops on
Newmarket Heath and often ends with a discussion of the day's
results over dinner in one of the many upmarket restaurants or
pubs – this is a town that lives and breathes all things equestrian.

Newmarket's page in racing history really began in 1604, when
James I went hunting in the area, and saw its potential for sporting
activities. Choosing Newmarket as his base, he leased a local inn,
creating what must have surely been the least glamorous of all of
Britain's royal palaces. The Griffin suffered from subsidence, and

eventually collapsed around 1614, with James I and several members of his court inside it at the time. Fortunately, they were all unharmed and were pulled free.

The King was not deterred, and both the Griffin and the nearby Swan Inn were demolished to make way for a much larger royal residence. With this, Newmarket's status as a sort of royal holiday resort was assured. The first recorded race here took place in 1622 – many more were to follow.

Charles I – who, in fact, was imprisoned in the royal palace at Newmarket before his execution – and his son Charles II were both keen horsemen. Charles II is said to have been interested in the breeding of racehorses and in improving the cavalry stock, which had been severely depleted during the Civil War. He is thought to have made at least two visits a year to the town to ride, during which time he set up both the July Course and the Rowley Mile. A pattern of spring and autumn race meetings was established, which continues to this day.

Newmarket was right at the centre of national horseracing again in 1750 when The Jockey Club set up shop there. This group of horseracing's elite members met to draw up the rules for horseracing, jockeys, trainers, owners and racecourses. Essentially a very exclusive gentleman's club at its inception – its members would largely have come from within the aristocracy – it conjures up delightful images of wealthy peers exchanging racing stories over a cigar in the billiards room; whether accurate or not, who can say? Its intriguing set up of privilege and power is one made use of by Dick Francis in his popular racing thrillers – well worth a read for anyone interested in horseracing.

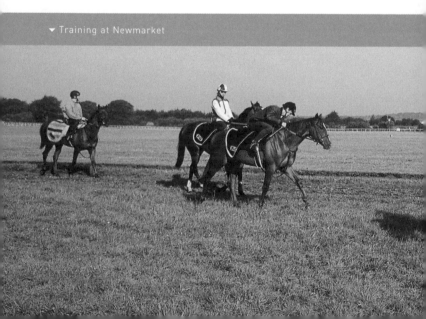

▼ Training at Newmarket

The Jockey Club moved to London in the 1960s and still owns 15 of Britain's racecourses, though racing itself is now governed by the British Horseracing Authority.

Back to Newmarket though. At any one time there are over 3,000 thoroughbred horses based here in training in the 50 or so stables, and almost as many owners, trainers, jockeys and stable hands, along with many breeding studs and veterinary practices – Newmarket is a world leader in horse health.

It is also the largest horse breeding and training centre in the country, and has two of the world's finest flat racing racecourses, the one mile, two furlong-long Rowley Mile and the mile-long Adnams July Racecourse. The latter is next to the National Stud, and is known for its summer party atmosphere. You can see the racecourses on your visit, along with huge swathes of flat greens neatly divided by fencing, where horses are trained.

To experience Newmarket at its best, try to plan your visit to coincide with a race day. In the morning, you may like to take a guided tour of the National Stud or join the popular Short Head tour, visiting the gallops and a trainer's yard. The Rowley Mile (spring and autumn) and the Adnams July Course (summer) have a programme of attractive meetings, or there are the QIPCO Guineas Festival in May and Dubai Future Champions Festival in October. Each summer the racecourse also hosts a series of Friday evening music nights on the July Course, with top name artists and bands, while Summer Saturdays feature family entertainment.

To splash out, buy a ticket that allows entry to the Premier Enclosure, which provides the best views of the Finishing Post, Parade Ring and Winners' Circle.

SUTTON HOO, LAND OF ANGLO-SAXON KINGS

One of the most important archaeological sites in Britain, Sutton Hoo, near Woodbridge in Suffolk, has revealed such astonishing treasures, befitting only a king, that its discovery in 1939 opened up a whole new chapter of English history.

The significance of the Anglo-Saxon finds, including a ship and priceless regalia, which had lain undisturbed since the early seventh century, is incalculable. It is an extraordinary site and well worth adding to your itinerary.

Sutton Hoo, a picturesque place surrounded by lovely walks with estuary views, is an Anglo-Saxon ship burial site. Excavation revealed an 89-foot-long heavy oak ship which, although its timbers had rotted, had moulded itself in the soil, together with

▲ The Sutton Hoo mask

its magnificent contents of jewellery, vessels and weapons, all beautifully preserved. Historians think that the ancient burial is probably that of King Raedwald, who reigned from around AD 599 to 624.

Among the treasures found in the burial chamber of the ship were a ceremonial warrior's helmet, shield, Byzantine silverware, a set of spears, a purse containing gold coins and a collection of gem-encrusted gold body ornaments, such as buckles, that were so fine as to suggest they could only have been the property of a great person. Particularly significant, and unusual, was a sceptre, traditionally carried only by a ruling monarch. No body was found, but soil analyses suggest that all traces of it would have long since disappeared in the acidic soil.

The Anglo-Saxons were a people from Denmark and Germany who settled in Britain after the Romans had left in the fifth century; 200 years later, Raedwald was one of the first rulers of the Kingdom of East Angles. Anglo-Saxon custom decreed that important people were buried beneath mounds, with precious goods as a sign of their wealth and importance. The burial of an entire ship is unique to East Anglia and Scandinavia, and signifies that the body was that of a prominent person. The ship would have been hauled up the hill from the river, and lowered into a trench with only its stem and stern posts visible above ground. The body and personal processions would have been placed in the ship, and then a mound of earth built around it.

Although few details of Raedwald's reign remain after the destruction of the monasteries, which held vital documents, by the Vikings in the ninth century, he was said to have been one of the most powerful kings of the period and Sutton Hoo would have been a fitting memorial to him.

You might be wondering how this extraordinary site was discovered. Well, at one time the land close to the River Deben was owned by amateur archaeologist Edith Pretty (1883–1942) who lived in a modern house on the site. She reported seeing ghostly warriors hovering over mounds on her land and sought the help of local archaeologist Basil Brown to start a dig here. Three of the mounds were empty, thought to have been robbed in the 16th or 17th century, but in the fourth he made the amazing discovery.

A treasure trove inquest declared Edith to be the owner of the finds, which she promptly donated to the British Museum in 1939, then the largest gift to the museum ever made by a living donor.

The National Trust now cares for Sutton Hoo and an exhibition houses some of the finds. There are replicas of the site's most fascinating treasures (which remain in the British Museum) and a full-sized reconstruction of the burial chamber, telling the story of how its treasures lay undisturbed for over 1,300 years.

LOCAL SPECIALITIES

When it comes to food and drink, you'd be hard pushed to find a region with quite so many specialities. Many of the recipes have been handed down through the generations and are supremely tasty with an exciting fusion of flavours.

TREATS

Norfolk's own treacle tart is made with lashings of black treacle, flavoured with lemon and topped with a gigantic blob of double cream. The tart, as well as Norfolk's version of bread pudding made with rum and dried fruit, locally known as Nelson slices, and Norfolk ginger biscuits, are eaten by households up and down the county and can usually be found in souvenir shops neatly packaged in portions for you to take home.

Cambridge has long been associated with puddings and cakes. Trinity College has served a baked cream custard with a burnt sugar topping since the 19th century; its college coat of arms was traditionally burnt into the top of the dessert with a branding iron. But Cambridge is probably best known for afternoon tea. At the Orchard Tea Garden in Grantchester, made famous in a poem by Rupert Brooke (1887–1915), tea with scones and cakes was served to students who had punted upstream from Cambridge. The tradition of serving afternoon tea, and other delicacies, in the Orchard continues to this day (see page 137).

ALE AND APPLES

Think of Suffolk pubs, and the smooth golden ale that has been brewed by Adnams of Southwold for the past 150 years springs to mind. This family business has been a constant in the town, and is its biggest employer. The range has grown over the years from the original cask ales to include bottled beers and lager, some of which are flavoured with banana and citrus, plus wines made from Merlot and Grenache grapes, and spirits such as barley vodka.

◀ Afternoon tea ▲ Cromer crabs

Suffolk is also famous for its acres of apple orchards and the excellent ciders they produce. The Chevallier family at Aspall Hall Farm has been making cider since 1728. It started out as a local brew, but is now an international brand that includes apple juice and vinegars available as far afield as the US and Australia.

In Bury St Edmunds, Greene King is an institution. The family business was founded in 1799 by Benjamin Greene and brews strong vintage ales. It's one of the largest British-owned breweries in the UK with many restaurants and pubs.

FOOD

To accompany all these fine ales and ciders, the area has plenty of food specialities too. Suffolk is known for its top-quality pork produced from herds throughout the county, and oysters from beds that dot the coastal creeks around Orford (see page 228). At Butley Creek, the beds yield oysters so fine that they have long been a delicacy on the menus of Suffolk restaurants. There's a smokehouse here too, founded by Richard Pinney, of Pinney's of Orford, where fishermen smoke trout and mackerel, kippers, eels and salmon over whole oak logs.

To follow, there are cheeses ranging from the delicately flavoured Suffolk Gold to the more robust Suffolk Blue. Then there are the pies and cakes, including medley pie, made from kidneys and apples, and Suffolk harvest cake with its spicy mix of fruit.

The coastline yields an abundance of delicacies. Be sure to try samphire, also known as sea asparagus, which grows in the tidal salt marshes off Norfolk; it can be pickled or steamed and served with a knob of butter. Don't miss Cromer crabs, whose habitat is the chalk reef just off the county's coastline, juicy Brancaster mussels from the creeks, or 'stewkey blue' cockles from Stiffkey.

Farmers' markets found throughout Norfolk, Suffolk and Cambridge provide the perfect opportunity to sample some of the finest specialities of the region and to chat with the producers.

BEFORE YOU GO

THINGS TO READ

Ask someone to name a classic novel set in Norfolk or Suffolk, and they might struggle; there's no dramatic heights to wuther, and no Jane Austen character ever went to Norwich – although David Copperfield was born near Great Yarmouth. But, and Dickens aside, that's not to say the area doesn't have its own share of great literature. George Orwell lived for a time in Southwold in Suffolk, while fantasy writers Philip Pullman and China Mieville were both born in Norwich – perhaps there's something in the water. One of the first graduates of the University of East Anglia's famous creative writing course was Booker Prize-winning novelist Ian McEwan – and he was taught there by Malcolm Bradbury (as was Kazuo Ishiguro). Diana Athill and *Black Beauty* author Anna Sewell were also Norfolk-born.

But one of the region's most famous literary connections isn't even a person: it's a line.

'The past is a foreign country: they do things differently there.' is the opening line of *The Go-Between* by L P Hartley. First published in 1953, and granted immortality by its induction to the hallowed halls of Penguin Modern Classics, *The Go-Between* is the story of a young boy's loss of innocence over a long, hot summer spent at the fictional Brandham Hall in Norfolk. Even if you've never read the novel, you'll almost certainly recognise the quote. The 1971 film adaptation was also made on location in Norfolk (the 2015 version was shot in Berkshire).

A Norfolk summer is also a feature of *The Accidental* by Ali Smith, when a family holiday is upended by the arrival of a mysterious stranger, while in Rose Tremain's *Restoration*, Norfolk is both exile and sanctuary for Charles II's foolish physician and sometime-favourite Robert Merivel.

Meanwhile, in Suffolk, childhood trauma with a

Martello tower in the starring role features in *The Twins* by Saskia Sarginson, a Richard and Judy book club pick and the type of holiday read to make you neglect all that actual sightseeing in favour of finding out just what happened...

It's probably against the rules to provide any sort of recommended reading for Cambridge without featuring that university, but *Porterhouse Blue* by Tom Sharpe and *The Liar* by Stephen Fry each take care of proceedings in suitably comedic fashion. If creepy multi-layered literature about science, religion and genius undergraduate musicians is more your thing – and why wouldn't it be? – *The Bellwether Revivals* by Benjamin Wood will have you sleeping a little less soundly in your bed at night.

Crime fans meanwhile should try Kate Atkinson's *Case Histories*, the first of her series of novels starring typically troubled private-investigator-with-a-past Jackson Brodie, as he attempts to solve three separate – but entwined – old cases in modern-day Cambridgeshire.

THINGS TO WATCH

Did you know that Harry Potter was from Suffolk? That's if you're watching *Harry Potter and the Deathly Hallows: Part I* (2010), at least – Harry's infant home 'Godric's Hollow', which Harry and Hermione visit in their search for the Deathly Hallows, is actually the Suffolk village of Lavenham. A lot of it was either re-created at Pinewood Studios or given a helping hand with CGI, but you'll recognise De Vere House, Harry's birthplace – said to be the second most photographed doorway in Britain, after 10 Downing Street.

Lavenham's medieval streets also featured in the British horror movie *Witchfinder General* (1968), starring Vincent Price. Less friendly to witches and wizards in this incarnation than in Harry Potter, the town square hosts a witch burning. The film, based on the true story of Matthew Hopkins in the 17th century, also used several other locations in the area, including Dunwich, Kentwell Hall and Orford Castle.

Plenty of properties in the area are well accustomed to pretending to be something else. Holkham Hall's Marble Hall stands in for the entrance hall of Devonshire House in *The Duchess* (2008) – and that wasn't Keira Knightley's only visit to Holkham. She can also be found hanging out on the estate's beach in *Never Let Me Go* (2010), while Gwyneth Paltrow washed up there at the end of *Shakespeare in Love* (1998). Fellow film star Elveden Hall's exotic interiors, meanwhile, host an orgy in *Eyes Wide Shut* (1999), a banquet in Bond movie *The Living Daylights* (1987), a king's bedchamber in *Stardust* (2007) and an evil villain's lair in *Lara Croft: Tomb Raider* (2001).

It's Ely Cathedral that's the real star, though – it has served as the backdrop for royalty three times in the last decade alone, as Henry VIII's palace, Whitehall and Westminster Abbey, respectively, in *The Other Boleyn Girl* (2008), *Elizabeth: the Golden Age* (2007), and *The King's Speech* (2010).

Incidentally, although largely set at Cambridge University, *Chariots of Fire* (1981) was refused permission to film on location at Caius College as the plot contained accusations of anti-Semitism against them. Eton College in Berkshire stood in, although there's a few establishing exterior shots of Cambridge itself. The film is largely based on true events, so still worth a watch even if you have to squint a bit to see a glimpse of the town.

If you prefer your scenery on the small screen, the roguish antiques dealer *Lovejoy* (1986–94) put Long Melford and nearby Suffolk towns on the tourist trail, while fans of *Dad's Army* (1968–77) will recognise much of the Norfolk town of Thetford as the fictional Walmington-on-Sea. Look out for the Guildhall, the flint cottages in Nether Row, the church and the Palace Cinema. Walmington-on-Sea's pier can be found at Great Yarmouth.

Stephen Fry's TV series *Kingdom* (2007–9) was both set and filmed in Norfolk, even if the town of Market Shipborough was fictional. It's actually Swaffham, though Wells-next-the-Sea, Hunstanton, Dereham, Thetford and – yes – Holkham's beach again all make appearances. The Norfolk accents have been criticised, but for pure East Anglian authenticity, it's still probably your best bet.

That's with one major exception, of course. Who could forget Norwich's most famous fictional son, Alan Partridge? In

▼ Church Bell Gate, East Bergholt

Alan Partridge: Alpha Papa (2013), look out for Cromer Pier and Norwich. You could also seek out *Alan Partridge: Welcome to the Places of My Life* (2012) and be taken by Alan on a tour of his beloved Norfolk.

THINGS TO KNOW

Norfolk, Suffolk and Cambridge have a few quirky tales. Legend has it that the church tower of St Michael in Beccles (see page 61), Suffolk, has clock faces on only three sides; the side facing Norfolk is blank because townsfolk didn't want to give their time for free to their neighbours.

It was the presence of ghostly warriors hovering over Sutton Hoo (see page 262) that led to the discovery of the ship burial containing priceless treasures belonging to the Anglo-Saxon King Raedwald.

If you thought the rolling fields surrounding the burial mounds at Sutton Hoo look like pristine fairways of the finest 18-hole golf course, you'd be right. Sutton Hoo turf is grown especially for golf courses, cricket grounds and sports pitches in dry countries such as Saudi Arabia.

Look out for the 500-year-old timber cage housing the bells of the church of St Mary the Virgin in East Bergholt (see page 125). They are believed to be the heaviest still rung in England, and are rare in that they are rung by hand by ringers who stand alongside.

Cambridge has one of the world's largest concentrations of sundials. The Old Court of Queens' College (see page 90) has a 17th-century moon-dial. It is one of the finest examples in Britain and one of only a few moon-dials in the world.

You are not allowed to walk on the colleges' grass in Cambridge – unless you are a senior member of the college,

▼ Burial mounds at Sutton Hoo

▲ Trinity College, Cambridge

that is, and only then on your own grass. For instance, Fellows of King's College can't walk on Trinity College's grass (see page 90).

Charles Dickens visited the Norfolk seaside town of Great Yarmouth (see page 139) in 1848, and the town appears in scenes in *David Copperfield*, among them the dramatic shipwreck in which David's boyhood friend Steerforth loses his life.

The Broads Reed and Sedge Cutters Association was formed to protect the age-old trade of reed and sedge cutting. The tall Norfolk reeds, which can grow up to 10 feet in height, are often used for thatching.

Wherry was the name given to the sailing boats that plied the Broads for centuries, carrying everything from timber to fish. Wherries were shallow-draughted, clinker-built, wooden boats powered by a large gaff sail, traditionally black in colour (see page 208).

Look out for Southwold Jack. Dressed in armour with a sword in one hand and an axe in the other, and standing next to a bell, the figure can be found in Southwold's church of St Edmund, King and Martyr (see page 247). He is incredibly rare. Today, as in medieval times, he is made to raise his axe, which rings the bell to tell the congregation the service is about to start.

THINGS TO PACK

The one thing you'll need to pack for a break in Norfolk, Suffolk and Cambridge is a good pair of walking boots.

▲ Moondial at Old Court, Queens' College

There's so much to see and do that your feet may take a bit of a pounding. But don't let all this talk of walking put you off visiting if you are a wheelchair user; East Anglia has been extremely conscientious in making many areas, including museums and churches, accessible for everyone. You'll find ramps, wide doors and so on to help you get about easily, with the exception of some of the old castle ruins and archaeological sites, although even these have been adapted reasonably well in recent years.

Clothing should be light and comfortable, especially in the summer. Take swimwear if you're planning to spend time on the beach or in a hotel with a swimming pool. Summer evenings can get a bit cooler so a jacket or jumper is advisable.

In winter, as in the rest of the UK, it's advisable to be mindful of weather conditions, and take note of forecasts that suggest heavy rain, frost or snow. Pack accordingly. Coastal areas can be extremely windy at any time of the year, so again you may need an extra layer of clothing. Evening dress should be smart casual, especially if you plan to dine in a restaurant or go to the theatre.

If you're planning to venture out into the countryside, you'll need waterproof clothes and suitable boots. Don't forget to carry your mobile phone, a torch and plenty of water. East Anglia has some wonderful walks, but always be mindful of a handful of risks, such as slippery cliff paths, tidal conditions if walking on the seashore, and farmyard machinery or livestock. Some areas, like heaths and marshland, can be tricky, especially in winter months when fog can descend quickly.

BASIC INFORMATION

It's easy to get about East Anglia, whether you are driving or planning to use the public transport network.

Driving from London and the south, you'll probably find yourself taking the M25 for a short while, before turning off on either the A12, which takes you into Essex and onwards to Suffolk and Norfolk as far as Great Yarmouth, or the M11/A11, on which you can easily reach Cambridge and the network of roads, including the A47, A10, A1065 and A14, that will take you into the heart of the region.

From the north of England and the Midlands, you'll need to navigate to the A14, which runs from Rugby in Warwickshire, right through to Felixstowe, passing through Cambridge and Ipswich.

The M25, M11, A12 and A14 are busy roads, especially at junctions and during rush hour and peak holiday times, when people are travelling to work. They all have service areas.

The region's main towns are well served by the railway network. Greater Anglia, for instance, connects the most northern regions of Norfolk – with stations at Sheringham and Cromer – with Ely, Cambridge and Newmarket to the west and with the eastern towns of Great Yarmouth, Lowestoft and Felixstowe, via Bury St Edmunds, Ipswich and Norwich, and many smaller stations along the routes. Great Northern operate a route from King's Lynn to Cambridge, while East Midlands Trains covers the stretch between Norwich and Peterborough. Community lines, such as the Bittern Line from Norwich to Sheringham, connect with local bus services, making car-free excursions straightforward.

Long-distance buses, such as National Express, operate out of major hubs, like Birmingham, Manchester and London Victoria, straight into the region's main towns and cities. In turn, local buses travel to smaller villages, or you could take a taxi.

Finally, the flatness of the countryside makes East Anglia ideal for exploring by bicycle, Key tourist areas like the Norfolk Broads all have cycle hire outlets, while Sustrans publish a range of route maps.

As far as accommodation goes, East Anglia has plenty to offer. There are city centre hotels, of course, while many on the coast, especially at popular destinations like Southwold, Aldeburgh, Lowestoft and Great Yarmouth, have fantastic views over the sea. You will find cosy guest houses and inns with rooms too. The region also has a good selection of campsites (see page 48).

FESTIVALS & EVENTS

The people of Norfolk, Suffolk and Cambridge will hold a festival at the drop of a hat, so there's always something going on if you fancy mingling with locals and having a fun day out. Here's a round-up of the best.

▶ **Beer festivals**
Beer festivals are a regular event in the Norfolk diary, as are the seafood festivals at Cromer and Sheringham, and folkloric events at Ludham, Cley, Holt, Wells and Worstead. Suffolk hosts the East Anglian Beer Festival in Bury St Edmunds in April.

▶ **Aldeburgh Festival**
The most famous classical music festival (snapemaltings.co.uk) in the region is held every summer at the Snape Maltings, a gorgeous 19th-century former granary on the Suffolk coast. Founded in 1948 by Benjamin Britten and Peter Pears, it now attracts world-class musicians.

▶ **Literature and Arts festivals**
Southwold, Stowmarket and Ipswich all host regular literature and arts festivals. Ip-Art (ipswichentertains.co.uk) in Ipswich stages acts ranging from top comedy performers to music, literature, film and theatre. Norwich, England's only Unesco city of literature, stages the Worlds Literature Festival (writerscentrenorwich.org.uk).

▶ **Music festivals**
The Wymondham Music Festival (wymfest.org.uk) mixes classical, choirs and jazz, while the WoW Music Festival (wow-arts.co.uk), held on fields near Diss, spans acoustic, roots, ska, bluegrass and more.

▶ **Cambridge festivals**
Cambridge hosts a Folk Festival (cambridgelivetrust.co.uk/folk-festival), a Jazz Festival (cambridgejazz.org), a Comedy Festival (cambridgecomedyfestival.com) and a Film Festival (cambridgefilmfestival.org.uk).

▶ **Summer in the City**
is a Cambridge favourite, and features a series of musical events held in the city's parks, while the Strawberry Fair transforms Midsummer Common into a fairground.

▶ **Ely Folk Festival**
In Ely, the Ely Folk Festival (elyfolkfestival.co.uk) attracts people from far afield, which is not surprising as the line-up includes jamming sessions, workshops and craft demonstrations.

▶ **Saints and harvest festivals**
East Anglia's many churches host a number of festivals. Norwich Cathedral and Ely Cathedral, in particular, are famous for their rich festival pageantry.

CAMPSITES

For more information on these and other campsites, visit theAA.com/self-catering-and-campsites

Cakes & Ale ▶▶▶▶▶
cakesandale.co.uk
Abbey Lane, Theberton, Leiston, IP16 4TE | 01728 831655
Open Apr–Oct (restricted service low season club, shop, reception limited hours)
A large, well spread out and beautifully maintained site on a former World War II airfield. The spacious touring area has plenty of hardstandings and super pitches, and there's a good bar.

Clippesby Hall ▶▶▶▶▶
clippesbyhall.com
Hall Lane, Clippesby, NR29 3BL
01493 367800 | Open all year
This lovely country house estate and its attached campsite has secluded pitches hidden among the trees or in sheltered sunny glades. There's a coffee shop with WiFi, a bar and restaurant and family golf. You can also try your hand at volley ball and table tennis, or hire a bike and take to the cycle trails. There are pine lodges and cottages available for holiday lets.

Haw Wood Farm Caravan Park ▶▶▶▶
hawwoodfarm.co.uk
Hinton, Saxmundham, IP17 3QT
01502 359550 | Open Mar–mid Jan
An unpretentious family-orientated park set in two large fields surrounded by low hedges. The amenity block is appointed to a very high standard - it includes an excellent reception with cafe, a good play area and excellent toilet and shower facilities.

Heathland Beach Caravan Park ▶▶▶▶
heathlandbeach.co.uk
London Road, Kessingland, NR33 7PJ | 01502 740337
Open Apr–Oct
A well-run and maintained park set in meadowland, with level grass pitches. There's direct access to the sea and beach, a heated swimming pool, three play areas, and a well-stocked fishing lake.

Moon & Sixpence ▶▶▶▶▶
moonandsixpence.eu
Newbourn Road, Waldringfield,

Woodbridge, IP12 4PP
01473 736650 | Open Apr–Oct
(restricted service low season – club,
shop, reception open limited hours)
This well-planned site is
located in a sheltered valley
around an attractive boating
lake with sandy beach. Toilet
facilities are housed in a smart
Norwegian-style cabin. Leisure
facilities include two tennis
courts, a bowling green, fishing,
boating and a games room. It
has an adult-only area, and a
strict 'no groups and no noise
after 9pm' policy.

The Old Brick Kilns ▶▶▶▶▶
old-brick-kilns.co.uk
Little Barney Lane, Barney,
NR21 0NL | 01328 878305
Open 15 Mar–2 Jan
A secluded and peaceful park
approached by a quiet, leafy
country lane. The site is on two
levels with its own boating and
fishing pool and plenty of
mature trees. There are two
excellent, well-appointed toilet
blocks, and a short dog walk.
Due to a narrow access road,
no arrivals are accepted until
after 1pm.

Rose Farm Touring & Camping Park ▶▶▶▶▶
rosefarmtouringpark.co.uk
Stepshort, Belton, NR31 9JS
01493 780896 | Open all year
A former railway line is the
setting for this very peaceful,
beautifully presented site,
which has some nice rural
views and many bright
flower beds. Customer care
is truly exceptional.

Run Cottage Touring Park
▶▶▶▶
runcottage.co.uk
Alderton Road, Hollesley, IP12 3RQ
01394 411309 | Open all year
Located in the peaceful
village of Hollesley, this
landscaped park with
generously sized pitches is set
behind the owners' house. It is
handily located for Sutton Hoo.

Seashore Holiday Park
▶▶▶▶▶ HOLIDAY HOME PARK
haven.com/seashore
North Denes, Great Yarmouth,
NR30 4HG
01493 851131
Open mid-Mar to Oct
Bordered by sand dunes
and with direct access to a
sandy beach, Seashore
Holiday Park is in Great
Yarmouth and close enough
to the Norfolk Broads for day
trips. Facilities include water
activities and bike hire for
children and lively evening
entertainment for adults.

Two Mills Touring Park
▶▶▶▶▶
twomills.co.uk
Yarmouth Road, North Walsham,
NR28 9NA | 01692 405829
Open Mar–3 Jan
This intimate, beautifully
presented park is set in
superb countryside. The
'Top Acre' section is maturing
and offers panoramic views
over the site. The very friendly
and helpful owners keep the
park in immaculate condition.
Please note this park is for
adults only.

VISIT THE MUSEUMS | GET OUTDOORS | EXPLORE BY BIKE | GO BACK IN TIME | TAKE A TRAIN RIDE | MEET THE WILDLIFE

TAKE IN SOME HISTORY | HIT THE BEACH | EAT AND DRINK | GET INDUSTRIAL | VISIT THE GALLERIES | GO CANOEING

SADDLE UP | PLACES NEARBY | CATCH A PERFORMANCE | GO ROUND THE GARDENS | TAKE A BOAT TRIP

A–Z of Norfolk & Suffolk

▶ **Aldeburgh** MAP REF 291 E4

With its timber-framed cottages dating back to Tudor times, many in shades of pink and yellow, Georgian houses and a shingle beach that stretches as far as the eye can see, Aldeburgh, in Suffolk, is every inch the quintessential sleepy English holiday resort. You'll start to relax the moment you arrive. Away from the coast, the town is surrounded by countryside, with neighbouring hamlets barely specks on the horizon. But don't mistake its importance – Aldeburgh is well and truly on the map, thanks to just one man.

Celebrated composer and conductor Benjamin Britten (1913–76), one of the most famous figures of 20th-century British classical music, adored Aldeburgh and made his home here. Born in Lowestoft, the son of a local dentist, he grew up a stone's throw from the sea. He began composing at the age of five. After studying at the Royal College of Music, he moved to the United States and, as coincidence would have it, began reading the works of Aldeburgh poet George Crabbe (1754–1832). Crabbe, who had lost two brothers to the sea, and whose father was a salt-master, wrote with passion about the lives of Suffolk fishermen. Inspired by Crabbe's work, Britten returned to Suffolk and purchased the Old Mill in Snape, which was to become his home. Here he wrote *Peter Grimes*, an opera based on Crabbe's 'The Borough'. The opera is magical and gritty; you can almost hear the waves breaking on Aldeburgh's shingle beach as the bitterly cold wind comes in on the tide, echoing the anguish of the fisherman Peter Grimes. Britten's lifelong partner, the operatic tenor Peter Pears, took the lead when it was first performed in 1945.

Britten and Pears founded the Aldeburgh Festival in 1948, which is considered one of the finest music festivals in the world. It is housed in former maltings at Snape. The couple lived in Aldeburgh for the rest of their lives, first on the seafront at 4 Crabbe Street – look out for the plaque which tells you that this was Britten's home from 1947 to 1957 – and then in the larger Red House, a farmhouse on the outskirts of town. They are buried side by side in St Peter and St Paul church.

This part of the Suffolk coast also held attractions for writers, including Daniel Defoe, Wilkie Collins and Edward FitzGerald, translator of the fatalistic *Rubaiyat of Omar Khayyam*. Thomas Carlyle wrote approvingly of Aldeburgh's shingly beach and clear water, and novelist E M Forster enjoyed the bleakness as well as the beauty of the place.

While you're in Aldeburgh, be sure to take a look at the Moot Hall, which is a glorious red-brick Tudor building on the seafront, containing a small museum telling the story of

▲ Aldeburgh beach

Aldeburgh. If you walk along the shingle beach from here you'll come to the Martello tower, which was one of a string of defensive towers built along the coast in the 19th century.

On the beach itself is a sculpture, entitled *The Scallop*, dedicated to Benjamin Britten. It's 12 feet high so you can't miss it, but don't mention it to the locals as it's not popular. Although you're encouraged to sit on it and look out to sea, many people consider it looks incongruous in the natural surroundings.

Aldeburgh, which means 'old fort', has a fascinating history. It was a bustling and prosperous medieval port with a flourishing fishing industry and shipbuilding workshops that were among the best in the country. It was here that Sir Francis Drake's ships, the *Greyhound* and the famous *Golden Hind*, were built. Like so many towns along the east coast, Aldeburgh fell into decline when the harbour silted up. Its fishing and shipbuilding days diminished to a point when only local fishermen, and smugglers, could navigate its waters in their tiny boats. In Victorian times its fortunes took a brief upwards turn when it became a fashionable, yet select, holiday resort.

Today, Aldeburgh lies on the banks of the River Alde, at a point where it diverts away from the sea and runs parallel with the coast, separated by the shingle ridge of Orford Ness. It is in an Area of Outstanding Natural Beauty. The shingle is home to many species of rare invertebrates, particularly spiders and beetles.

TAKE IN SOME HISTORY
Martello Towers
visit-aldeburgh.co.uk
Slaughden Road, IP15 5NA
The area's Martello towers date from around 1810, built to defend against a Napoleonic invasion. The largest, now converted into a holiday home, stands on Orford Ness shingle spit, a short walk along Aldeburgh's seafront. There's another at Bawdsey cliffs.

VISIT THE MUSEUMS
The Red House
brittenpears.org
Red House, Golf Lane, IP15 5PZ
01728 451700 | Open Apr–Oct
Tue-Sat 1–5, guided tours 2pm
(book in advance)
You can join a tour at the Red House, once the home of Benjamin Britten and Peter Pears and now headquarters of the Britten-Pears Foundation. See their house; the gallery, which has an exhibition that gives you a wonderful introduction to their music; the Archive, purpose built to house Britten's significant collections; and their studio, cleverly created with excellent acoustics within a former hayloft.

The Aldeburgh Museum
aldeburghmuseumonline.co.uk
Moot Hall, Seafront, IP15 5DS
01728 454666 | Open daily Apr–May, Sep–Oct 2.30–5, Jun–Aug 12–5
The little museum inside the Moot Hall on Aldeburgh's seafront tells the fascinating story of the town's history. This Grade I listed timber-framed, flint-and-brick hall was built in Tudor times and would have been the focal point of Aldeburgh's market square. It now stands in isolation, almost on the shingle beach where fishermen draw up their boats, but would almost certainly have once been surrounded by similar Tudor buildings that have vanished into the sea. On its gabled wall is a sundial with the date 1650; it was added around 130 years after the hall was built. The building was restored in 1854 and Jacobean-style chimneys added. As well as the museum, it houses the council chamber, as it has for the past 400 years.

ENTERTAIN THE FAMILY
Kids' Treasure Trail
treasuretrails.co.uk
Starts at Fort Green car park, IP15 5DR
Allow at least two hours for this circular, self-guided, 2-mile walk exploring the highlights and hidden treasures of Aldeburgh. Suitable for pushchairs and wheelchairs, it's available to buy online.

PLAY A ROUND
Aldeburgh Golf Club
aldeburghgolfclub. co.uk
Saxmundham Road, IP15 5PE
01728 452890 | Open daily all year
Good natural drainage provides year-round golf in links-type conditions on this well-bunkered heathland course. There are fine views over the Suffolk Coast and Heaths to be had.

EAT AND DRINK
Regatta Restaurant ◉
regattaaldeburgh.com
171 High Street, IP15 5AN
01728 452011

A nautical-themed mural and piscine prints leave no doubt that fresh local seafood, often landed on the beach, is the main thrust of this High Street restaurant. It's a cheery, relaxed sort of place, with brown leather-look banquettes and upholstered dining chairs at plain wooden tables, and a blackboard of daily specials padding out the carte. Featuring seasonal ingredients, the frequently changing menu includes poultry, meat and vegetarian dishes and some memorable desserts.

Wentworth Hotel
wentworth-aldeburgh.com
Wentworth Road, IP15 5BD
01728 452312

A grand country house in a peaceful location overlooking Aldeburgh's pebble beach, the Wentworth is one of the town's premier hotels and restaurants. Oozing tradition, its restaurant has claret-coloured walls hung with portraits, a thickly carpeted floor, crisp napery and sea views. The cooking has its roots in the traditional English repertory, with local produce the mainstay – think meat from Suffolk farms and fish landed on the beach that morning.

The White Lion Hotel ◉
whitelion.co.uk
Market Cross Place, IP15 5BJ
01728 452720

Unpretentious brasserie dining is the deal at the White Lion, Aldeburgh's oldest hotel, sitting in prime beachfront splendour by the shingle banks of Aldeburgh's strand, and

▼ The Moot Hall, Aldeburgh

it's all built on fine Suffolk ingredients. In fact, sourcing doesn't get more local than the fish landed just a few steps away, which turns up on the plate in dishes suchs as exemplary haddock in Adnams beer batter with crisp golden

10 top experiences

▶ Take a punt on the **River Cam** and see the **Mathematical Bridge,** page 90

▶ Stroll along **Britannia Pier** in **Great Yarmouth** and experience the wind in your hair, page 145

▶ Enjoy the tranquillity and wildlife of the **Norfolk Broads,** page 203

▶ Let your imagination take you back to Anglo-Saxon times at **Sutton Hoo,** page 262

▶ See seals bobbing in the waters off **Blakeney Point,** page 62

▶ Wonder at **Ely Cathedral,** rising like a massive ship from the flat landscape of the Fens, page 126

▶ Pass under the magnificent gatehouse and stroll around **Abbey Gardens** in Bury St Edmunds, page 77

▶ See a Norfolk windmill – one of the prettiest is **Bircham Windmill** with its massive white sails, page 138

▶ The sunset from **Hunstanton beach,** page 162

▶ Follow in the footsteps of royalty at **Sandringham House,** page 236

chips and chunky tartare sauce. The sparkling-white building revels in a fresh contemporary look inside, done out in cheery colours that let you know you're at the seaside.

▶ **PLACES NEARBY**

Thorpeness is a five-minute drive along the coast and is a lovely place in which to unwind (see page 271), while Orford lies to the south of Aldeburgh and is an important wildlife area (see page 228). The Minsmere RSPB Nature Reserve is close by (see page 238), and the small village of Leiston – where you can visit the Long Shop Museum and abbey ruins – is a short drive inland. No visit to Aldeburgh would be complete without a visit to the Snape Maltings, home of the Aldeburgh Music Festival. For refreshments, try the Parrot and Punchbowl Inn in Aldringham or the Crown Inn in Snape.

Leiston Abbey

english-heritage.org.uk
Leiston, IP16 4TD | 0370 333 1181
Open at any reasonable time
For hundreds of years this mostly 14th-century abbey – originally founded in 1182 by Henry II's chief justiciar, Ranulf de Glanville – was used as a farm and its church became a barn. A Georgian house, now used as a school for young musicians, was built into its fabric and remains of the choir, the church transepts and parts of the cloisters still stand.

Long Shop Museum

longshopmuseum.co.uk
Main Street, Leiston, IP16 4ES
01728 832189 | Open Apr–May, Oct
Tue–Sat 10–5, Sun 11–3, Jun–Sep
Mon–Sat 10–5, Sun 11–3
Discover the magic of steam
with a visit to the world-famous
traction engine manufacturers,
Richard Garrett Engineering.
See the traction engines and
road rollers in the very place
that they were built. Soak up
the atmosphere of the Long
Shop, built in 1852 as one of the
world's first production line
engineering halls. This is an
award-winning museum with
five exhibition halls full of items
from the glorious age of steam,
covering 200 years of local,
social and industrial history. It
is very family-friendly and the
talks are fascinating.

Snape Maltings

snapemaltings.co.uk
Snape, Aldeburgh, IP17 1SP
01728 688303 | Open Mon–Sat
10–5.30, Sun 10.30–4.30
The former 19th-century
maltings complex at nearby
Snape has been turned into one
of the country's leading music
venues and a smart shopping
outlet. Here you can buy
upmarket goodies, and take a
break in the tea room or the
pub. The concert hall is housed
in a converted red-brick
warehouse and hosts a regular
programme of classical, jazz
and folk concerts, featuring the
world's finest musicians. Here,
too, the famous Aldeburgh
Music Festival, founded by
Britten and Pears in 1948,
takes place every June. The
complex stands amid reeds
and marshes on the outskirts
of Aldeburgh.

**The Parrot and Punchbowl
Inn and Restaurant**

aldringhamparrot.com
Aldringham Lane, Aldringham,
IP16 4PY | 01728 830221
If you thought bizarre pub
names were a late 20th-century
fad, think again. Originally
called The Case is Altered, this
16th-century white-washed
smugglers' inn became The
Parrot and Punchbowl in
1604 when Aldringham was
a centre for smuggled
contraband. East Anglian-
brewed ales from Adnams and
Woodforde's, and Suffolk's
Aspall cider all feature in the
bar line-up. The good-value
menu includes daily specials
and vegetarian meals. There
are hearty roasts with all the
trimmings on Sundays.

The Crown Inn

snape-crown.co.uk
Bridge Road, Snape, IP17 1SL
01728 688324
Getting on for 600 years old and
once the haunt of smugglers
using the nearby River Alde,
this village stalwart shelters
beneath a most extraordinary
saltbox pantile roof. Inside, the
public area threads beneath
vast old beams and across
mellow brick floors to cosy
corners and an inglenook
enclosed by the arms of a huge
double settle. Both pre- and

post-concert meals are available for those going to Snape Maltings (when booking is advisable). The Crown's owners run their own livestock smallholding behind the pub, ensuring a very local supply chain, enhanced by locally sourced Limousin beef, Orford seafood and game from nearby shoots. Menus change frequently, but catch of the day or their own rare-breed pork sausages may feature.

▶ Baconsthorpe   MAP REF 294 B2

Baconsthorpe is a sleepy village that lies just a few miles from Holt and the coastal town of Sheringham in one of Norfolk's wildest and most remote spots. Here, huge skies and an ever-changing landscape provide interest for its 250 or so inhabitants. The village is perhaps best known for the remains of its once magnificent 15th-century castle, now owned by English Heritage. It once formed part of fortified quadrangle-style manor house built by Sir John Heydon, a wealthy landowner and political ally of William de la Pole, the first Duke of Suffolk, during the Wars of the Roses (1455–85). In the village, the medieval church of St Mary contains a magnificent 16th-century glass window and artefacts dating back six centuries.

TAKE IN SOME HISTORY
Baconsthorpe Castle
english-heritage.org.uk
NR25 6LN | 0370 333 1181
Open at any reasonable time during daylight hours

Baconsthorpe Castle was the home of wealthy Sir John Heydon, who had it built around the 1460s to protect himself and his family during the Wars of the Roses. He was a supporter of the first Duke of Suffolk, but is said to have changed his allegiance a few times for his own gain, thus upsetting a number of influential people. The exact date when work started on the castle is not known, since Sir John did not apply for the statutory royal licence necessary to construct a fortified house. He built the house anyway, to a quadrangle design with towers and a collection of buildings around an inner courtyard, with the fortification added later. A three-storey gatehouse was built as a focal point in the middle of the south wall, and an outer gatehouse had a drawbridge over which visitors could cross the moat. It was a lavish home, built to display the family's status. In the 1560s, Sir John's grandson added the outer gatehouse, which was inhabited until the 1920s, when one of the turrets fell down.

Visiting the site today, you can see many of the walls and the gatehouses, which remain in fairly good condition and give an insight into how grand this house once was. The red-brick and knapped-flint remains are reflected in the lake, which still partly embraces the castle as a moat, offering a dramatic view and a great photo op.

▶ **PLACES NEARBY**
Be sure to visit Holt (see page 155) and Sheringham (see page 239), two of the prettiest places in the Norfolk coastal region, and the Blakeney National Nature Reserve for great views (see page 62).

▶ Banham MAP REF 290 B1

Banham lies in the southernmost regions of Norfolk, not far from Diss (see page 117), in an area rich in forest and agricultural countryside. This historic, yet modern, town with plenty of amenities such as shops and schools, revolves round its parish church of St Mary the Virgin. An impressive Grade I listed building made of Norfolk flint, its construction began in the early part of the 14th century, but it took many decades for it to be completed because a huge number of local masons died in the Black Death of 1349 and a shortage of the craftsmanship and skills needed ensued. Banham is also the home of Banham Zoo, which you'll find has everything for a great day out from tigers and leopards, zebras and horses to an adventure playground and restaurants.

ENTERTAIN THE FAMILY
Banham Zoo
banhamzoo.co.uk
Kenninghall Road, NR16 2HE
01953 887771 | Open Jan–Mar, Nov–Dec daily 9.30–4, Apr–mid-Jul, mid-Sep–Oct 9.30–5, mid-Jul to mid-Sep 9.30–6

Set in 50 acres of magnificent parkland and gardens complete with winding pathways, rest areas and lakes, Banham Zoo is one of the best in the region. You can see hundreds of animals ranging from big cats, such as cheetahs, ocelots and the gorgeous snow leopard, to birds of prey; and from giraffes, zebras and red kangaroos to shire horses, snakes and monkeys. Tiger Territory is a purpose-built enclosure for Siberian tigers, including a rock pool and woodland setting; you can also visit Lemur Island and Tamarin and Marmoset Islands, or take the woodland walk to see the flamingoes. The Farm Barn, with its domestic animals, is popular with children, as is the adventure play area, though the skytrek – aerial trekking on zipwires – is not for the faint-hearted. The zoo has restaurants, baby-changing facilities, locker hire, a Natural World art gallery, activities, an education centre and a souvenir shop to complete your day out.

▶ Bawburgh MAP REF 294 C4

Bawburgh, a few miles outside Norwich in Norfolk, is associated with St Walstan who, legend has it, was responsible for many miracles. A special day of celebration is held every year at the village's Church of St Mary and St Walstan, on the nearest Sunday to 30 May, the day he died.

As the story goes, St Walstan was a charitable man who is said to have given his belongings to those less fortunate than himself. He dedicated his life to farming and livestock, and his knowledge became legendary. When he died in 1016 he was brought to Bawburgh from the village of Taverham, where he worked, on a cart pulled by two white oxen. Along the route, springs bubbled up to provide water for the animals. Walstan's shrine at Bawburgh's church became a place of pilgrimage for farmers. Throughout medieval times the cult grew and extended to counties beyond Norfolk, and eventually he was declared a patron saint of farmers and husbandry.

The church of St Mary and St Walstan, a Grade I listed building, is unusual in having a round tower.

Bawburgh's other claim to fame is a mill in the centre of the village that was formerly managed by Jeremy Colman, the creator of Colman's mustard, famously made in Norwich.

PLAY A ROUND
Bawburgh Golf Club
bawburgh.com
Glen Lodge, Marlingford Road,
NR9 3LU | 01603 740404
Open daily all year
A challenging 18-hole course with its mixture of parkland and heathland, Bawburgh Golf Club's main feature is a large hollow that meanders down to the River Yare, creating many interesting tee and green locations.

EAT AND DRINK
The Kings Head
Bawburgh ◉◉
kingshead-bawburgh.co.uk
Harts Lane, NR9 3LS
01603 744977
Old English roses and lavender fragrance the lanes in front of this low, rambling 17th-century inn, set in the cosy village of flint and brick cottages beside the River Yare. Leather sofas and a vaguely rustic mix of furnishings add to the charm that attracts customers keen to sample the enticing menu of pub favourites and something that little bit special. The busy kitchen team relies on East Anglian suppliers for virtually all the ingredients. There's plenty of seafood on the à la carte menu, which changes every month; and vegetarian and gluten-free options, plus a daily-changing specials boards, add to the choices. The pub offers an extensive range of local real ales, lagers and a good selection of European and New World wines.

▶ Beccles MAP REF 295 E6

As you stand in the centre of Beccles it's hard to believe that this historic – it was given its charter by Elizabeth I in 1584 – yet modern community-minded market town was once a thriving Saxon port. That's because it now lies some 6 miles from the sea. Beccles was at one time on the coast and all that could be seen looking east was water. In time, land was reclaimed and wherries plied up and down the waterways.

Beccles lies in the Waverley Valley at the southernmost extremity of the Norfolk Broads, although the town itself is rooted across the county border in Suffolk. The name Beccles is a combination of 'beck', a Scandinavian word meaning stream, and 'leas', meaning meadow. In fact, that's what medieval Beccles must have been for many years – largely a beautiful meadow by a stream.

The attractive parish church, St Michael's, has a 97-foot bell tower, which dates from the 16th century and is Perpendicular Gothic in style. Interestingly, it is not actually attached to the church building, but stands independently. Locals have dubbed it Beccles Bell Tower, and whenever you're arranging to see someone in town, you will almost always set the meeting place as the tower. The church tower has clock faces on only three sides; according to legend, the side facing Norfolk is blank because the inhabitants of Beccles did not want to give the time to their neighbours for free.

Horatio Nelson's mother, Catherine Suckling (1725–67), married his father, the Reverend Edmund Nelson, curate of Beccles, at St Michael's church in May 1749. Horatio was born in Burnham Thorpe, Norfolk, the sixth of 11 children, in 1758 and is best known for his naval career that ended with his death at the Battle of Trafalgar in 1805. Suffolk poet and doctor George Crabbe (1754–1832) was also married in St Michael's, in the 18th century.

PLAY A ROUND

Beccles Golf Club
becclesgolfclub.co.uk
Common Lane, NR34 9BX
01502 712244 | Open all year
8am–dusk, Sat members only
Beccles' heathland course was founded in 1899 and welcomes visitors. A nine-hole course with fast greens, it has gorse bushes, but no water hazards or bunkers to hinder you.

▶ PLACES NEARBY

Two exotic surprises lie within a 20-minute drive towards the coast: a garden and a wildlife park, both well worth a detour.

Henstead Exotic Garden
hensteadexoticgarden.co.uk
Church Road, Henstead, NR34 7LD
07715 876606 | Open Jun–Sep
Wed 2–5 plus some Sun in Jul, Aug and Sep

The Henstead Exotic Garden really lives up to its name. For years, Andrew Brogan's 400-year-old cottage had been sheltered by a 10-foot yew hedge on one side and dense ancient woodland on the other, so when he moved here in 2000 a microclimate was already established. Andrew wanted to create an exotic garden in which all the plants – with the sole exception of a red ensete banana – would be left outside to survive the fierce East Anglian winters. As much as 50 tons of rocks, stones and hardcore were needed to create the foundation of the garden and the volume of plants he has established since then is impressive: 10 large tree ferns,

Dicksonia antarctica, which grow 12 inches every 10 years, 15 large bananas, 50 large palms, including six different types, all growing in the ground unprotected, over 100 bamboos and countless yuccas, puyas and ferns that cover tiers of rocks, low stone walls and curved paths.

The garden now extends into part of the adjoining ancient woodland, which is full of huge oak, yew and holly trees. Three large ponds, one stocked with koi carp and golden orfe, attract dragonflies. Pheasants strut around the garden as if it were their own.

Africa Alive!
see highlight panel opposite

▶ **Blakeney** MAP REF 294 A1

Blakeney is one of the many brick-and-flint villages that line the North Norfolk coast in an Area of Outstanding Natural Beauty. It is an important area for birds and wildlife, especially around the harbour, known as Blakeney Haven, and Blakeney Point, a strip of shingle where grey and common seals can often be seen bobbing in the waters.

The town was mentioned in the Domesday Book of 1086. At that time it was a small harbour, but from early medieval times through to relatively recently it has been a prosperous port, trading in grain and fish, and later in gold and silver. Sadly, like so many ports in the region, it went into decline when its sea channels began to silt up. Only small boats can now navigate the waters from the quayside out past Blakeney Point. While merchants decried the slow accumulation of salt marsh and sand bars over the decades, birds began to flock here in their thousands – so much so that by Victorian times Blakeney had become known as the place to go shooting.

Today, Blakeney's harbour and the surrounding marshes from Cley Beach to the tip of the sand and shingle peninsula of Blakeney Point are owned by the National Trust; it was one of the first nature reserves to be safeguarded in Britain.

▶ Africa Alive! MAP REF 291 F1

africa-alive.co.uk

Whites Lane, Kessingland, NR33 7TF | 01502 740291

Open daily from 9.30. Check website for seasonal opening hours

Set in 100 acres of dramatic parkland in Kessingland, a few miles from Beccles towards the coast, Africa Alive! is one of Suffolk's most exotic wildlife parks. Here you can explore the sights and sounds of Africa, see giraffes, rhinos, cheetah and hyenas, and get a bird's-eye view of the lion enclosure. Animal experiences, bookable on the day, include Meet the Meerkats and a Plains of Africa safari guided by one of the senior animal keepers.

▲ Blakeney harbour

Among the bird species found here, including some that are
vulnerable and rare, are Pallas' warbler, yellow-breasted
bunting, subalpine warbler and red-spotted bluethroat. Various
companies run boat trips from Morston Quay to see the birds
and spot seals, which usually bask on the sandbanks at
Blakeney Point. If you enjoy walking, the Norfolk Coastal Path,
from Hunstanton (see page 162) to Cromer (see page 103),
runs along Blakeney's quayside. A bright summer day will
show you glittering streams, grasses waving gently in the
breeze and yachts bobbing in the distance, while a wet and
windy day in winter will reveal the stark beauty of this place,
with the distant roar of waves pounding the beach.

In the centre of the village, look out for the large Gothic-
style church of St Nicholas, with its two huge towers, the most
westerly of which has mighty flint buttresses. The towers are
landmarks; the smaller one is lit at night and has long been
used as a beacon to guide boats past the Point to the harbour.

SEE A LOCAL CHURCH
St Nicholas' Church

A landmark Grade I listed church and one that has especially interesting architectural features, St Nicholas can trace its origins back to the 13th century when it was built at around the same time as Blakeney friary. The earliest part of this church is its deep, two-bay chancel, which dates from the period, while its 100-foot-long nave and its west and east towers are 15th century.

Take a look inside: it has the most beautiful hammerbeam rib-vaulted roof. There are only a handful of other churches with a roof built to this style, and few that look quite so dramatic. There's a seven-light window too, which is rare, and on the walls you can make out pre-Reformation graffiti that would have been done by the hand of merchants. The east tower is lit up at night and has an almost ghostly presence. It's very dramatic.

GET OUTDOORS
Blakeney National Nature Reserve

nationaltrust.org.uk/blakeney
Morston Quay, Quay Road,
NR25 7BH | 01263 740241
Open daily dawn–dusk

Join the many walkers who flock to the Blakeney National Nature Reserve to enjoy the exercise, the peacefulness and the sweeping, uninterrupted views of the unspoilt coastline with its changing tides and abundance of coastal plants and wildlife. If you're lucky you may see Arctic terns, skylarks, redshanks, oystercatchers and the thriving colonies of seals.

EAT AND DRINK
The Blakeney Hotel ®

blakeneyhotel.co.uk
The Quay, NR25 7NE
01263 740797

Those who like to be by the sea need look no further: this hotel is in a perfect spot on the quay, with magnificent views over the estuary to Blakeney Point. Well-sourced raw materials underpin the operation, while a sure-footed handling of ingredients gives dishes layers of flavours.

The White Horse Blakeney
adnams.co.uk
4 High Street, NR25 7AL
01263 740574

Since the 17th century, this former coaching inn has been tucked away among Blakeney's flint-built fishermen's cottages, a short, steepish amble up from the small tidal harbour. The tastefully appointed, Adnams-stocked bar is stylish yet informal, the conservatory is naturally bright – both are eating areas, where the same menu and daily specials apply. Locally sourced food is a given, especially the lobster, crab and mussels from village fishermen, meats and game from Norfolk estates, soft fruit, salads, asparagus and free-range eggs from local smallholders, while rod- and line-caught mackerel and sea bass find their way into the kitchen in summer. For lunch, there's a more casual menu with filled bagels, baguettes and pie of the day, and more formal fare in the evening.

The Kings Arms
blakeneykingsarms.co.uk
Westgate Street, NR25 7NQ
01263 740341

Tucked away in a popular fishing village close to North Norfolk's coastal path (Peddars Way), this thriving free house is the perfect refreshment stop following an invigorating walk, time spent birdwatching, or a boat trip to the nearby seal colony. Open all day and run by the same family for almost 40 years, it serves an excellent selection of real ales, including Norfolk-brewed Woodforde's Wherry, backed by menus featuring locally caught fish and seasonal seafood.

Morston Hall ⊛⊛⊛⊛
morstonhall.com
Morston, NR25 7AA
01263 741041

Morston stands on the A149 coastal road across alluring North Norfolk. It's a handsome enough house, dating back to the Jacobean period, with generous glassed-in spaces at the front to take advantage of the maritime vistas. The place is run with warmth and easygoing charm, and a considerateness that extends to plenty of room between tables in the dining areas, from the main restaurant to the orangery and conservatory. Dinner is a fixed tasting menu of seven courses, from soup to cheese. The wine choices to go with these dishes bear all the hallmarks of thoughtful selection based on testing and tasting. Afternoon tea is served in summer in the sun lounge or walled garden, in winter indoors by a log fire.

▶ **Blickling**
see **Cromer**, page 108

▶ **Blythburgh** MAP REF 291 E2

Blythburgh lies on the Suffolk coast in an Area of Outstanding
Natural Beauty. An old Saxon town, it is quiet and peaceful,
and surrounded by a tidal river, marshes, heathland, small
woodlands, pastures and arable fields. The tidal section of the
River Blyth flows just to the north of the village, reaching the
sea at Southwold. Over the years, the sea walls have been
breached and the land not reclaimed, creating a tidal lagoon,
Blythburgh Water, which is immensely popular with coastal

▼ River Blyth, Blythburgh

birdlife as a safe habitat. The town is probably best known for the goings-on at its cathedral-like 15th-century church – which is often used as a venue for the Aldeburgh Festival (see page 52) – and for being the birthplace of actor Ralph Fiennes.

SEE A LOCAL CHURCH
Holy Trinity Church
holytrinityblythburgh.org.uk
Church Lane, IP19 9LL

Holy Trinity Church in Blythburgh has a mixed history. Famously, it was hit by a bolt of lightning in August 1577, bringing its steeple crashing to the ground. The devil was blamed for this deed. On the same day, the legendary devil-dog of the marshes, Black Shuck, is said to have run through the church, killing two parishioners. The damage to the roof meant that for a time congregations had to worship beneath umbrellas.

On a happier note, the church is sometimes referred to by locals as the Cathedral of the Marshes, lending credence to the claim that Blythburgh was once much larger than it is today. But even though Blythburgh has always been small, it attracted sufficient wealthy piety to build a large church. It also had an important Augustinian priory founded here in 1130, which probably accounts for the size and splendour of the church.

In 1412, Henry IV granted permission for the church to be rebuilt, transforming it into one of Suffolk's finest Perpendicular churches. The tower remains from the earlier building. The exterior is an amazing mix of flint and glass, with intricate decorative stonework and carving along the parapets of the porch and south aisle. Set into the east end are enigmatic carved letters.

If you step inside you'll see the aged wooden roof, still with its original faded paintwork, stretching the entire length of the church. On it are the 12 wooden angels celebrated in Blythburgh's town sign. There used to be more, and some of those that remain have had to be repaired or renewed.

One story tells that they were fired at by Puritans trying to dislodge them. Shot has been found in the roof timbers, but this probably dates from the 18th century, when people were paid to shoot at the jackdaws that inhabited the church.

In the chancel are stalls carved with figures of saints and the Apostles, which may have been part of the base of the rood screen. Each carries his own symbol so that he can be recognised. The figures are beautifully made and very sophisticated, with neatly combed beards and hair.

Look out for the clock jack, which rings to signal the start of services; it dates from 1682 and stands on a shelf near the altar.

▶ Brancaster   MAP REF 293 D1

Brancaster, together with the villages of Brancaster Staithe and Burnham Deepdale, form a community that hugs the North Norfolk coastline, on the edge of the protected Brancaster Manor salt marsh owned by the National Trust.

Each has stunning vistas over glorious tidal marshes to Scolt Head Island, a 4-mile-long sandbar that is home to a nature reserve rich in birdlife. The villages are peaceful and picturesque with lots of brick-and-flint cottages that give this area its distinct look.

Many of this region's unspoiled villages have imposing, often circular, church towers, such as St Mary's in Burnham Deepdale – one of six medieval churches found within two miles of each other.

The reason for the distinctive round towers, which are so common in Norfolk, was not, as is often stated, that they were a form of defence against invaders, but simply because the absence of any other workable building stone made local flint the best available material. This knobbly and uneven stone is usually hammered and split open to reveal its black interior, a process known as knapping. The demands of working with this stone meant that it was easier to build circular towers than masonry-faced square ones.

Brancaster is said to have been where Horatio Nelson (1758–1805), the famous admiral noted for his bravery in the Napoleonic wars of the 19th century, learned to sail as a boy. He was born in the nearby village of Burnham Thorpe. Local folklore says his nurse haunts the village's pub, The Ship.

ENTERTAIN THE FAMILY
Brancaster Estate
nationaltrust.org.uk/brancaster-estate
Brancaster Beach, PE31 8BW
0344 800 1895
Part of the National Trust's coastal estate, which includes Brancaster Staithe Harbour and the site of Branodunum, a third-century Roman fort, the four-mile-long golden sands of Brancaster beach are perfect for summer sandcastles and winter kite flying. Fun events and free activities are organised every Wednesday and Thursday throughout the school holidays.

PLAY A ROUND
Royal West Norfolk Golf Club
rwngc.org
PE31 8AX | 01485 210087
Open Sep–Jul Mon–Fri
A fine links laid out in grand manner characterised by sleepered greens, superb cross bunkers and salt marshes. The tranquil surroundings include a harbour, the sea, farmland and marshland, inhabited by many rare birds. Both the 8th and 9th holes are affected by the tide (check the tide table before play), and the clubhouse is inaccessible by car at high tide.

EAT AND DRINK
The Jolly Sailors
jollysailorsbrancaster.co.uk
Brancaster Staithe, PE31 8BJ
01485 210314

The focal point of the village, the 18th-century 'Jolly' is the brewery tap for the Brancaster microbrewery, both run by father-and-son team, Cliff and James Nye. In the Harbour Snug you can look out over the water, read local books, and play darts and board games. The Nyes' Brancaster ales aren't obligatory – you'll also find Woodforde's, 13 wines by the glass and 30 rums. Pub food is typified by open-fired pizzas, pie of the day, deep-fried whitebait and spiced veggie burger. The beach-themed ice cream hut in the garden is an attraction. A beer, real cider and music festival begins in mid-June.

The Ship Hotel
shiphotelnorfolk.co.uk
Main Road, Brancaster, PE31 8AP
01485 210333

Set in a prime coastal location close to Brancaster beach, TV chef and hotelier Chris Coubrough's stylish gastro-pub continues to attract walkers, beach lovers and families with its appealing menus of modern pub food prepared from fresh produce sourced from local farmers and fisherman. Wash your meal down with a pint of Bitter Old Bustard and relax in the bar and dining rooms,

which offer rug-strewn wood floors, wood-burning stoves, shelves full of books, scrubbed wooden tables and a distinct nautical feel.

The White Horse ●●
whitehorsebrancaster.co.uk
Main Road, Brancaster Staithe, PE31 8BY | 01485 210262

The White Horse offers stunning vistas over glorious tidal marshes across to Scolt Head Island, a 4-mile-long sandbar that's home to a nature reserve rich in birdlife. Reflecting the view, interior colours are muted and natural, with scrubbed pine tables and high-backed settles in the bar creating a welcoming atmosphere, while alfresco dining in the sunken front garden is a popular

▶ The coast at Brancaster

warm-weather option. While the bar menu lists grills, salads and sandwiches, the extensive, daily-changing menu in the airy conservatory restaurant champions the freshest local seafood, delivered directly to the kitchen door by the fishermen.

▶ **PLACES NEARBY**

Pop into The White Horse or The Jolly Sailors at Brancaster Staithe for a bite, and take in Scolt Head Island, Wells-next-the-Sea (see page 275) and the magnificent Holkham Estate (see page 152). In North Creake you can visit the ruins of Creake Abbey; and a few miles away are the RSPB Titchwell Marsh reserve and the old church of St Mary's in Burnham Deepdale.

10 top nature reserves

20 North Street Cafe/Bistro

20northstreet.co.uk
20 North Street, Burnham Market,
PE31 8HG | 01328 730330
Open Wed, Sun 12–4, Thu–Sat 12–4,
6–10.30

Behind its smart pebbled facade, this small bistro with its friendly atmosphere has quickly become so popular with locals that booking is essential. Inspired by Norfolk's bountiful produce, the weekly changing menu features British dishes with some European influences that reflect the background and experience of the classically trained chef.

Church of St Mary

Main Road, Burnham Deepdale,
PE31 8DD | Open daily

The highlights of this little church are the Saxon round tower, its collection of medieval stained glass and its stone Norman font. The font is a gem. Carved on three sides, each side has four panels representing the months of the year, each filled with a figure engaged in farming activities. Look for workers pruning a vine, weeding out thistles, scything hay, binding a sheaf of corn and filling a wine barrel. December shows a group of four men at a table feasting. In the porch, look for the delightful windows featuring the medieval faces of the sun and the moon in their top lights. The ancient window glass throughout the church has recently been restored, bringing its delicate colours and fascinating detail to vibrant life.

Creake Abbey

english-heritage.org.uk
North Creake, NR21 9LF
0370 333 1181 | Open at any
reasonable time in daylight hours

The ruins at North Creake once formed part of an Augustinian abbey founded here in 1206. They stand in 40 acres. The abbey was originally founded as a hospital by local landowners Sir Robert and Lady Alice de Nerford; it later became a priory. Henry III elevated the priory to an abbey. Today, the ruins, which are beautifully preserved – albeit smaller than they once were due to a massive fire in 1484 that saw much of the building collapse – provide a backdrop to a monthly farmers' market, and a food hall, cafe, craft workshops and studio complex.

Scolt Head Island

naturalengland.org.uk

This shingle and sand offshore barrier island between Brancaster and Wells-next-the-Sea (see page 275) is a nature reserve of national importance. The salt marshes are considered to be among the finest in Britain and hold some uncommon species of plant, including rare matted sea lavender and sea heath. Roughly 4 miles long, the island supports internationally important numbers of breeding terns, including common, arctic, sandwich and little terns, as well as shelduck, widgeon, teal, curlew and wintering wildfowl, especially pink-footed geese. A seasonal ferry operates between April and September from Burnham Overy Staithe.

RSPB Nature Reserve Titchwell Marsh
rspb.org.uk
PE31 8BB | 01485 210779
Open daily Mar–Oct 9.30–5, Nov–Feb 9.30–4
Titchwell Marsh is one of the RSPB's most popular reserves. Here, hundreds of thousands of migrating birds pass through in spring and autumn and many stay during winter, providing an opportunity to see various species of ducks, waders, seabirds and geese. If you are really lucky you may catch sight of the RSPB emblem, the avocet. The reserve, which lies on the coast, is a great day out for the entire family.

Titchwell Manor Hotel ⊛⊛⊛
titchwellmanor.com
Titchwell, Brancaster, PE31 8BB
01485 210221
The Snaith family created this elegant boutique hotel out of a Victorian farmhouse that enjoys unbroken views across the marshes to the North Sea. Dining fills two spaces; the pick of them a light conservatory room overlooking the walled garden. The menus merely list the principal ingredients, leaving you to discover what's been done with them when the plate turns up. A skill with novel combinations produces starters such as roasted quail with watermelon, while locally sourced meats and fish make up the main courses. With its light-giving terrace and bold decor, the more informal Eating Rooms offers an array of tapas and traditional dishes simply presented, as well as the restaurant menus that span classic favourites and a seven-course taster menu.

▶ Bressingham
see **Diss**, page 118 see **Diss**, page 118

▶ Bungay MAP REF 295 D6
The small market town of Bungay occupies a hilltop location surrounded by marshes and the valley of the River Waveney, which means you'll get fabulous views from here across the Suffolk countryside towards the sea. The Anglo-Saxons and Romans identified it as an excellent spot from which to defend their territories, and the Normans went a step further and built a castle. You can visit Bungay Castle (see page 74), which was built in 1165 and dominates the centre of the town. It is the focus for Bungay Festival, held in July.

TAKE IN SOME HISTORY
Bungay Castle
bungay-suffolk.co.uk
6 Cross Street, NR35 1AU
01986 896485 | Open Mon–Sat
9.30–5, also Apr–Oct Sun 10–4
A Norman castle with a large square keep added in 1165 and gate towers and curtain walls erected in 1294, Bungay was constructed by the powerful Bigod family, whose members had a habit of falling out with the ruling kings. Learn about its history at Jesters, the castle's visitor centre.

VISIT A BREWERY
St Peter's Brewery
stpetersbrewery.co.uk
St Peter's Hall, St Peter South Elmham, NR35 1NQ | 01986 782322
Check website for opening times
Award-winning craft beers and traditional ales are brewed, using locally malted barley and Kentish hops, in former agricultural buildings next to the medieval, moated St Peter's Hall. The hall now houses a restaurant serving lunches and afternoon teas. Tours of the brewery take place on weekends from Easter to end-Dec.

PLAY A ROUND
Bungay and Waveney Valley Golf Club
club-noticeboard.co.uk
Outney Common, NR35 1DS
01986 892337 | Open daily all year
The heathland course of this golf club, which was founded in 1899, is lined with fir trees and gorse, and has excellent greens all year round, with easy walking.

▶ PLACES NEARBY
In the nearby village of Flixton, the Norfolk and Suffolk Aviation Museum is well worth a visit to see its remarkable collection of aircraft and war memorabilia. A little further afield, the Halesworth Airfield Museum offers a smaller collection.

Halesworth Airfield Museum
halesworthairfieldmuseum.co.uk
Sparrowhawk Way, Upper Holton
Halesworth IP19 8NH | 01986 875084 | Open Apr–Oct Sun, bank holidays 2–5
This interesting museum has at its heart a collection of memorabilia dedicated to the period it served as an airfield during World War II.

Norfolk and Suffolk Aviation Museum
aviationmuseum.net
The Street, Flixton, NR35 1NZ
01986 896644 | Open Apr–Oct Sun–Thu 10–5, Nov–Mar Tue–Wed, Sun 10–4
Situated in the Waveney valley, East Anglia's Aviation Heritage Centre contains collections from, among others, the 446th Bombardment Group USAAF, RAF Bomber Command and the Royal Observer Corps. It houses over 60 historic aircraft. A section is dedicated to the RAF Air Sea Rescue and Coastal Command. Among the displays are Decoy Sites and Wartime Deception, and Fallen Eagles – Wartime Luftwaffe Crashes. A former Ipswich Airport hangar made by Norwich company Boulton and Paul is a feature.

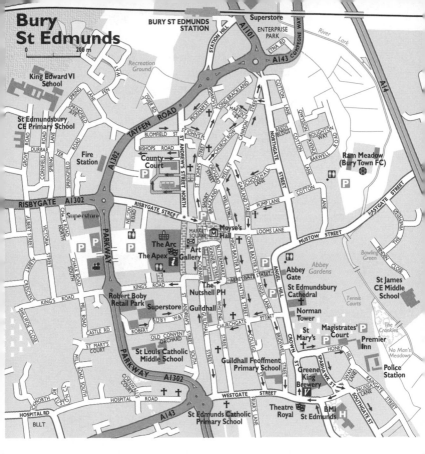

▶ Bury St Edmunds MAP REF 289 E3

Bury St Edmunds is one of Suffolk's most prominent, elegant
and imposing towns. It has a long and prosperous history
dating back way before Saxon times when it was a royal town.
Sigebert, the Saxon King of the Angles (East Anglia), and later
a saint, lived here for a time, and founded a monastery in 633.
The town grew in stature, and remains significant to this day.

The town takes its name from Edmund, also King of East
Anglia from around 855 until 869. It is said he loved the town
and was a popular king, but few documents relating to his reign
remain since the Vikings destroyed much of the region,
including the churches where important documents were kept.

When Edmund died, an abbey was built in his honour,
housing his tomb, and became a place of pilgrimage. Miracles
were attributed to him and he became patron saint of England
in the Middle Ages. The abbey, along with the town, grew to
become one of the most powerful and wealthiest in Europe.

Take a stroll around Bury, as it's affectionately known. The
centre is quite compact, although a little steep in places. You'll
be able to see the remains of the abbey and its magnificent

gatehouse, its cathedral and leafy streets lined with the most beautiful Norman flint, Elizabethan timber-framed, elegant Georgian brick and Victorian Bath stone houses.

There are several museums for you to visit, including Moyse's Hall Museum, glorious gardens that are ablaze with colour all year round, and walks alongside the River Lark. Look out, too, for St Mary's Church, the burial place of Mary Tudor, Queen of France and the younger sister of Henry VIII. Just beyond the church is the Norman Tower, part of the original abbey and now the bell tower for St Edmundsbury Cathedral.

▼ Abbey Gardens and St Edmundsbury Cathedral

▲ Inside the Cathedral

TAKE IN SOME HISTORY
St Edmundsbury Cathedral
stedscathedral.co.uk
Abbey House, Angel Hill, IP33 1LS
01284 748720 | Open daily 8.30–6;
guided tours May–Sep Mon–Sat at 11
St Edmundsbury Cathedral
began life as the parish church
of St James and was upgraded
when the diocese of St
Edmundsbury and Ipswich was
created in 1914. A popular
setting for concerts, it is a
major venue for the Bury St
Edmunds Festival in May.

VISIT THE MUSEUM
Moyse's Hall Museum
moyseshall.org
Cornhill, IP33 1DX | 01284 706183
Open Mon–Sat 10–5 (last entry at
4), Sun 12–4
Moyse's Hall is a 12th-century
Norman house built of flint and
stone which now serves as a
local history museum. Among
the fascinating exhibits are
memorabilia of the Murder in
the Red Barn, an infamous
crime of 1827 that took place
in nearby Polstead. Other
collections include the history
of Bury St Edmunds, the Suffolk
Regiment, fine art, toys, clocks
and timepieces.

GO ROUND THE GARDENS
Abbey Gardens
westsuffolk.gov.uk
Mustow Street, IP33 1XL
01284 757490 | Open Mon–Sat
7.30–dusk, Sun 9–dusk
You'll enter the gardens
through the magnificent
gatehouse of the abbey
dedicated to St Edmund. There
are herb and sensory gardens
to explore, a rose garden, a
children's play area and a
delightful riverside walk.

10 top cathedrals and churches

CATCH A PERFORMANCE
Theatre Royal
theatreroyal.org
Westgate Street, IP33 1QR
01284 769505 | Open daily
The Theatre Royal, which dates from 1819, is owned by the National Trust and is the only surviving Regency playhouse in Britain. It's still in daily use and you can catch a theatrical experience here most evenings. Hour-long guided tours of the theatre take place between February and July, and there are regular 'Self Explore' sessions held on weekdays. All are dependent on rehearsal schedules, so do check before your visit.

SEE A LOCAL CHURCH
Church of St Mary
wearechurch.net
Honey Hill, IP33 1RT
01284 754680 | Open Mon–Sat 10–4 (10–3 in winter)
Mary Tudor (1496–1533), the younger sister of Henry VIII and grandmother of Lady Jane Grey, was reburied in St Mary's after being moved from Bury St Edmunds abbey when her brother announced the Dissolution of the Monasteries. You might think the church is named after her, which is a popular misconception. In fact, it refers to the Virgin Mary. The church dates from the 12th to the 16th centuries, and has one of the finest hammerbeam angel roofs in the country.

PLAY A ROUND
All Saints
allsaintshotel.com
Fornham St Genevieve, IP28 6JQ | 01284 706777
Open daily all year
Here you can stay in style, play the pretty 18-hole parkland course with the River Lark running through it and take advantage of the gym and spa treatments.

Bury St Edmunds Golf Club
burystedmundsgolfclub.co.uk
Tut Hill, IP28 6LG | 01284 755979
Open daily all year
The nine-hole pay-and-play undulating course has some challenging holes. It consists of five par 3s and four par 4s with modern-construction greens.

EAT AND DRINK

The Angel Hotel ◉◉

theangel.co.uk
Angel Hill, IP33 1LT
01284 714000

With a prime position overlooking the cathedral and the old abbey walls, The Angel is a quintessential Georgian coaching inn. Its brickwork facade is suitably curtained with creepers, while the inside has a contemporary boutique look, especially in The Eaterie, with its pale wood tables, high-backed chairs and statement chandelier. The kitchen reveals equally 21st-century sensibilities in its repertoire of Mediterranean-influenced brasserie food, using top-notch local produce.

The Bannatyne Spa ◉

bannatyne.co.uk
Horringer Court, Horringer Road, IP29 5PH | 01284 705550

Health and fitness are top of the agenda at this impressive neo-Jacobean mansion in a parkland setting, with its spa, swimming pool and gym. So there's no excuse for not shedding the calories gained in the restaurant, where menus steer a broadly European course. Main courses are a mixed bag, taking in burger with fries as well as the healthier options such as steamed fish.

The Nutshell

thenutshellpub.co.uk
17 The Traverse, IP33 1BJ
01284 764867

Measuring just 15 feet by 7 feet, this unique pub has been confirmed as Britain's smallest by Guinness World Records; yet somehow more than 100 people and a dog managed to fit inside in the 1980s. It has certainly become a tourist attraction and there's lots to talk about while you enjoy a drink – such as the mummified cat and the bar ceiling, which is covered with paper money. No food is available, though the pub jokes about its dining area for parties of two or fewer.

The Old Cannon Brewery

oldcannonbrewery.co.uk
86 Cannon Street, IP33 1JR
01284 768769

Brewing started at this Victorian pub over 160 years ago. Today it's brewing still, the only independent brewpub in Suffolk where you can see beer being brewed on a regular basis. Indeed, dominating the bar are two giant stainless steel brewing vessels, fount of Old Cannon Best Bitter, Gunner's Daughter and seasonal and special occasion beers. The decor and furnishings are easy on the eye, with rich, earth-coloured walls, wooden floors and scrubbed tables. The 'Cannon Fodder' menu offers starters, light dishes and mains made from freshly prepared from local produce, and the daily-changing specials board offers at least three more options. Since the pub is tucked away in the back streets, follow the website directions carefully.

Pea Porridge ◉◉

peaporridge.co.uk

28–29 Cannon Street,

IP33 1JR | 01284 700200

Two cottages dating from 1820 have been converted into this refreshingly unpretentious restaurant of three rooms with wooden floors, pine tables, exposed brick, beams and a baker's oven (the premises used to be a bakery). Guests are greeted warmly and nothing is too much trouble for the friendly front-of-house staff. 'Simplicity' is the kitchen's buzzword, which denies the level of thought and expertise that goes into the cooking.

▶ PLACES NEARBY

Bury St Edmunds is in the heart of Suffolk and as such is within easy reach of some fabulous places of interest. You could visit Ickworth House in the village of Horringer and Wyken Hall, a wonderful medieval house standing in an estate that was occupied by the Romans. In nearby West Stow, you'll find an Anglo-Saxon village. If you fancy a game of golf, head for nearby Flempton Golf Club, or for a bite to eat try Theobalds in Ixworth, the White Horse in Whepstead, the Cadogan Arms in Ingham, the Leaping Hare in Stanton or the Plough in Rede.

Ickworth House

nationaltrust.org.uk/ickworth

The Rotunda, Horringer,

IP29 5QE | 01284 735270

Open Mar–Nov daily 11–5, parkland 9–5.30 or dusk if earlier

This beautifully elegant neoclassical country house is set in acres of parkland. Its unusual rotunda effortlessly dominates the landscape. Owned by the National Trust, the house gives you the chance to see restored rooms, including the servants' quarters. An exhibition hall above the rotunda contains priceless treasures collected over centuries by the succession of owners, which have included the Marquises of Bristol. The Georgian silver collection is considered the finest in private hands. The 1,800 acres of parkland, some landscaped in the 'Capability' Brown style, features Italianate and kitchen gardens, cycle trails, walking trails and a children's playground. Outdoor and indoor events are planned throughout the year – see website for details.

West Stow Anglo-Saxon Village

weststow.org

West Stow Country Park, Icklingham Road, West Stow, IP28 6HG

01284 728718 | Open daily 10–5

Located in the 125-acre West Stow Country Park with many trails and paths and children's play areas, this interesting centre on the site of an excavated Anglo-Saxon settlement makes a fine day out. The village is a reconstruction of the settlement, which dates from around AD 450–650. There are seven buildings on the site,

▲ West Stow Anglo-Saxon Village

including the Anglo-Saxon
Centre displaying some of the
finds, such as tools and pots,
unearthed here. The visitor
centre houses a west Suffolk
archaeology exhibition. A full
programme of special events
runs throughout the year.

Wyken Hall

wykenvineyards.co.uk
Wyken Road, Stanton, IP31 2DW
01359 250287 | Garden open
Easter–Sep Sun–Fri 2–6
Wyken Hall is a half-timbered
medieval manor house with
multiple gables, banks of
octagonal brick chimneys and

an almost indefinable roof line.
The garden is a plant-lover's
dream, its mood changing from
restrained to wild in areas that
blend seamlessly into the
surrounding meadows and
woodland of the Suffolk
countryside. Wyken Hall is also
famous for its wines, and a
woodland walk takes you to the
south-facing vineyard. It was
planted in 1988 and now
produces award-winning wines.

The house is private, but you
are free to wander around the
garden. You will see low,
clipped diamond-shaped box
hedges, sculptural topiary

pyramids and cubes, all planted as focal points. There are lawns and a rose garden planted with a collection of old-fashioned blooms. A lake offers a different environment again. Rocking chairs and benches are dotted around, allowing you to relax in this most perfumed and peaceful of gardens.

Flempton Golf Club

flemptongolfclub.co.uk
Flempton, IP28 6EQ
01284 728291 | Open daily all year
The course here has very little water but it's surrounded by woodland and Suffolk Wildlife Trust lakes.

Theobalds Restaurant ◉◉

theobaldsrestaurant.co.uk
68 High Street, Ixworth,
IP31 2HJ | 01359 231707
A Tudor inn in a village to the north of Bury St Edmunds, Theobalds has an abundance of uneven oak timbers, an inglenook fireplace and plain whitewashed walls. Simon Theobald is an assiduous country chef, seeking out the best of seasonal produce, so the menu changes monthly.

The White Horse ◉

whitehorsewhepstead.co.uk
Rede Road, Whepstead, IP29 4SS
01284 735760
Stylishly made over in recent years, this mustard yellow village inn now sits comfortably at the gastropub end of the spectrum, but without losing any of its charm. The large, copper-topped bar, open fire and comfortable wooden chairs make you feel instantly at home, while nostalgic touches like the Tuck Shop – which sells ice cream, sweets and chocolate – appeal to adults and children alike. The award-winning menus change on a daily basis. Quality seasonal ingredients are locally sourced where possible, and everything is made from scratch – even the sausages.

The Cadogan Arms ◉

thecadogan.co.uk
The Street, Ingham, IP31 1NG 01284 728443
A friendly and inviting pub with bedrooms for those who want to stay longer, the Cadogan is just 4 miles from the centre of Bury St Edmunds. The kitchen places an emphasis on seasonality and local produce; for something lighter there are grazing boards at both lunch and dinner (cheese, seafood, deli and puds). The pub has a large garden with a children's play area, perfect for alfresco dining.

The Leaping Hare Restaurant & Country Store ◉◉

wykenvineyards.co.uk
Wyken Vineyards, Stanton,
IP31 2DW | 01359 250287
The Leaping Hare occupies a splendid 400-year-old barn, with a high-beamed and raftered ceiling and polished wooden floor, on a 1,200-acre farm complete with a flock of Shetland sheep and Red Poll cattle, plus a vineyard. What the

farm doesn't provide is grown or farmed locally too, often within 5 miles, with fish landed at Lowestoft. The kitchen follows a straightforward route along classical lines, with a bias towards meat dishes.

The Plough
Rede, IP29 4BE | 01284 789208
Tucked away on the village green is this part-thatched, 16th-century pub, easily identified by an old plough and a weeping willow at the front. Long-standing landlord Brian Desborough's ever-changing blackboard menu offers interesting choices, while the bar serves Fuller's, Adnams, Ringwood and Sharp's ales and a choice of 10 wines by the glass. At 420 feet above sea level, Great Wood Hill near Rede is actually Suffolk's highest point (and a good place for walking) – a fact verified by Guinness World Records.

▶ Caister-on-Sea MAP REF 295 F4
One of Norfolk's most popular seaside destinations, located just up the road from Great Yarmouth, Caister-on-Sea is lively yet refined. Known simply as Caister by locals, it dates back to Roman origins and was a naval base from around AD 200 through to the end of the fourth century. There are Roman remains, now owned by English Heritage, if you fancy delving into the town's ancient past. Caister is also famous for its

▼ Caister Castle

lifeboat station – there's been one here since the 1790s and its crews have saved thousands of lives. The phrase 'never turn back' has been attributed to Caister's lifeboat crews following a thwarted rescue in dangerous seas in 1901. Caister is also home to Great Yarmouth's racecourse.

VISIT THE MUSEUM
Caister Castle Car Collection
caistercastle.co.uk
Castle Lane, NR30 5SN
01664 567707 | Open mid-May to
Sep Sun–Fri 10–4.30
The car enthusiasts in your family will be thrilled by the exhibits on show in this lovely museum housed in the moated 15th-century Caister Castle. The museum's display of rare vintage, classic and sports automobiles and motorcycles dates from the late 19th century to the 1990s and is the largest private collection in Britain. It includes the first real motor car in the world, the 1893 Panhard et Levassor. There is also the first Ford Fiesta off the production line and the Lotus belonging to British Formula One racing driver and world champion Jim Clark (1936–68). The castle itself was built in 1432 by English knight Sir John Fastolf (1378–1459) and is notable for being one of the earliest brick constructions in

▼ Thrigby Wildlife Gardens

the country. You can climb to the top of its 90-foot-high tower. The spectacular castle and countryside view is worth the effort.

GO BACK IN TIME
Caister Roman Fort
english-heritage.org.uk
0370 333 1181 | Open at any reasonable time in daylight hours
The Caister Roman Fort remains give a fascinating insight into the town's defence connections. Here, a Roman naval base stood for some 150 years or so until the Romans withdrew from Britain. Infantry and cavalry personnel would have been stationed here, as well as sailors. It occupied an island that has since been covered with silt, at a point where four rivers, including the Waveney and Yare, met. There would have been barracks, workshops and stables. Now managed by English Heritage, the partially excavated site includes the south gateway, a town wall built of flint with brick courses and part of what may have been a seamen's hostel.

GO TO THE RACES
Great Yarmouth Racecourse
greatyarmouth-racecourse.co.uk
Jellicoe Road, NR30 4AU
01493 842527
Located on the fringes of Caister towards Great Yarmouth, this racecourse holds flat-racing fixtures from late April to October. It's a left-handed, oblong course with races of up to a mile run on the straight. There is a full range of hospitality for race days. The complex is also used for a variety of events.

▶ **PLACES NEARBY**
Visit the remains of Burgh Castle (see page 148), a fort built by the Romans overlooking Breydon Water to the ever-cheerful and lively Great Yarmouth (see page 139). In nearby Filby you can see wildlife at the Thrigby Wildlife Gardens.

Thrigby Wildlife Gardens
thrigbyhall.co.uk
Thrigby Hall, Filby, NR29 3DR
01493 369477 | Open daily from 10 (closing times vary)
Located in the grounds of one of Norfolk's most attractive country houses, the 18th-century Thrigby Hall, this wildlife garden has tigers, primates and reptiles. There are hundreds of birds, from cockatoos and owls to wetland species; there is even a red panda. There are tropical bird houses, a unique blue willow-pattern garden and tree walk, and a summer house as old as the park. The enormous jungle swamp hall has special features such as underwater viewing of large crocodiles. The garden has an animal and tree adoption scheme, with all money going to its Thrigby Conservation Fund, which supports leading environmental projects around the world.

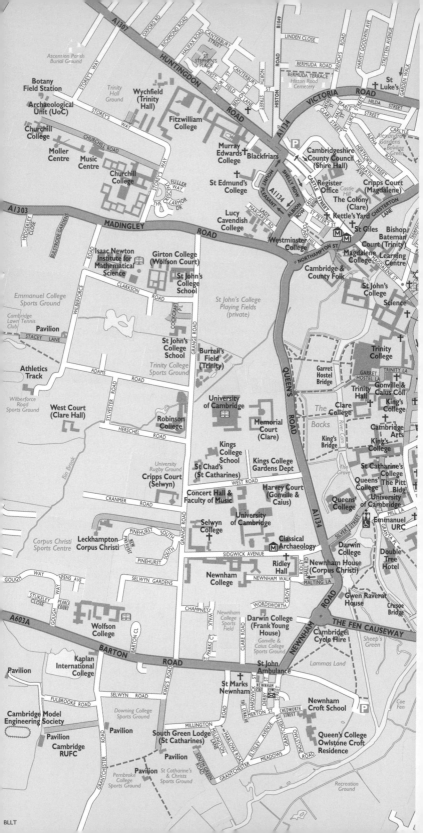

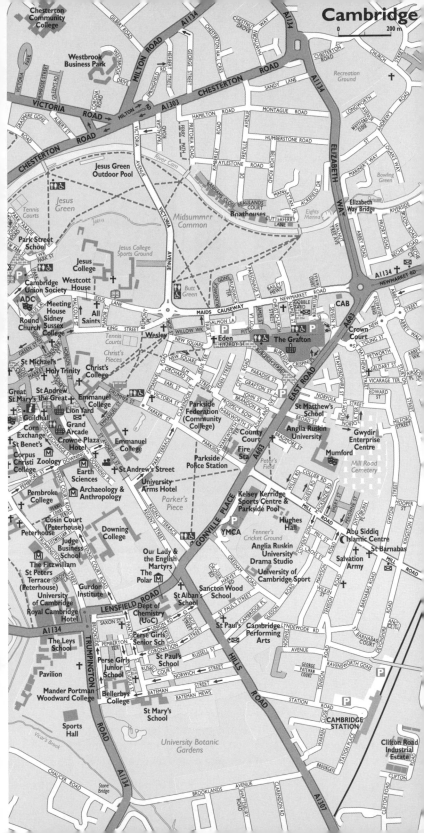

Cambridge

0   200 m

▶ Cambridge MAP REF 288 A4

You could be forgiven for feeling overwhelmed by Cambridge.
With its hauntingly beautiful Gothic architecture displayed in
grand style on the facades of most of its colleges and chapels,
its vast open areas, fabulous shopping and cafes, its energetic
arts scene and busy streets that will leave you breathless,
Cambridge is a pulsating fusion of the traditional and the
contemporary. It has played a major role in English history
and world academia since before the Roman Empire, when a
humble farmstead occupied the site of Fitzwilliam College.

A prosperous and influential market town occupying an
elevated location – something of a curiosity in the famously
flat fenlands of Cambridgeshire – the city was one of the first
in England to be granted a town charter, while the University
of Cambridge and its illustrious alumni have pioneered
advances in the fields of medicine, astronomy, architecture,
the arts and sciences.

Yet Cambridge, a pretty place with the River Cam snaking
its way through the city centre, manages to retain a feeling
of peaceful friendliness. You'll be sure to find this comforting
if it's your first visit and even just a little bit bizarre, given the
city's huge importance.

▲ Left to right: King's College; the River Cam; Christ's College gates

It's easy to explore the city centre on foot or bicycle. Hours spent slowly browsing in its cobbled streets and passageways could be one of the most relaxing experiences of your holiday. It's a great way to see the city's amazing architecture up close. Some of the university buildings were the work of the famous 18th-century architect Sir Christopher Wren, whose other great claim to fame is St Paul's Cathedral in London.

Another good way of seeing Cambridge is to join walkers and joggers along the banks of the River Cam, an area affectionately known as the Backs. Early morning is a lovely time of day to be here. A thin mist often blankets the area, lending the river and the back of the college buildings an eerie half-light, until the sun rises high enough to illuminate the building in shafts of clear light. From here you can see the much-photographed King's College and King's College Chapel, which together dominate the city and could be considered the iconic view of Cambridge – it's certainly the view that appears in all the brochures.

Cambridge's atmosphere is refined without doubt, but it is lively and entertaining too. Most evenings you'll find small groups of students singing in harmony and dancers or jugglers

▲ The Mathematical Bridge, Queens' College

bringing a smile to the faces of passersby. The joviality around Silver Street, where students help excited visitors into punts on the River Cam, is an experience in itself. You'll catch yourself beaming from ear to ear.

Hopping aboard a punt is one of the 'must have' experiences of a visit to Cambridge. The River Cam has busy stretches of water and quiet, almost hidden, places where you can easily dream away a few wistful hours. You can hire a punt and set out on your own – it's not easy to steer a punt, though – or you can hire one that is 'chauffeured', usually by a student, leaving you free to sit back, enjoy the atmosphere and see the city from a whole new perspective.

From the river, you'll see colleges and bridges, including Queens' College's Mathematical Bridge, which got its name from its geometrical construction. It was widely thought to have been designed by Sir Isaac Newton, who studied at Trinity College in the late 17th century. He was said to have built it without nails, but when students disassembled it for a jest they found they couldn't put it together again and so had to use

bolts. It is, however, one of the more fanciful yarns told in Cambridge, not least because Newton had been dead for over 20 years when the bridge was first built.

Around 3.5 million visitors a year are drawn to the city, but far from frowning upon the invasion, you'll find residents helpful and pleased to point you in the direction of the best cafe, gallery or market stall. The city offers lots to do, from browsing in the secondhand bookshops that seem to occupy a prime spot at every turn, to visiting museums and galleries, enjoying the theatre, taking a sightseeing tour or having a long leisurely break at any one of the many pubs, buzzy cafes and multicultural restaurants that befit a university city.

The Fitzwilliam Museum in Trumpington Street holds an exhaustive collection of antiquities found in and around the city, and is a must-see if you want to learn more about Cambridge's ancient history; while the Museum of Cambridge covers more recent local history. If studying the flora of Cambridgeshire is your passion, then head for the Cambridge University Botanic Museum. You may prefer to visit an art gallery or exhibition hall or discover handmade jewellery, organic produce or designer goodies in and around the city's centuries-old market square.

▲ Trinity College

Music, theatre and live entertainment are popular in Cambridge. The Cambridge Corn Exchange and the Cambridge Arts Theatre promote the more traditional arts, the emphasis being on ballet, opera and orchestral concerts. More contemporary works are performed at the La Raza, the Cambridge Junction and the West Road Concert Hall, plus the ADC Theatre, famously the home of the Cambridge Footlights comedy troupe that has had actress Emma Thompson, comedians Alexander Armstrong, Peter Cook and John Cleese and television's *Downton Abbey* creator and writer Julian Fellowes treading its boards.

Whatever you do during your stay in Cambridge, you will inevitably succumb to the fascination of the colleges and want to know more about them. There are 31 colleges making up the University of Cambridge, all dotted around the city centre. Dating from the 13th century, Peterhouse is the oldest college building, but it is perhaps the predominantly Tudor colleges along King's Parade and Trinity Street, and King's College, together with King's College Chapel, that dominate the city. The Chapel is famous the world over for its superb choir and the Christmas Eve Festival of Nine Lessons and Carols.

You will find that many of the colleges welcome visitors out of study and exam times and the tourist information centre at the Guildhall, Peas Hill, just off the Market Square, has leaflets with information and routes around the city for you to follow. It's open year round Mon–Sat 10–5 (also Sun Apr–Oct 11–3). Joining students and Fellows in the courtyards of the colleges, engaging in stimulating conversation and admiring the architecture and achievements of Cambridge, is what time spent in this beautiful city is all about.

▶ Fitzwilliam Museum

fitzmuseum.cam.ac.uk
Trumpington Street, CB2 1RB | 01223 332900 | Open Tue–Sat 10–5, Sun 12–5

Cambridge's foremost museum with over a half a million exhibits, the Fitzwilliam is one of the finest in Europe. It was founded in 1816 by the wealthy musical antiquarian and art collector, Richard Fitzwilliam, the seventh Viscount Fitzwilliam of Merrion (1745–1816), who was an alumnus of Trinity College. He felt the university needed its own art museum and library, and on his death donated a priceless collection of works including Renaissance pieces by Italian painters Palma Vecchio, Titian and Veronese, 144 rare Dutch paintings, engravings by artists such as Rembrandt and sheet music signed by German composer Handel.

The Fitzwilliam became the museum of the University of Cambridge, and remains to this day one of the oldest public museums in Britain. You'll easily find it along the main thoroughfare, Trumpington Street, for it is housed in a monumental neoclassical mansion, a Cambridge landmark. Its magnificent collection has grown over the years and spans centuries and civilisations from as far back as 2500 BC to the present day. Among the exhibits are works by Rubens, Constable, Picasso and Monet, along with antiquities from Ancient Egypt, Greece and Cyprus, rare Oriental works of art and medieval coins.

The museum's own Courtyard Cafe serves morning coffee, light lunches and afternoon tea, and is sure to provide a welcome break.

10 famous colleges in Cambridge

▶ Clare College
▶ Corpus Christi College
▶ Girton College
▶ Gonville and Caius College
▶ Jesus College
▶ King's College
▶ Pembroke College
▶ Peterhouse
▶ Queens' College
▶ Trinity College

VISIT THE MUSEUMS

Kettle's Yard

kettlesyard.co.uk
Castle Street, CB3 0AQ
01223 748100

The fresh and bright interior of this fine country house-turned-gallery on the outskirts of the city centre provides the perfect backdrop to a varied collection of contemporary art. After a major building project, Kettle's Yard reopened in 2018 to reveal a four-floor education wing including an archive and project space, more galleries, a new entrance area and a cafe.

The Museum of Cambridge

museumofcambridge.co.uk
2–3 Castle Street, CB3 0AQ
01223 355159 | Open Tue–Sat 10.30–5, Sun 2–4

A pretty 17th-century timber-framed former inn houses the Museum of Cambridge, one of the city's most popular museums. A country and folkloric museum, it aims to present a glimpse of the everyday lives of the county's people from early times through to the present day, with nine room settings, including a kitchen and a playroom. There are more than 20,000 exhibits amassed from private homes. Children, especially, will love the display of toys that would have been an essential part of youngsters' lives centuries ago. This delightful museum was founded in 1936 to help generations understand their local heritage and is particularly family friendly with plenty of hands-on experiences and games for children. There are temporary exhibitions too, talks, events and kids' activities, plus a shop featuring locally hand-crafted gifts, toys and jewellery.

The Polar Museum, Scott Polar Research Institute

spri.cam.ac.uk
Lensfield Road, CB2 1ER
01223 336540 | Open Tue–Sat 10–4

Located within this international centre for polar studies, the museum has one of the best collections of journals, photographs, maps and even items of clothing that chronicle the most important Arctic and Antarctic expeditions ever undertaken. Special emphasis is placed on Captain Scott and on the exploration of the Northwest Passage. Other exhibits include Inuit work and the art of the polar regions, as well as displays on current scientific exploration. The museum has a regular programme of exhibitions in addition to its permanent displays. Public lectures run from October to December and February to April.

University Museum of Archaeology and Anthropology

maa.cam.ac.uk
Downing Street, CB2 3DZ
01223 333516 | Open Tue–Sat 10.30–4.30 Sun 12–4.30

The museum is part of the Faculty of Archaeology and Anthropology of the University of Cambridge and houses exhibits spanning two million years of human civilisation. It was established in 1884 and has been in its present location in the city centre since 1913. Some of the highlights are Pacific material collected on Captain Cook's voyages of exploration, a 46-foot-high totem pole from Canada and some of the earliest stone

tools ever found. Housing a million artefacts made by people from all over the world, as well as exploring our ancient past, the museum also exhibits work by today's indigenous communities.

GO ROUND THE GARDENS
Cambridge University Botanic Garden

botanic.cam.ac.uk
1 Brookside, CB2 1JE
01223 336265 | Open daily, Apr–Sep 10–6, Feb–Mar, Oct 10–5, Nov–Jan 10–4

The university's Botanic Garden comes as something of a surprise. This 40-acre oasis of beautifully landscaped gardens and glasshouses is close to the bustle of the city centre and yet if it's peace you're after then you'll find it here. The garden opened on its present site in 1846, and showcases a collection of some 8,000 plant species, including nine national collections, among them geraniums and fritillarias. This Grade II heritage

▼ Cambridge University Botanic Garden

landscape features rock gardens full of alpine species, winter and autumn gardens, and even a tropical rainforest. You can relax in the Scented Garden, enjoy beds of herbaceous varieties and, best of all, see the finest collection of trees in the east of England.

CATCH A PERFORMANCE
Cambridge Corn Exchange
cambridgelivetrust.co.uk/cornex
Wheeler Street, CB2 3QB
01223 357851 | Box office open Mon–Sat 10–6, Sun performance days only
Just minutes from the market square the Corn Exchange hosts around 300 performances a year, so whatever your preference you'll be sure to find the perfect evening out, from stand-up comedians and contemporary singers to symphony orchestras and ballet companies.

Cambridge Arts Theatre
cambridgeartstheatre.com
6 St Edwards Passage, CB2 3PJ
01223 503333 | Box office open Mon–Sat 12–8
If you're visiting over the festive season, be sure to take the family to the theatre's pantomime. It's a Cambridge institution. Alternatively, try to catch a touring musical show fresh from the West End. Comedy dramas and plays featuring top international actors, and concerts and dance performances are held here throughout the year.

ADC Theatre
adctheatre.com
Park Street, CB5 8AS
01223 300085 | Open Mon–Sat 1–7. During university term time the main show commences at 7.45 Tue–Sat, followed by a late show at 11
If you fancy finding out how the likes of actors Sir Ian McKellen, Emma Thompson, Stephen Fry and Hugh Laurie, to name but a few, came to get the performing bug, then book a show at the ADC. This pretty, white- and blue-washed period building, a few minutes' walk from the city centre, has hosted the university's Amateur Dramatic Club (ADC) since the late 1800s. The club itself was formed in 1855. Shows are a superb mix of comedy sketches, stand-up, music, drama and satire.

PLAY A ROUND
The Gog Magog Golf Club
gogmagog.co.uk
Shelford Bottom, CB22 3AB
01223 247626 | Open Mon–Tue, Thu–Fri, Sun all year
Founded in 1901, Gog Magog Golf Club has two well-established courses, each with plenty of hazards to present a challenge. Both are chalk downland courses and, because they are at such a high elevation, afford panoramic views of the countryside surrounding the city. The view of Ely Cathedral in the distance is mesmerising. The nature of the ground ensures good winter golf too. The area has been designated a Site of Special Scientific Interest.

EAT AND DRINK

The Anchor Pub, Dining & River Terrace

anchorcambridge.com
Silver Street, CB3 9EL
01223 353554

Bordering Queens' College is a medieval lane, at the end of which stands this attractive pub, right by the bridge over the River Cam. Head for the riverside patio with a local real ale or a Hazy Hog cider, and watch rookie punters struggling with their tricky crafts – another definition of pole position, perhaps. A good choice of food includes classic pub fare as well as more adventurous dishes.

Fitzbillies

fitzbillies.com
51–2 Trumpington Street, CB2 1RG
01223 352500

From its art nouveau shop front to the famously sticky Chelsea buns that have been made and sold here since 1921, Fitzbillies is a Cambridge institution. Inside you'll find the charming original cake shop, a restaurant with waiter service and a separate coffee bar. It is open daily for cakes, coffee, sandwiches, scones, ice creams, lunch and traditional afternoon tea and serves a full brunch menu every day until 4pm.

Hotel Felix ◎◎

hotelfelix.co.uk
Whitehouse Lane, Huntingdon Road, CB3 0LX | 01223 277977

This lovely bow-fronted Victorian mansion is home to a sleek

10 comedians who studied at Cambridge

▶ Clive Anderson
▶ Alexander Armstrong
▶ David Baddiel
▶ John Cleese
▶ Peter Cook
▶ Jimmy Edwards
▶ Eric Idle
▶ Hugh Laurie
▶ Bill Oddie
▶ Griff Rhys Jones

boutique hotel that combines elegant period features with a contemporary sheen. The Graffiti restaurant sports abstract modern art on battleship-grey walls, burnished darkwood floors, and unclothed tables, while the large terrace is a crowd puller for alfresco aperitifs and fair-weather dining. Like the decor, the food is vibrant and sets off along a modern British road with plenty of sunny Mediterranean flavours along the way.

Midsummer House ◎◎◎◎◎

midsummerhouse.co.uk
Midsummer Common, CB4 1HA
01223 369299

The Victorian villa that houses Midsummer House restaurant enjoys an idyllic setting: on the edge of Midsummer Common (where cows do actually freely roam as if they own the place) with the River Cam flowing by. The conservatory looks over the

10 famous Cambridge alumni

▶ **Charles Babbage**, computer inventor

▶ **Cecil Beaton**, photographer

▶ **Anthony Blunt**, Soviet spy

▶ **HRH Prince Charles**

▶ **David Frost**, television presenter

▶ **Germaine Greer**, writer

▶ **Sam Mendes**, film director

▶ **Isaac Newton**, mathematician

▶ **Vladimir Nabokov**, writer

▶ **Emma Thompson**, actress

pretty garden and there's a small bar upstairs with a terrace looking out over the river. The conservatory looks over the pretty garden (where apples from its trees feature on the highly respected Chef Patron Daniel Clifford's signature dish of scallop, truffle and apple) and there's a small bar upstairs with a terrace looking out over the river. A five-course menu features at lunch on Wednesday to Friday; the eight-course main menu is served at dinner on Tuesday and lunch and dinner Wednesday to Saturday. Featuring beautifully presented dishes, this is very fine special occasion dining.

The Old Spring

theoldspring.co.uk
1 Ferry Path, CB4 1HB
01223 357228

You'll find this bustling pub in the leafy suburb of De Freville, just a short stroll from the River Cam and its many boatyards, which makes its splendid decked patio popular as a post-workout refreshment spot for rowers. The bright and airy interior offers rug-covered wooden floors, comfy sofas and large family tables. Sip a pint of Abbot Ale, one of several real ales on tap, or one of 20 wines by the glass, while choosing from over a dozen main courses plus specials.

The Punter

thepuntercambridge.co.uk
3 Pound Hill, CB3 0AE
01223 363322
Two minutes' walk from the city centre, this former coaching house is popular with post-grads, locals and dog lovers alike. The interior is an eclectic mix of previously loved hand-me-downs: comfy sofas, sturdy school chairs, and an assortment of pictures and painting jostling for space on the walls. Drinkers can enjoy local ales but it seems it's the tasty seasonal food that draws people in. The modern menu offers classic dishes such as risotto and beef bourguignon.

Restaurant Alimentum ⊛⊛⊛

restaurantalimentum.co.uk
152–4 Hills Road, CB2 8PB
01223 413000
If your Latin's a bit rusty, the name of this operation, in a modern building near the city's leisure park, means 'food', and

the place comes with bags of contemporary swagger. It has seats upholstered in red at black-lacquered tables, scarlet padded walls and an open-to-view kitchen. Ethics and sustainability are at the top of the agenda when it comes to sourcing ingredients, while the cuisine follows a broadly modern European path. Chef Patron Mark Poynton favours slow cooking techniques to accentuate flavour in his contemporary, imaginative and elegantly presented dishes. For lunch and dinner there's both a la carte, from which to choose two or three courses, and a seven-course tasting menu 'Taste of Alimentum' (designed to be taken by the whole table).

Restaurant 22 ⬡
restaurant22.co.uk
22 Chesterton Road, CB4 3AX
01223 351880
The converted Victorian townhouse near Jesus Green conceals a discreetly elegant and comfortable dining room done out in shades of fawn, brown and beige. The menu follows a monthly-changing, set-price formula of three courses with a sorbet following the starter. The cooking is driven by market-fresh ingredients, and the unfussy dishes have an appealing contemporary European feel.

▶ **PLACES NEARBY**
Madingley, an unassuming village on the outskirts of Cambridge, has two sites of particular interest: Madingley Hall, an elegant 16th-century country mansion that houses Cambridge University's Institute of Continuing Education, and which is not open to the public, and the Cambridge American Cemetery and Memorial.

Cambridge is ideally located for visiting so many great places. There's heritage at Ely (see page 126) and Houghton Mill, the idyllic country houses at Anglesey Abbey in Lode and Hemingford Grey, and wildlife at Wicken Fen National Nature Reserve (see page 279). Or you can see the planes at Duxford (see page 124), take afternoon tea in Grantchester (see page 137) or enjoy a traditional pub lunch at the Queen's Head in Newton.

Also nearby is Wandlebury, an area of beautiful grasslands, and chalk slopes that is heaven for walkers and nature lovers. You can see the remains of the Wandlebury Ring, an Iron Age fort on the Gog Magog Downs.

Anglesey Abbey, Gardens and Lode Mill
nationaltrust.org.uk/angleseyabbey
Lode, CB25 9EJ | 01223 810080
House open daily Apr–Oct 11–5, Nov–Mar 11–4, garden 10–5.30 (4.30 Nov–Mar), mill Tue–Sun 10.30–3.30 (times can vary)
This Jacobean-style house, standing in c.115 acres of landscaped gardens just a few miles outside Cambridge, dates from 1600 and is built on the site of a 12th-century Augustinian priory. It contains

an idiosyncratic collection of art depicting the tastes of wealthy politician Urban Huttleston Broughton (1896–1966), the first Baron Fairhaven, who purchased the Abbey in 1926.

Among the many paintings you'll see works by Claude Lorraine, set alongside fine examples of furniture, silver and tapestries and one of the largest collections of clocks found in any National Trust property. In the domestic quarters of the house, exhibits offer a glimpse of how the belowstairs staff would have lived and where they worked.

The priory is surrounded by a landscaped garden that has been designed to provide year-round floral interest and contains an arboretum with more than 100 sculptures, most of which take the form of mythical or biblical characters. The garden is famous for its drifts of snowdrops and its summer roses.

The watermill in the grounds, Lode Mill, has milling days on the first and third Saturday of each month, provided the water levels are adequate. You can see how wheat has been ground in the same way here for around a 1,000 years, and then buy some to take home to make bread. Anglesey Abbey has its own restaurant, Redwoods, in the grounds, which serves light meals and snacks, including scones made with flour ground at Lode Mill.

Cambridge American Cemetery and Memorial

abmc.gov

Madingley Road, Coton, CB23 7PH

01954 210350

This sprawling, peaceful memorial garden, framed by woodland, commemorates predominantly American servicemen who died in World War II. Most were killed in the Battle of the Atlantic or the strategic air bombardment of northwest Europe. You can find it along Madingley Road, a main thoroughfare out of Cambridge, between Coton and Madingley.

▼ Cambridge American Cemetery and Memorial

Castle Acre
see **Swaffham**, page 265

Castle Rising
see **King's Lynn**, page 181

Cley next the Sea MAP REF 294 B1

Cley next the Sea is a curiosity in so far as it's nowhere near the sea. To be fair, it was once. Up until about the 17th century its quayside on the River Glaven was a bustling place of boats laden with wool and cloth; then marshland was reclaimed to provide pastures, and its harbour silted up. There's still a little quayside next to the river, but no boats now of any size. You can see the brick-and-flint cottages that once lined the quayside, but now they stand a mile or so from the coast.

▼ Cley Windmill

Cley, as it's commonly abbreviated, or Cly as it's pronounced, lies in the Norfolk Coast Area of Outstanding Natural Beauty. It's on a strip of land along the sea's edge, no more than two miles long, built up along the North Norfolk coast over the past thousand years by sediment brought down by the rivers. Creeks wind their way muddily to the sea among banks of shingle and sand. Birds haunt the area in multitudes, and almost the entire coastline is protected by nature reserves. Here, you may catch sight of rough-legged buzzards and little terns, avocets and even the odd oystercatcher.

The most prominent feature of the landscape here is the white-sailed windmills, such as the village's own 18th-century red-brick tower mill with its brilliant sails and conical wooden cap. These windmills were often used not to grind corn, as is usually assumed, but to drain the salt marshes to create more land for agriculture. Cley Windmill is now one of East Anglia's more unusual bed-and-breakfast places.

Among the attractive houses in the village is Whalebone House, with panels of flint in the walls framed by whale vertebrae. To the south, where the old harbour stood, the medieval church of St Margaret is one of Norfolk's finest, built on a grand scale and a witness to Cley's prosperity at that time.

In the centre are shops selling local foods and crafts. Look out for Cley Smokehouse for food and Made in Cley, which has some contemporary souvenirs. Both are in the High Street.

Cley is a great place if walking is your passion. A minor road runs northwards from the village through the marshes and takes you to Cley Eye on the coast. From here there is a walk of 3 miles or so along a narrow shingle spit to the National Nature Reserve at Blakeney Point (see page 65), which is best known for its colonies of seals.

SEE A LOCAL CHURCH
Church of St Margaret
Holt Road, NR25 7TT

Church of St Margaret is a richly decorated Grade I listed church dating from medieval times when Cley was a prosperous and thriving port. It overlooks the village green, which is one of the largest in the region.

The tower, which can be seen from almost everywhere in Cley, remains from the 13th century and there are large 15th-century windows in the aisles. Take a minute to look at the 15th-century two-storey south porch's beautiful fan-vaulted roof with carved bosses. Inside, you can see its 500-year-old bench ends depicting mythical creatures, its seven sacraments font, and, from the 17th century, the pulpit and altar table. The royal arms dates from Charles II's reign and was repainted for Queen Anne.

EAT AND DRINK
The George Hotel
thegeorgehotelatcley.co.uk
High Street, NR25 7RN
01263 740652

The George's beer garden backs on to the salt marshes of the North Norfolk coast, which prove a paradise for birders. Indeed, this old hotel has been an ornithological focal point for many years. Ask to see its 'bird bible', a record of sightings kept by visiting observers. The welcoming bar is home to several real ales, including Yetman's from just along the coast at Holt. You can snack in the lounge bar or dine in the light, painting-filled restaurant. The daily-changing menu offers only the best of local fresh ingredients, and fish and seafood are a real strength. The village's famous mill is next door and Blakeney Haven is just over a mile away.

▶ PLACES NEARBY
The Salthouse Dun Cow
salthouseduncow.com
Coast Road, Salthouse,
NR25 7XA | 01263 740467

Situated in a quiet coastal village within an Area of Outstanding Natural Beauty, this traditional brick-and-flint pub probably originated as a cattle barn built around 1650. Today it overlooks some of Britain's finest salt marshes, so expect to share it, particularly the front garden, with birders and walkers. The interior decor reflects the surrounding farmland and seascapes, with brick walls, bare floorboards and a wood-burning stove. Local suppliers provide high-quality produce for select menus prepared from scratch, especially fresh shellfish and game from local shoots. Samphire, asparagus and soft fruit are all sourced from within 5 miles.

▶ Cromer MAP REF 294 C1

Cromer, known as the Gem of the Norfolk Coast – a motto you will see everywhere you go – is an ancient town best known for its superb crabs. Cromer crabs are caught on long lines from little clinker-built boats that chug out to sea regardless of the weather. Once the pots are out, the fishermen must collect them the following day, even when a gale is raging. Tractors haul the boats to and from the water's edge. You can spend some time here watching them; it makes for an interesting diversion. The crabs are said to be the best in the country and every traditional Cromer restaurant, bar none, has them on the menu. Be sure to have a taste.

Cromer has long been a fashionable sort of place. It is said that when a bathing machine was advertised at Cromer in 1779, word got round and soon wealthy Norwich families, including the banking families of Gurney and Barclay, bought holiday homes here. The Victorian era brought even more wealth, aided by the railway in 1877. As now, families would think nothing of spending days on the sandy beach, eating the local crab.

Walking around Cromer, especially along its quintessential English seafront, is a delight. The Pavilion Theatre is one of only a few surviving end-of-the-pier theatres in the country. Original fishermen's cottages have been turned into a history and geology museum. Look out, too, for the RNLI's museum near the pier that tells the amazing story of Coxswain Henry Blogg (1876–1954), who served as a lifeboatman for 53 years and was awarded more medals and commendations than any other in Britain. Cromer's fine 14th-century church, St Peter and St Paul, which has Norfolk's tallest tower, is worth a visit.

VISIT THE MUSEUMS
RNLI Henry Blogg Museum
rnli.org/henryblogg
The Rocket House, The Gangway,
NR27 9ET | 01263 511294
Open Apr–Sep Tue–Sun 10–5,
Oct–Nov, Feb–Mar 10–4

The Royal National Lifeboat Institute's Henry Blogg was an old man when he died, but when you hear about his exploits in plucking imperiled sailors from the treacherous seas you'll wonder how he managed to cheat death for so long. His bravery is legendary; he launched 387 times and was awarded more medals and commendations than any other lifeboatman in Britain. You can learn more about Blogg at the museum dedicated to him. A lifeboat has been stationed at Cromer since 1804, and this museum at the bottom of The Gangway covers local lifeboat history and the RNLI in general too. The main exhibit is the Watson-class lifeboat *HF Bailey*, the boat Henry Blogg coxed.

Cromer Museum

museums.norfolk.gov.uk
East Cottages, Tucker Street,
NR27 9HB | 01263 513543
Open Mar–Oct Mon–Fri 10–4,
Sat–Sun 12–4

A handful of 19th-century fishermen's cottages, one of which has period furnishings, have been turned into a museum of the area's history and geology. There are pictures and exhibits from Victorian Cromer, with collections illustrating local natural history, social history, archaeology and geology. A highlight is the collection of bones from the West Runton elephant – a 600,000-year-old fossilised mammoth discovered in the crumbling cliffs nearby. There are a number of guided walks that start at the museum.

▼ Cromer beach and pier

CATCH A PERFORMANCE
Pavilion Theatre
cromerpier.co.uk
Cromer Pier, NR27 9HE
01263 512495

From good old-fashioned seaside specials with belting singers, family-fun comedians and a bevy of colourfully costumed dancers, concerts and events, the Pavilion Theatre at the end of Cromer Pier is the place to go for a lively night out. You'll often find entertainers on the pier itself. Walking along the 496-foot-long pier before and after the show, or simply to take in the bracing air, is an experience in itself.

SEE A LOCAL CHURCH
Church of St Peter and St Paul
Church Street, NR27 9HA

The impressive church of St Peter and St Paul, whose 160-foot tower is Norfolk's tallest by far, was built in the 14th century at a time when Cromer was hugely prosperous. The town later went through a period of decline, during which time the chancel was demolished and by the 19th century the church was almost derelict. Respected Victorian architect Sir Arthur Blomfield came to the rescue in the 1880s when Cromer had regained its prosperity, and rebuilt the chancel and repaired the nave and tower.

Today, the church is a popular, friendly place, its enormous nave full of light and space. There is excellent glass at the east end made by the English Arts and Crafts movement's designer William Morris's company, and modern glass elsewhere celebrates and commemorates local places and people. The outside of the church is magnificent, with superb architectural detailing, and the great tower is an attraction in its own right because of the available views from the top.

PLAY A ROUND
Royal Cromer Golf Club
royalcromergolfclub.com
145 Overstrand Road, NR27 0JH
01263 512884 | Open daily all year

This challenging course has spectacular views out to sea and overlooks the town. Strong sea breezes affect the clifftop holes, the most famous being the 14th, which has a green in the shadow of a lighthouse.

EAT AND DRINK
Buttercups Tearooms
5 High Street, NR27 9HG
01263 510990

Drop into this friendly little family-run cafe, a local favourite, for coffee and homemade cakes, tea and scones, Cromer crab salad, soup, sandwiches or a baguette – all freshly made on the premises.

The Red Lion Food and Rooms
redlioncromer.co.uk
Brook Street, NR27 9HD
01263 514964

Guests can gaze through the inn's front windows directly over the fine beach to the sturdy pier.

Fishing boats drawn up on the shingle bank may provide the wherewithal for the pub's renowned seafood dishes, whilst sharing platters overflow with produce from Norfolk's generous inland larder. The playful menu has suggestions for wines to accompany dishes, while beer-lovers will delight at a choice that includes cutting edge local breweries like Wolf and Cromer's own Poppyland. There are bedrooms here if you want to stay longer.

The Grove @@

thegrovecromer.co.uk
95 Overstrand Road, NR27 0DJ
01263 512412

The award-winning restaurant at The Grove would be the place to go for a special dinner, served in either the oak-panelled study or the original Georgian dining room. Norfolk ingredients features strongly on the seasonally inspired menu, with fruit, vegetables and herbs plucked from the hotel's own kitchen gardens Many dishes have a gluten-free option. Traditional Sunday lunch is family-friendly but still stylish.

▶ PLACES NEARBY

The Amazona Zoo, with its collection of unusual species, the grand Felbrigg Hall, and the impressive Blickling Estate, owned by the National Trust, are all a short drive from Cromer. If you fancy playing golf, Mundesley Golf Club is a 10-minute drive, while the

Links Country Park Hotel and Golf Club is a little further in West Runton. For refreshments en route, try The Gunton Arms in Thorpe Market, the Walpole Arms in Itteringham, or Sea Marge Hotel or the White Horse, both in Overstrand, which is also home to a pleasant arts centre.

Amazona Zoo

amazonazoo.co.uk
Hall Road, Cromer NR27 9JG
01263 510741 | Open daily 10–5
(can close earlier in winter)

On the outskirts of Cromer lies one of the area's most endearing animal complexes. The Amazona Zoo presents rainforest creatures in an idyllic wooded setting created on the site of former brick kilns. Home to over 200 animals, the zoo is devoted to the conservation of rare species and habitats.

The Belfry Centre

thebelfrycentre.co.uk
23A Cromer Road, Overstrand, NR27 0NT | 01263 579196
Open Mon–Fri 8.45–4, Sat 10–1

A music and arts centre with recitals, concerts, exhibitions and classes for adults and children, plus a good cafe.

Felbrigg Hall

nationaltrust.org.uk
Felbrigg, NR11 8PR | 01263 837444
Hall open daily Feb–Mar 12–3, Apr–Oct 12–5

Set in the tranquil Norfolk countryside, this great 17th-century house is one of the best in East Anglia. It was begun in the 1620s by a lawyer, Frances Windham, whose grandson William filled the rooms with pictures, including many seascapes, he had acquired on a tour of Italy. Intricate plaster ceilings and a fine library are further highlights of the interior. Less grand but equally fascinating is the kitchen, with its array of household implements, utensils and gleaming copper pots and pans.

Outside, the walled garden contains a functioning dovecote and the National Collection of Colchicums. There is free access to the estate, where waymarked trails thread their way past venerable trees. The nearby 15th-century parish church, standing alone, has box pews, memorial brasses and interesting family monuments.

Blickling Estate

nationaltrust.org.uk/blickling
Blickling, Aylsham, NR11 6NF
01263 738030 | House open daily
Jan–mid-Mar, Nov–Dec 10.30–3,
mid-Mar–Oct 12–5, park dawn–dusk

There are 55 acres of grounds for you to wander in on the sprawling Blickling Estate, including woodland and a lakeside walk, a formal parterre, topiary yew hedges, a Secret Garden, an orangery, and a dry moat filled with roses, camellias and other plants. Its focal point in the resplendent Blickling Hall, a red-brick country mansion flanked by dark yew hedges and topped by pinnacles. It is one of the great houses of the region and once home to the Boleyn family in the early 16th century. It is a magical sight.

Inside, you can visit the Great Hall where stunning reliefs of notable residents, including Anne Boleyn and her daughter, Elizabeth I, adorn the staircase. In the Long Gallery ladies of the court once walked for exercise when the weather was bad in the days before it was transformed, in 1745, into what is today one of the country's finest country house libraries. It contains a remarkable collection of some 12,000 books.

More highlights include the spectacular Jacobean plaster ceiling and fireplace in the South Drawing Room; the tapestry, a gift from Empress Catherine the Great, in the Peter the Great Room; and the exquisite Chinese Bedroom with its authentic Oriental furniture and decorations amassed by owners since the 18th century. Throughout the hall are some quite stunning paintings and tapestries.

You could easily make a day of it at Blickling Estate. There's the Hobart Restaurant, where light meals are produced almost entirely from produce grown or reared on the estate, and the Muddy Boots Cafe for light snacks and drinks.

Links Country Park Hotel and Golf Club

links-hotel.co.uk
West Runton, NR27 9QH
01263 838383 | Open daily all year

This parkland course has superb views of the North Norfolk coast and is ideal for all levels of golfer.

Mundesley Golf Club

mundesleygolfclub.com
Links Road, NR11 8ES
01263 720095 | Open daily all year
This club has an undulating downland course with panoramic views, a mile from the sea. The small, fast greens and tight fairways make for a pleasurable visit.

The Walpole Arms

thewalpolearms.co.uk
Itteringham, NR11 7AR
01263 587258
Owned by a local farming family, this renowned rural dining venue is tucked away down narrow lanes on the edge of sleepy Itteringham, close to Blickling Hall. Its oak-beamed bar offers local Woodforde's and Adnams ales on tap, while menus champion top-notch meats and produce from the family farm and local artisan producers.

The Gunton Arms

theguntonarms.co.uk
Cromer Road, Thorpe Market,
NR11 8TZ | 01263 832010
Warm and inviting, this stylishly restored pub with a fortune of contemporary art on its walls stands in a 1,000-acre deer park. It builds its menus on tradition and hearty but modern British cooking, and spit-roasts meat (including its own venison) over an open fire in the Elk Room. There are 12 cosy bedrooms should you be tempted to stay.

Sea Marge Hotel ❀❀

mackenziehotels.com
16 High Street, Overstrand,
NR27 0AB | 01263 579579
On the edge of Overstrand, the Sea Marge is a family-run Edwardian hotel of great charm. Its terraced lawns sit just above the coastal path, with marine views from the panelled dining room, Frazer's, where pastel hues and linen-clad tables create a restful ambience. The kitchen does a skilful job of incorporating touches of British modernism into what are essentially traditional haute cuisine dishes. This is very much fish and seafood territory, but there may also be creative variations on classic meat dishes.

The White Horse ❀❀

whitehorseoverstrand.co.uk
34 High Street, Overstrand,
NR27 0AB | 01263 579237
Just a short walk from the sea, this Victorian inn pulls in the punters, with a bar (serving real ales and its own menu), a games room, garden and guest accommodation as well as the restaurant in a converted barn, given a sleek look within flint walls and oak ceiling trusses. The kitchen makes everything on the premises, from excellent breads to ice creams, and produces a range of ambitious, assertively flavoured dishes.

▶ **Dedham Vale** MAP REF 290 A6

With endless rural landscapes that so inspired 19th-century artist John Constable (1776–1837), the Dedham Vale is a 35-square-mile designated Area of Outstanding Natural Beauty on the Suffolk–Essex border. At its heart you can see the wide, meandering River Stour dotted with sailing boats of all shapes and sizes. Sometimes you will even spot an old Thames barge with its deep red sails straining against the power of the wind. These magnificent vessels were used to transport goods on the River Thames in London during the 19th century, and some have been preserved to provide pleasure tours.

The Stour runs inland from its estuary at Manningtree and at this point marks the counties' boundaries. On the Suffolk side, you can visit the pretty village of East Bergholt (see page 125), where the famed 19th-century painter John Constable was born in June 1776. A plaque marks the spot where his family home, East Bergholt House – the subject of several of Constable's works – once stood.

Once you've found the plaque, walk the few yards to the village's church, the 16th-century church of St Mary the Virgin where the painter was baptised. Wander around the gardens and you will find the tomb of his parents, Golding and Ann Constable. Don't miss the timber cage just off to the left which houses the bells of this spire-less church. It was built in 1531 as a temporary home for the bells, which are thought to be the heaviest still rung in England at approximately 4.25 tons, and remains their home to this day.

▼ Cloth Hall, Dedham   ▶ The River Stour

Almost opposite the church you'll see Flatford Road and, if you head down here and park where indicated, you can visit Flatford Mill. This large, red-brick 18th-century watermill was once owned by Constable's wealthy father and was made famous in the painter's work *The Hay Wain*. You can't go in, sadly, as today it is an environmental studies centre, but you can see how beautifully the Grade I listed building has survived the ravages of time. Then gaze across the mill pond to the whitewashed Willy Lott's cottage.

Willy Lott was a local farmer who lived here for 84 years and is said to have never travelled further than the churchyard of East Bergholt, where he is buried. You can walk to his cottage, and also to Bridge Cottage, which appears in many of Constable's paintings. Both are owned by the National Trust and open for you to visit. Times vary so do check before setting out if you want to go in. Constable tours by volunteer guides take visitors on an artistic journey through favourite views.

On the Essex side of the river you can visit Manningtree, one of Constable's favourite places – he painted *The Ascension* for its church; it now hangs in nearby Dedham's church – and the village of Dedham itself, where he went to school.

Dedham is a picture postcard village dominated by its church, St Mary the Virgin. A mighty structure with a 131-foot-high tower and a lavishly carved Galilee porch, the church towers above the village and was the focal point in many of Constable's paintings. It has stood on the site since 1492 and was built through the efforts of two leading wool merchants of the time. Dedham was a prosperous village in the 13th and 14th centuries, and had a thriving weaving industry so the church was built, to some extent, as a consequence of the village's wealth.

▶ Willy Lott's Cottage, East Bergholt

You can visit the church before enjoying an afternoon cream tea – Dedham is famous for its cream teas. Look out for the church's interior features; many are quite extraordinary, including its octagonal font engraved with emblems of the Four Evangelists, the Lion, Man, Bull and Eagle, with angels and little cherub heads around its edge. If you ask the vicar he'll tell you it dates from the 14th century. Behind the font is a rare window depicting Faith, Hope and Charity, and if you look up you will see a wonderful wood ceiling.

The Dedham Vale, which also includes the villages of Stratford St Mary (whose church stands isolated across the busy dual carriageway of the A12), Polstead, Nayland and Stoke-by-Nayland, is an important RSPB breeding ground. If you have a keen eye for spotting birds you'll see blackcaps, nightingales and grey plovers; at low tide waterfowl tread delicately among the precariously lopsided yachts.

Unspoiled areas like the valley of the River Stour are rare in East Anglia, yet here you can see the landscapes that so captured the imagination of one of the country's foremost artists.

VISIT THE MUSEUM AND GALLERY
Flatford Mill, Willy Lott's Cottage and Bridge Cottage
nationaltrust.org.uk/flatford
East Bergholt, CO7 6UL
01206 298260 | Open all year, check website as times vary
An 18th-century watermill once owned by the John Constable's father, Flatford Mill lies next to the River Stour and is at the heart of the Dedham Vale. Nearby are Willy Lott's Cottage and Bridge Cottage – which you can visit – made famous in the painter's works. Displays tell the story of Constable's life.

Dedham Art and Craft Centre
dedhamartandcraftcentre.co.uk
High Street, Dedham, CO7 6AD
01206 322666 | Open daily 10–5
Housed in a converted church, this centre has three floors of artisans' displays. You can see demonstrations of woodturning and pottery, painting and glass decorating, and buy the perfect souvenir to take home. Its tea room specialises in local vegetarian dishes.

TAKE A WALK
If you head for East Bergholt you can take a leisurely walk along its main street and see where John Constable was born. His childhood home, East Bergholt House, is no longer there but a plaque on railings marks the spot. His first studio is nearby and further along is the church where his parents are buried.

On the opposite side of the road you'll see a signpost to Flatford. Head down here for Flatford Mill, Bridge Cottage and Willy Lott's Cottage. The highlight of walking around here is that you get to stand in the places where Constable produced some of his finest paintings, such as *The Cornfield*, *The White Horse* and *Boat-Building Near Flatford Mill*.

EAT AND DRINK
Marlborough Head Inn
Mill Lane, Dedham CO7 6DH
01206 323250
Tucked away in glorious Constable country, this 16th-century building was once a clearing house for local wool merchants. In 1660, after a slump in trade, it became an inn. Today it is as perfect for a pint, sofa and newspaper as it is for a home-cooked family meal. There is a terrace and walled garden.

Le Talbooth ☺☺
milsomhotels.com
Gun Hill, Dedham, CO7 6HP
01206 323150
This former toll house by the River Stour dates from Tudor times and oozes period character. Alfresco dining is possible whatever the weather, thanks to an impressive sail canopy above the waterside terrace. Inside, the look is slick and contemporary, and the kitchen stays abreast of culinary trends while paying attention to the seasons and local materials.

▲ St Mary the Virgin church, Dedham

milsoms ◉
milsomhotels.com
Stratford Road, Dedham, CO7 6HN
01206 322795
The old creeper-covered house
in its neat garden may look like
a bastion of traditional values,
but this place offers a little
piece of boutique glamour. The
bar and brasserie strike a
contemporary pose, the latter
with its split-level dining room
opening out onto a beautiful
(and large) terrace. The menu
– which is available all day –
sticks to the modern message
and offers everything from posh
lunchtime sandwiches to steaks
and burgers cooked on the grill.

The Sun Inn ◉◉
thesuninndedham.com
High Street, Dedham,
CO7 6DF | 01206 323351
The setting may be in the heart
of Constable country, but The
Sun Inn's culinary leanings are
distinctly Mediterranean. The
place is a proper 15th-century
village inn, revamped, but

retaining its open fires, doughty timbers and panelling. Food is taken seriously, combining fresh locally sourced produce and quality Italian ingredients, such as cured meats, cheeses and oils, in uncomplicated, well-executed dishes.

▶ Denver   MAP REF 292 C5

The village of Denver, which lies on the banks of the Great Ouse in Norfolk, has some really pleasant walks for you to enjoy, including one that takes you past its beautifully restored 19th-century windmill, a landmark of the village, and the mighty sluice gate on the river.

In fact, Denver's claim to fame is that it was the first village to have a sluice, in 1651. This area of the Fens is extremely flat and sluices are essential for drainage and to stop villages like Denver being flooded. If you're feeling active, there are boats to hire on the river or you can play a round of golf at the Ryston Park Golf Club.

Denver's most famous resident was Captain George Manby, who was born in the village in 1765 and is best remembered for his work in establishing the forerunner of the modern fire extinguisher. The village lies on the Fen Causeway, a 24-mile-long Roman road that runs between Denver and Peterborough.

PLAY A ROUND
Ryston Park Golf Club
club-noticeboard.co.uk
Ely Road, PE38 0HH | 01366 382133
Open Mon–Fri all year
This mature nine-hole parkland course has two challenging par fours to open. Water features come into play on holes five, six and seven. The course is well wooded with mature trees and an abundance of wildlife. The club house is well equipped for refreshments.

▶ Dereham   MAP REF 294 A4

Dereham (officially East Dereham) can trace its roots back to Neolithic times. Most of its earliest buildings were lost in fires, but look for Bishop Bonner's cottage, built in 1502 and said to have been the home of the notorious Edmund Bonner (1500–69), Bishop of London, who persecuted heretics relentlessly in Mary I's time and died as a prisoner of Elizabeth I.

PLAY A ROUND
Dereham Golf Club
derehamgolfclub.com
Quebec Road, NR19 2DS
01362 695900 | Open daily all year
On the outskirts of Dereham this friendly club has a nine-hole parkland course and 17 different tees. There's a lounge bar and dining area.

▶ PLACES NEARBY

The Gressenhall Farm and Workhouse is a great destination for a family outing just outside Dereham – follow the brown signs from the town centre. If you like country golf courses, then head for the Mattishall Golf Course.

Gressenhall Farm and Workhouse

museums.norfolk.gov.uk
Gressenhall, NR20 4DR
01362 869263 | Open Mar–Oct
daily 10–5
This superb museum of Norfolk life provides plenty for families to do: there's a woodland adventure playground, a working farm with rare breed animals, a dairy complete with a milking machine and a workhouse where daily Victorian life is re-created by costumed guides and stories told of the people who lived there. All this is set in 50 acres of pristine parkland, criss-crossed by trails.

Mattishall Golf Course

mattishallgolfclub.co.uk
South Green, Mattishall,
NR20 3JZ | 01362 850111
Open daily all year
Mattishall has the distinction of having the longest hole in Norfolk, at a very demanding 638 yards par five. This nine-hole course can be played as 18 holes. Facilities include a large practice putting green next to the main course.

▶ Diss MAP REF 290 B2

Diss is a delightful Norfolk market town that almost straddles the county's border with Suffolk. Timber-framed cottages and smart Georgian properties line many of its town-centre streets. The town can trace its roots back to the time of Edward the Confessor (c.1003–66), one of the last Anglo-Saxon kings of England, when daily life revolved around a wealthy Crown estate. Over the centuries Diss became a centre for the wool industry and enjoyed great prosperity; some of grand wool merchants' houses remain to this day.

Look out for the 14th-century church of St Mary the Virgin in the area of the Market Place, and then turn to see Dolphin House. This lavishly timbered house is one of the finest period properties in Diss.

CATCH A PERFORMANCE
Diss Corn Hall

thecornhall.co.uk
St Nicolas Street, IP22 4LB
01379 652241
From music and dance to comedy, theatrical performances and films, Diss's Corn Hall is the place to head for an evening out. By day it hosts exhibitions featuring the work of local artists, and there are displays about the building's history on loan from

the award-winning Diss Museum, which is housed in a building called The Shambles in the Market Place (open mid-Mar to late Nov, daily 11–3).

PLAY A ROUND
Diss Golf Club
dissgolf.co.uk
Stuston Common, IP21 4AA
01379 641025 | Open daily all year
The heath and parkland course of the Diss Golf Club, which is located alongside the River Waveney, provides challenging golf for all standards of player. Holes range from the scenic but difficult 468-yard par 4 13th hole to the pretty 15th at 146 yards.

▶ PLACES NEARBY
Children will jump at the chance to ride on the steam trains at Bressingham, which you'll find two and a bit miles away. Diss has a number of fine restaurants, and you'll be spoilt for choice but, if you fancy venturing a little further afield, then head for the Fox and Goose in Fressingfield, or the Crown in Burston.

Bressingham Steam Museum and Gardens
bressingham.co.uk
Low Road, Bressingham, IP22 2AB
01379 686900 | Open daily
end-Mar–May, Sep–Oct 10.30–5,
Jun–Aug 10.30–5.30
Alan Bloom is an internationally recognised nurseryman and a steam enthusiast, and has combined his interests to great effect at Bressingham. There are three miniature steam-hauled trains, including a 15-inch gauge called 'Waveney Valley Railway' running through two and a half miles of the wooded Waveney Valley.

A steam roundabout is another attraction, as is the steam museum. There is also a museum of props and vehicles from *Dad's Army*. See the website for events that are held throughout the year.

The Dell Garden has 5,000 species of perennials and alpines; Foggy Bottom has wide vistas, pathways, trees, shrubs, conifers and winter colour (restricted opening).

Fox & Goose Inn ❀❀

foxandgoose.net
Church Road, Fressingfield,
IP21 5PB | 01379 586247
Hard by the medieval church,
Fressingfield's timber-framed
Tudor guildhall serves the local
community as the village inn.
The pub part of the equation
pulls a fine pint of real ale and
sports a spruced up modern
look with old beams, open fires,
church pews at pale wood
tables, and slate and quarry tile
floors. If you want something
more ambitious than well-
crafted pub classics, head
upstairs to the beamed
restaurant for creative modern
cooking driven by Suffolk's
abundant larder.

The Crown

burstoncrown.com
Mill Road, Burston, IP22 5TW
01379 741257
Steve and Bev Kembery have
transformed their 16th-century
pub by the green into a cracking
community pub, drawing locals
in for top-notch ale and food,
organising the village fete,
hosting three beer festivals a
year, and offering a weekly
buskers' night and regular
theme nights.

▼ Diss Mere

▶ Dunwich

Dunwich was an important port in Saxon and Norman times, exporting wool and grain to Europe and importing cloth and wine. It boasted a population of 5,000 and had at least three churches plus many monastic buildings, a mint, a large guildhall, alehouses, farmhouses and mills.

The sea was the making and breaking of Dunwich. It was the sea that provided the reason for its existence, supporting its industries of shipbuilding and fishing, and bringing its most famous figure, St Felix of Burgundy, to preach Christianity to

▼ The Dunwich coastline

the pagans of East Anglia in the 7th century. He became Bishop of Dunwich and gave his name to Felixstowe.

And it was the sea that silted up the harbour in a terrible storm in 1286, leading to its inevitable decline. Further storms followed. A particularly fierce one in 1328, which diverted the River Blyth northwards, effectively obliterated the settlement. The crashing North Sea breakers left a couple of solitary gravestones from the former church of All Saints, near the cliff, and the crumbling walls of the Greyfriars friary, as the only evidence of the medieval town lost beneath the waves. Ever since, the sea has been reclaiming Dunwich, a process that continues at the rate of around one yard each year.

The Roman town here extended a mile beyond the present coastline. Half of this had disappeared by the time of the Norman Conquest, but the worst was yet to come. The remains of the last church tumbled over the cliffs as recently as 1920; Dunwich Museum has a series of dramatic photographs showing it collapsing year by year.

According to local legend, you can still hear the bells of the sunken churches pealing beneath the sea on a stormy night. A pioneering underwater survey has recently mapped the lost areas, and confirmed that many of the larger stone structures are still standing.

Just south of Dunwich is Dunwich Heath, belonging to the National Trust. Beyond is the Minsmere RSPB Nature Reserve (see page 238), an area of marshes and lagoons that attracts many wading birds.

VISIT THE MUSEUM
Dunwich Museum
dunwichmuseum.org.uk
St James Street, Dunwich, IP17 3DT
01728 648796 | Open Mar Sat–Sun 2–4, Apr–Oct daily 11.30–4.30
The Dunwich Museum tells the fascinating story of this once bustling medieval seaport through narratives, including a series of dramatic photographs showing it falling into the sea over the centuries. A scale model also features and there are changing exhibitions.

GET OUTDOORS
Dunwich Heath
nationaltrust.org.uk/dunwichheath
Saxmundham, IP17 3DJ
01728 648501 | Open daily, tea room open Mar–early-Nov
Dunwich Heath is run by the National Trust and is a quiet and peaceful place, ideal for leisurely coastal walks. From July to September it is especially colourful with its carpet of purple heather and bushes of yellow gorse.

EAT AND DRINK
The Ship at Dunwich ☻
shipatdunwich.co.uk
Saint James Street, IP17 3DT
01728 648219
Two minutes' stroll from the beach, the Ship at Dunwich is a well-loved old smugglers' inn overlooking the salt marshes and sea, and is popular with walkers and birders visiting the nearby reserves. The Ship keeps Dunwich on the map with hearty meals, ales from Adnams and a range of guest ales from local breweries. Its delightful, unspoiled public bar offers nautical bric-a-brac, a wood-burning stove in a huge fireplace, flagged floors and simple wooden furnishings. It is locally renowned for its fish and chips. Look for the ancient fig tree in the garden, and take note of the inn's beer festivals that take place on bank holiday Sundays. Accommodation, including family rooms, are available if you want to stay over.

▶ Duxford MAP REF 288 B5

Duxford is a small village a few miles south of Cambridge and is best known as the airfield home of RAF Duxford during the Battle of Britain. In the centre of the village are cottages that sit snugly with Georgian country houses, two somewhat stately medieval churches, St Peter and St John the Baptist, and a gorgeous chapel, but it is the Imperial War Museum Duxford on the former RAF site that most people head for when visiting the village. The museum is well signposted and easy to find just off the main road from Essex into Cambridge. It's the largest aviation and war museum in the country, so you can't miss it.

VISIT THE MUSEUM
Imperial War Museum Duxford
see highlight panel overleaf

EAT AND DRINK
Duxford Lodge Hotel
duxfordlodgehotel.co.uk
Ickleton Road, CB22 4RT
01223 836444
Just a few minutes from the famous airfield and its museum, Edwardian Duxford Lodge Hotel is steeped in wartime history, having played host in the 1940s to stars and big names such as Bing Crosby, Winston Churchill and Douglas Bader. With views of the secluded gardens, its Le Paradis restaurant is a soothing, pastel-hued venue offering a European-influenced menu.

The Duxford Plough
theduxfordplough.co.uk
57 St Peter's Street, CB22 4RP
01223 833170
In this cosy traditional pub with beams and an open fire, five real ales, four draught ciders and various guest ales are always on tap and the menu is varied and interesting. The Sunday roasts are so popular that it's advisable to book ahead.

10 top museums

▶ **Bressingham Steam Museum and Gardens**, Bressingham, page 118

▶ **Dunwich Museum**, Dunwich, page 122

▶ **Fitzwilliam Museum**, Cambridge, page 93

▶ **Gainsborough's House**, Sudbury, page 257

▶ **Imperial War Museum Duxford**, Duxford, page 124

▶ **Moyse's Hall Museum**, Bury St Edmunds, page 77

▶ **National Heritage Centre for Horseracing and Sporting Art**, Newmarket, page 198

▶ **Norfolk and Suffolk Aviation Museum**, Flixton, page 74

▶ **RNLI Henry Blogg Museum**, Cromer, page 104

▶ **Time and Tide Museum**, Great Yarmouth, page 143

▶ Imperial War Museum Duxford

MAP REF 288 B5

iwm.org.uk
CB22 4QR | 01223 835000
Open mid-Mar to late-Oct
daily 10–6, late-Oct to
mid-Mar 10–4
This remarkable museum
tells the story of the
impact aviation had on the
nature of war, on people's lives and on the history of the region.
Duxford is Britain's best-preserved World War II fighter station, and
has seven impressive hangars – some with listed building status
– filled with an extraordinary collection of aircraft and vehicles.
Here you can see around 200 aircraft, naval vessels and military
vehicles, plus sections dedicated to the Parachute Regiment and
the Royal Anglian Regiment. Books and photographs help tell the
story of Britain at war. If you are lucky, you may catch an air show;
they are a regular feature among the special events.

▼ Imperial War Museum Duxford

chmitt Bf 109E

German fighter of the Second World War. This example actually flew in the

The John Barleycorn
johnbarleycorn.co.uk
3 Moorfield Road, CB22 4PP
01223 832699

This thatched and whitewashed former coach house was built in 1660 and took the name John Barleycorn in the mid-19th century. During World War II, it was a favourite watering hole for the brave young airmen of Douglas Bader's Duxford Wing. Step through the door into the softly lit bar with a rustic mix of country furniture, large brick fireplace, old tiled floor, cushioned pews and hop-adorned low beams. It's a cosy place in which to enjoy a hearty home-cooked meal, or a lighter lunch of jacket potato or sandwiches, washed down with a refreshing pint from the range of real ales. Summer alfresco eating can be enjoyed on the flower-festooned rear patio.

▶ East Bergholt   MAP REF 290 B6

East Bergholt in Suffolk is famous for being the birthplace of 19th-century landscape painter John Constable. His childhood home, East Bergholt House, is no longer there but a plaque on railings marks the spot where it once stood; you can find it a few minutes' walk from the village's church of St Mary the Virgin. Constable moved to London to join the Royal Academy, but he is said to have returned to East Bergholt every summer to draw fresh inspiration from the bucolic scenery of meadows, valleys, rivers and farmland – several well-known works of his feature landscapes from the surrounding area. His parents are buried in the churchyard, and there is a memorial to his wife, Maria, inside the church (Constable himself, along with Maria, is buried in the churchyard of St-John-at-Hampstead in Hampstead, London).

Flatford Mill, which was owned by Constable's wealthy father, Willy Lott's Cottage and the Bridge Cottage were all painted by Constable and can be visited in the village. You can take a tour of these sites and enjoy some of the best walks you could wish for in the beautiful unspoiled countryside of the Dedham Vale.

The village has fine examples of half-timbered and thatched cottages and magnificent churches, reflecting its heyday during the 14th century when this part of East Anglia was one of the richest parts of England and the base of the wool industry. See also Dedham Vale (page 110).

▶ Easton

see **Framlingham**, page 136

▲ Ely Cathedral

▶ Ely MAP REF 288 B2

You will be bowled over by Ely. It has a real sense of harmony, with its vast cathedral, one of the most beautiful buildings you're ever likely to see, towering over the rustic cottages and elegant homes that surround it. Ely's history is awesome.

It has its origins in the foundation of an abbey in 673 on the Isle of Ely, which was under the protection of Saint Etheldreda. Destroyed by Danish invaders in 870 and then not rebuilt for over a century, the site was one of the last places in England to hold out against the rule of William the Conqueror.

The stunning cathedral is known as the Ship of the Fens for the distant views of the 170-foot-tall Octagon that dominates the surrounding low-lying wetlands. Oliver Cromwell lived in Ely for several years after inheriting the position of local tax collector. His former home dates from the 16th century and is now used as the tourist information office and a museum, with rooms displayed as they would have been in Cromwell's time.

Today, Ely has some attractive Georgian buildings and a large park that, together with the cathedral and its history, make this an appealing place to visit.

TAKE IN SOME HISTORY
Ely Cathedral
elycathedral.org
CB7 4DL | 01353 667735
Open summer daily 7–6.30, winter
Mon–Sat 7–6.30, Sun 7–5.30

The present cathedral dates from 1083 and is a magnificent example of Romanesque architecture. You can take a tour of the cathedral, including the Octagon Lantern Tower, and visit the museum of stained glass inside. Choral music is a big attraction at the cathedral; there are concerts throughout the year and you can hear Evensong every day at 5.30 (4 on a Sunday).

VISIT THE MUSEUMS

Ely Museum

elymuseum.org.uk
The Old Gaol, Market Street, CB7 4LS | 01353 666655
Open summer Mon–Sat 10.30–5, Sun 1–5, winter Mon, Wed–Sat 10.30–4, Sun 1–4

Ely Museum is housed in a building dating from the 13th century that has been a private house, a tavern, a register office and, most famously, the Bishop's Gaol. It was sensitively renovated in 1997 and you can see much of the building's history, including prisoners' graffiti, hidden doorways and original planking on the walls. Telling the story of the area from prehistoric times to the 20th century, the museum is a history centre for the Isle of Ely and the Fens.

Oliver Cromwell's House

olivercromwellshouse.co.uk
29 St Mary's Street, CB7 4HF
01353 662062 | Open daily Apr–Oct 10–5, Nov–Mar 11–4; last admission 1 hour before closing

Politician Oliver Cromwell (1599–1658) inherited this fine timber-framed house and local estates from a maternal uncle and moved here in 1636, along with his mother, sisters, wife and eight children. There are displays and period rooms dealing with his life, the English Civil War and domestic life in the 17th century, as well as the history of the Fens and the house itself, from its medieval origins to its role as an inn in the 19th century. Various special events are held during the year.

▼ Oliver Cromwell's House

Stained Glass Museum

stainedglassmuseum.com
The South Triforium, Ely Cathedral,
CB7 4DL | 01353 660347
Open Mon–Sat 10.30–5, Sun
12–4.30. Check the website for
closures due to special events

It's fascinating to see stained glass up close, albeit in protective cabinets. Some 800 years of stained-glass history are illustrated in this unique museum inside Ely Cathedral, displaying over 125 panels of original windows rescued from Britain and abroad. The medieval section includes important loans from the Victoria and Albert Museum in London. There are also exhibits from Buckingham Palace and Windsor Castle, work by William Morris and John Piper; and changing exhibitions of contemporary work are held throughout the year.

PLAY A ROUND

Ely City Golf Club

elygolf.co.uk
107 Cambridge Road, CB7 4HX
01353 662751 | Open daily all year

The slightly undulating parkland with water hazards formed by lakes and natural dykes ensure that the course here presents a challenge. There's a demanding par 4 5th hole (467 yards), often into a headwind, and a testing par 3 2nd hole (160 yards) played over two ponds. The clubhouse offers meals, and there are magnificent views over the cathedral.

EAT AND DRINK

Peacocks

peacockstearoom.co.uk
65 Waterside, CB7 4AU
01353 661100

The owners of Peacocks add a little extra to the traditional tea room experience with their homemade specialities. Light meals such as Norfolk ham salad and cakes are available all day, with both soup and a dish of the day offered. A treat are the freshly baked scones served with Cornish clotted cream. The choice of teas is remarkable, with 70 listed, so try something different – maybe the Chocolate Imperial from Paris.

▶ PLACES NEARBY

The enthralling Wildfowl and Wetlands Trust's Welney Wetland Centre as well as Cambridge (see page 88) and the Wicken Fen National Nature Reserve (see page 279) are all within easy reach of Ely. En route you might like to take a refreshment stop at the Lazy Otter in the village of Stretham.

Welney Wetland Centre

wwt.org.uk
Hundred Foot Bank, Welney,
PE14 9TN | 01353 860711 | Open
Mar–Oct daily 9.30–5, Nov–Feb
Mon–Wed 10–5, Thu–Sun 10–8

This important wetland site on the beautiful Ouse Washes, managed by the Wildfowl and Wetlands Trust, is famed for the breathtaking winter spectacle of wild ducks, geese and swans. Impressive observation facilities, including hides and a heated main observatory, offer outstanding views of the huge numbers of wildfowl, which include Bewick's and whooper swans, wigeon, teal and shoveler. Floodlit evening swan feeds take place between November and February. In summer, the reserve is alive with over 40 per cent of all British wetland plant flowers. Butterflies, dragonflies and damselflies are in abundance, and the available summer walk gives visitors unique access to the wetland habitat.

The Lazy Otter
lazy-otter.com
Cambridge Road, Stretham,
CB6 3LU | 01353 649780
A pub here has served fenland watermen for centuries; today's incarnation is popular with leisure boaters on the River Ouse, which glides past the extensive beer garden. As well as overlooking the river, the garden has views over the rich farmland. Barley from these acres goes into a wide range of East Anglian beers, including the house ale from Milton Brewery. The pub hosts an annual beer and cider festival.

▶ Fakenham MAP REF 293 F2

The market town of Fakenham lies at the heart of Norfolk's flat open countryside and seems to be miles from anywhere. It's mentioned in the Domesday Book and was awarded its charter in 1250. It is best known locally for its racecourse. On race days people come from miles around and the town is bustling. There's a museum, too, dedicated to gas and local history, and a nature reserve and gardens at Pensthorpe which are worth a visit.

VISIT THE MUSEUM
Fakenham Museum of Gas and Local History
fakenhamgasmuseum.com
Hempton Road, NR21 7LA
01553 762151 | Open Thu 10–12
Housed in a building that is the only surviving town gasworks in England, complete with all the apparatus needed to turn coal into gas, this museum offers a fascinating account of local social history. You can see original purifiers and condensers, and displays about heating, lighting and cooking

through the decades. The town's gasworks closed in 1965, having been in operation providing gas since 1846.

GET OUTDOORS
Pensthorpe Natural Park
pensthorpe.co.uk
Pensthorpe, NR21 0LN
01328 851465 | Open daily Jan–Feb 10–4, Mar–Dec 10–5
You can explore the beautiful lakes, nature trails and gardens designed by Chelsea Flower Show gold medalists at award-winning Pensthorpe,

which was home to BBC TV's popular *Springwatch* series from 2008 to 2010. Look out for red squirrels and the large collection of cranes in the Conservation Centre. There are purpose-built hides, daily bird feeds and warden-guided walks. Children can enjoy exploring the bug walks and discovering underwater wildlife or playing in the WildRootz adventure playground or state-of-the-art Hootz House indoor play centre.

In spring and summer, the hour-long Wensum Discovery Tour in a specially designed Land Rover and trailer weaves a way through remote parts of the Wensum Valley. The three gardens here, all designed to attract wildlife, are spectacular through the seasons. There's a lovely wildflower meadow too, grazed by Norfolk long horn sheep in autumn, with a boardwalk nature trail through it. The diverse range of habitats at Pensthorpe means it's an important breeding site for many species of bird and insect.

You can easily spend a day here and the Courtyard Cafe has plenty on the menu to suit all tastes.

GO TO THE RACES
Fakenham Racecourse
fakenhamracecourse.co.uk
The Racecourse, NR21 7NY
01328 862388

Race days at the Fakenham Racecourse are friendly affairs. It doesn't have a dress code so there's no stuffiness and everyone's welcome, including children. You can visit the paddocks and see the horses before they race. There are two restaurants and afternoon tea is available too. Check the website for racing dates, which are predominantly in the spring, autumn and winter.

EAT AND DRINK
The Wensum Lodge Hotel
wensumlodge.co.uk
Bridge Street, NR21 9AY
01328 862100

Located in an idyllic spot by the River Wensum, just 3 minutes' walk from the centre of Fakenham, this lovely pub has a stream flowing through its garden and offers guests free fishing on the river. The building dates from around 1700 and was originally the grain store for the adjoining mill. The fine ales are complemented by home-cooked food prepared from locally supplied ingredients, with baguettes, jacket potatoes and an all-day breakfast on the light bites menu and an à la carte menu for heartier fare. The hotel is an ideal base for cycling, birding, fishing and horseracing.

▶ PLACES NEARBY

Just 6 miles or so from Fakenham is Thursford Green village, where you can visit the wonderful Thursford steam and mechanical collection and perhaps indulge in a behind-the-scenes tour and dine in the Old Forge Seafood Restaurant.

Thursford Collection

thursford.com
Thursford, NR21 0AS
01328 878477 | Open Apr–mid-Sep
Sun–Thu 11–4 (last entry 3pm)
The Thursford Collection is
famous for being the world's
largest collection of steam
engines and mechanical
organs. You can see Wurlitzer
shows, silent movies, old-
fashioned fairground carousels
and static displays of both
fairground and road engines,
along with all kinds of related
memorabilia. There are two
behind-the-scenes tours: the
first goes backstage, taking
in dressing rooms, costume
stores, and the wardrobe
department; while the second
visits the old forge and a
re-creation of an engine yard
of the 1940s. During November
and December, people flock
from miles around to the huge
Christmas Spectacular shows
and to take the children on
Santa's Magical Journey.
There's free entry to the
shops between April and
December and the Thursford
restaurant offers a full range
of hot food and snacks.

The Old Forge Seafood Restaurant

seafoodnorthnorfolk.co.uk
Fakenham Road, Thursford,
NR21 0BD | 01328 878345
This whitewashed former
coaching station and forge
used to be a resting place
for pilgrims heading to
Walsingham, and even merits
a name-check in *The Pilgrim's
Progress* (1678). A sympathetic
refurbishment means that
the beams, the York stone
floor and walls, and even the
original iron hooks where the
horses were shod are in
evidence in the cosy, buzzy
restaurant. It's all about the
seafood here – why not, when
you can get it in fresh every day
from nearby Blakeney and
Wells-next-the-Sea. Expect
good, honest, rustic cooking,
often with Spanish influences
and using spices grown in The
Old Forge's garden.

▶ Felbrigg

see **Cromer**, page 103

▶ Felixstowe MAP REF 291 D6

Felixstowe, whose name means 'happy place', is a traditional
Edwardian seaside resort on Suffolk's coast that continues to
provide families with buckets of summer fun. Here, your
children can ride bumper boats, go fishing for crabs and buy
sticks of rock from kiosks on the pier, while older folk stroll
along the promenade and drink tea at seafront cafes.

Yes, the character of Felixstowe, which is all rather genteel,
hasn't changed much over the decades – the exception being

its port. In the days of press gangs, Felixstowe was not a place to drop your guard. If you did so you risked spending the next few months or years sailing and fighting on the high seas. The town became a major port in 1886, and in recent years has grown to become Britain's largest container complex. A village has stood on the site since before the Norman Conquest. Its location made it a lynchpin in England's defences, most notably in 1667 when Dutch soldiers landed and failed to capture Landguard Fort.

During the late Victorian era, with the opening of the railway station, Felixstowe became a fashionable resort.

Today, despite the size of the port, Felixstowe retains its attractiveness. It has a long sand and shingle beach and extensive gardens line the promenade. Some of the gardens, such as those by the Spa Pavilion and Town Hall, have been listed on the English Heritage Register of Parks and Gardens of National Importance.

Just along the beach, Landguard Peninsula is a nature reserve with an historic fort and the Felixstowe Museum, and a passenger ferry links Felixstowe with Harwich in Essex, on the other side of the River Stour (sailing times vary according to the season and weather).

TAKE IN SOME HISTORY
Landguard Fort
discoverlandguard.org.uk
View Point Road, Landguard
Peninsula, IP11 3TW | 01394
675900 | Open Apr–Oct daily 10–5
Visit the site of the last seaborne invasion of England in 1667. There's a maze of rooms and bastion viewing platforms.

PLAY A ROUND
Felixstowe Ferry Golf Club
felixstowegolf.co.uk
Ferry Road, IP11 9RY
01394 286834 | Open Mon–Fri
all year
The Felixstowe Ferry Golf Club is the fifth oldest such club in England. It has a seaside links with pleasant views and easy

▼ Landguard Fort

walking, and a nine-hole pay-and-play course. Both courses offer a good challenge.

EAT AND DRINK
The Regal Fish Bar
and Restaurant
theregalrestaurant.com
Sea Road, IP11 2DH | 01394 273977
There's nothing quite like dining on the freshest fish and chips in a restaurant right on the seafront of a traditional town like Felixstowe. The Regal, housed in a glorious Victorian building looking out over the sea, where fish brought ashore just hours before is delivered daily, offers exactly that. Dine in the large restaurant or take away for chips by the sea – it's up to you.

▶ Framlingham MAP REF 291 D3

You will adore the gorgeous Suffolk market town of Framlingham, or Fram as it's referred to by locals. Dominated in alarming fashion by its remarkably well-preserved fortifications that date from around the reign of King John (1166–1216), it is steeped in royal history. It was here at the castle, in 1553, that Mary Tudor gathered her supporters around her as she waited anxiously to learn whether she or Lady Jane Grey would be declared Queen.

Framlingham Castle is today in the care of English Heritage, and is one of the most important and beautiful medieval castles in the country. It simply oozes 800 years of history at every turn. Its unusual curtain wall, one of the earliest in England, is topped by 13 defensive towers. Unlike in other castles, it is possible to walk the full length of the battlements. Little remains of the interior of the castle, however, except a 17th-century poor house and medieval headstones.

A walk around Framlingham – it is nice and compact, if a little steep in places – will show you attractive houses and shops that gather around the triangular Market Hill. In a county replete with glorious church architecture, the parish church of St Michael is especially pleasing. The roof is resplendent with intricate fan tracery, which conceals hammerbeams. There is also a splendid collection of 16th-century tombs belonging to members of the Howard family – John Howard (c.1425–85) was the first Duke of Norfolk – at the time when they owned the castle.

The town has many quaint buildings dating from the 17th, 18th and 19th centuries, the best examples of which can be found on Market Hill. Framlingham is surrounded by the villages of Sweffling, Kettleburgh, Earl Soham and Saxtead, and country lanes that are ideal for walking and cycling. It is an excellent base from which to explore this part of Suffolk.

▲ Framlingham Castle

TAKE IN SOME HISTORY
Framlingham Castle
english-heritage.org.uk
IP13 9BP | 01728 724189
Open Apr–Sep daily 10–6, Oct daily
10–5, Nov–Mar Sat–Sun 10–4; check
website for school holiday events

The attractive, mellow-hued
battlemented towers and walls
of Framlingham Castle have
had some notable owners. The
Earl of Norfolk, Roger Bigod,
built the castle somewhere
between about 1189 and 1200
on the site of an earlier castle.
The Bigods traditionally had
tempestuous relationships with
their kings – Hugh Bigod
supported Henry II's eldest son
when he rebelled against his
father in 1173, Roger Bigod II
held Framlingham against King
John in 1216, and Roger Bigod
IV refused to go to Flanders to
fight for Edward I in 1297.

Framlingham Castle was
also owned by the Mowbray
family, one of whom was
engaged to marry one of the
unfortunate princes in the
Tower; and the Howard family,
members of which were dukes
of Norfolk in Henry VIII's time.
It was at Framlingham that
'Bloody' Mary learned that she
had become Queen of England
in 1553. Later, Elizabeth I used
the castle as a prison for priests
who refused to accept the new
Church of England.

Framlingham Castle has 13
towers, all connected by walls,
and you can walk right round
the castle. There are beautiful
views over the mere. When the
castle was no longer used as a
ducal residence, it took on
several different roles through
the ensuing centuries, including
a poor house – the buildings for

which survive in the courtyard – a parish meeting place, dance hall, courtroom, drill hall and a fire station.

You can learn more about the castle's colourful past from the new walk-through exhibition and interactive games that bring history to life.

SEE A LOCAL CHURCH
St Michael the Archangel
Church Street, IP13 9BJ
01728 621255

Known affectionately as St Mike's, the church of St Michael the Archangel is not far from the town centre, almost at the foot of the castle. You can see fabulous tombs and the 500-year-old nave roof, which is a masterpiece of carpentry. The hammerbeams are concealed behind timber vaulting. A masterpiece of a different kind is the ornate organ, built in 1674 by Thomas Thamar and still in use. Its case may be older, and is a rare survivor of the destruction of such organs ordered by Oliver Cromwell during the English Civil War.

This Perpendicular-style church was built by the third Duke of Norfolk, Thomas Howard, in 1550 as a family mausoleum, and it incorporates some remains of an earlier church. Look out for the capitals of the chancel arch which date from the 12th century. The church holds the tombs of the Howard family from before the Reformation. Some of the remains had to be moved to the church from Thetford Priory when Henry VIII dissolved the monasteries. They were joined by later family tombs of increasingly extravagant design, such as the gilded tomb of Henry Howard, Earl of Surrey, who was beheaded, aged 30, in 1547.

EAT AND DRINK
The Station Hotel
thestationframlingham.com
Station Road, IP13 9EE
01728 723455

Built as part of the local railway in the 19th century, The Station Hotel has been a pub since the 1950s, outliving the railway, which closed in 1962. Inside, you will find scrubbed tables and an eclectic mix of furniture. During the last decade it has established a reputation for its earthy, gutsy food, listed on the ever-changing blackboard menu. Many of the beers are brewed in Suffolk, and the pub hosts a beer festival in mid-July.

▶ **PLACES NEARBY**

A 5-minute drive away is the village of Cretingham, where locals will tell you the tale of a grisly murder at the vicarage in 1887, when the elderly Reverend Farley had his throat cut by his apparently mentally unstable curate. Today, it is a quiet, unassuming little place, with one of the area's finest golf courses. The quiet village of Easton is also close by; this was an estate up until the end of World War I, when it was sold and divided into plots for new homes. Here you'll find Easton Farm Park, one of the best places in the region for seeing rare breeds of farm animals. The village of Saxtead Green is known for its gorgeous windmill; the green itself is also a haven for beautiful wild flowers.

Cretingham Golf Club
cretinghamgolfclub.co.uk
Cretingham, IP13 7BA
01728 685275 | Open daily all year

Cretingham Golf Club has a tree-lined parkland course with many water features, including the River Deben, which runs through it. The par 4s are described as a mixture of risk and reward, with some proving deceptively challenging. This course offers lovely Suffolk views and the clubhouse has a bar and restaurant area.

Easton Farm Park
eastonfarmpark.co.uk
Easton, IP13 0EQ | 01728 746475
Check website for opening times

An award-winning farming museum and park, Easton Farm Park lies on the banks of the River Deben. There are plenty of breeds of farm animals, including Suffolk Punch horses, ponies, pigs, lambs and calves, goats, rabbits, guinea pigs and poultry. Children love to see the chicks hatching, and to join in the daily egg collecting, plus free hug-a-bunny and pony rides.

Saxtead Green Post Mill
english-heritage.org.uk
The Mill House, Saxtead Green, IP13 9QQ | 0370 333 1181
Open Apr–Sep Fri–Sat 12–5

With its massive sails silhouetted against the sky and its brilliant white round house that revolves on its base, you will adore the post corn windmill at Saxtead Green. It dates from the late 1790s and, although commercial milling ceased in 1947, is still in working order. You can climb the wooden stairs of this three-storey mill; each floor is full of fascinating machinery, such as millstones and the massive oak brake wheel. At the top you can see the windshaft, on which the sails and their fantail are fixed. The mill is classed as an Ancient Monument and is cared for by English Heritage. An audio tour explains the workings of the mill.

▶ Grantchester MAP REF 288 A4

Grantchester, on the outskirts of Cambridge, conjures up images of jolly young men and winsome girls enjoying picnics next to the river, which flows gently between flower-strewn meadows. Bicycles are propped up against trees and poetry is in the air. Except that Grantchester is an altogether busier place today than as portrayed in the poems of Rupert Brooke (1887–1915), who was a student at King's College before World War I. His 1912 poem 'The Old Vicarage, Grantchester', in which he recalls happy days in the idyllic English surroundings of Cambridgeshire, immortalised a particular view of 'Englishness'. Brooke lived at the Orchard (tea gardens) for a couple of years, and then next door at the Old Vicarage, the present home of author Jeffery Archer and his wife Mary.

Within walking distance of Cambridge, Grantchester is a lovely village of black-and-white half-timbered buildings, thatched cottages, a pretty church and meadows. The village is a favourite among both tourists and students who travel upstream from Cambridge by punt to eat a picnic in the meadows or at the Orchard, as they have done since the 19th century.

EAT AND DRINK
Orchard Tea Garden
theorchardteagarden.co.uk
45–7 Mill Way, CB3 9ND
01223 840230 | Open daily all year, check website for seasonal timings
The tradition of serving afternoon tea at the Orchard began in 1897, when a group of students punted up the river and asked for refreshments. It soon became a regular thing. Among the famous people who have taken tea there are James Mason, Norman Hartnell, Emma Thompson, John Cleese, Peter Cook, Stephen Fry, Hugh Laurie, Griff Rhys Jones, King George VI, Prince Charles and Clive James. Poets Ted Hughes and Sylvia Plath often walked to Grantchester from their city-centre home for tea in the 1950s. Although famed for cakes, scones and afternoon

cream teas, it does a good breakfast and serves light lunches, too.

▶ **PLACES NEARBY**
Head off to see beautiful Anglesey Abbey (see page 99), Duxford (see page 123) and the delights of Cambridge (see page 88), which are 10 minutes or so away by car, or the enchanting Wicken Fen National Nature Reserve (see page 279).

▶ Great Bircham MAP REF 293 D2

Great Bircham, together with the villages of Bircham Tofts and Bircham Newton, make up a community that sprawls over several miles of the flat north Norfolk countryside. It is best known for its windmill, which you can see for miles around.

GET INDUSTRIAL
Bircham Windmill
birchamwindmill.co.uk
PE31 6SJ | 01485 578393
Open late Mar–Sep daily 10–5
This gorgeous, moody, grey tarred-brick windmill with huge white sails and a white cap is one of the last remaining purpose-built windmills in Norfolk. If you visit on a windy day, you'll see the sails turning at an alarming speed. It's a spectacular sight. There are five floors, which you can climb and, when the sails are turning, you can see the milling machinery working.

Next to the windmill is a bakery – simply follow the aroma of freshly baked goods. There's also a tea room, built on the site of the granary, which, along with 17 blends of tea, also serves light lunches, scones and cakes.

You could make a trip to the windmill part of a day out as it stands in a complex with ponies, sheep, chickens and guinea pigs for children, a lovely garden to wander around and, at weekends, workshops where local craftspeople demonstrate their skills.

EAT AND DRINK
The Kings Head Hotel
thekingsheadcountryhotel.co.uk
Bircham, PE31 6RJ
01485 578265
Built during the Edwardian era, the Kings Head mixes tradition with boutique styling in its 12 individually designed rooms. The bar stocks more than 60 different gins alongside real ales and a good wine list. The team in the kitchen covers a lot of bases and there's a pleasing lack of stuffiness all round, so you can pop into the bar for posh scampi and chips or head into the restaurant with its gently contemporary decor and tuck into something a little more creative. The kitchen makes good use of Norfolk's plentiful larder and has a regularly changing specials menu.

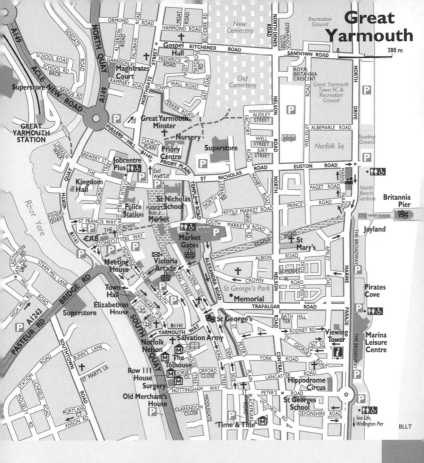

▶ Great Yarmouth MAP REF 295 F4

From modern theme parks and amusements set in gardens to miles of golden sands that hug the promenade, Great Yarmouth in Norfolk is every inch a modern seaside resort; in fact, it's the largest in East Anglia.

You'll find family attractions from carousels to one-armed bandits, from end-of-the-pier shows to zoos, rollercoasters, spas, trendy cafes and gardens to keep everyone amused for hours, even interactive amusements and arcades so all the family are catered for.

Great Yarmouth has been a prosperous seaside resort since 1760 when George II was on the throne – in its heyday, it was one of the wealthiest towns in the country. It has seen wars – being bombed in both World Wars I and II – flooding, the collapse of its fishing industry and the heyday of the music hall, and also had one of the first electric tramway systems in England. Today, it celebrates its heritage as one of the country's foremost maritime centres and Victorian seaside resorts while embracing the 21st century with aplomb.

Ancient peninsula

Great Yarmouth, or simply Yarmouth to locals, occupies a strategic location on the Norfolk coast, which has ensured its prosperity since Roman and Norman times. Remains of early settlers and their large communities can still be seen here today. Like the River Alde to the south, the Yare heads for the sea only to be deflected to the south by a narrow spit of land. It was on this peninsula that the port of Yarmouth developed over millennia – with, as was fashionable, its buildings facing away from the sea.

For centuries Yarmouth's prosperity grew, resting mainly on the vast shoals of herring in the North Sea. Merchants from all over Europe and Scandinavia would come to the medieval Free Herring Fair, which was held in the town and lasted 40 days from Michaelmas (29 September) to Martinmas (11 November). Before World War I, more than 1,000 fishing boats plied their trade from Yarmouth, but overfishing eventually took its toll and the port turned to gas and oil.

You can see reminders of Yarmouth's one-time immense fishing industry. A few houses still stand that were once part

▼ Great Yarmouth harbour

of the 'Rows' – small passageways running inland from the quayside lined with fishermens' houses. They were so narrow that a special horse-drawn vehicle known as a troll cart, which was only 3 feet wide, was developed for moving goods in the town. Today, you can visit the Old Merchant's House, owned by English Heritage, which has been converted into a museum. Yarmouth's Time and Tide Museum, housed in a converted fish-curing works, also celebrates the town's maritime history.

Wide boulevards

Yarmouth today is an elegant place of wide boulevards and handsome buildings. Contemporary architecture sits comfortably with Tudor and Victorian merchants' houses and mansions, especially around the trendy quayside area and along the promenade. The buildings now face the sea; Yarmouth 'turned round' in the 19th century when it became fashionable for Victorian families to visit the seaside, and the ever-resilient town was able to exploit its beach.

The beach and promenade remain the highlight for many visitors. Dominating the scene are Yarmouth's two piers, the Wellington Pier, which opened in 1853 (see page 145), hotly followed five years later by the Britannia Pier, where evening

band performances drew record numbers of people
(see page 145). The late 1800s through to the turn of the
century was a particularly prosperous time for Yarmouth, and
musical and theatrical evenings were the highlight of most
prosperous families' week.

Landmark piers

Both piers are landmarks. The Wellington Pier, and the Winter
Gardens that form part of its complex, has been turned into
a huge family entertainment centre with bowling alleys and
interactive gadgetry, while on the Britannia Pier you can still
catch a show; comedies are popular, as are magic and dance
shows. It also has two amusements arcades where you can
challenge a one-armed bandit, before heading off for a spot of
rifle shooting, bingo or hopping aboard the ghost train. You can
buy multicoloured rock and enjoy doughnuts. Yes, it's good old
family seaside fun.

Along Marine Parade, between the piers, you'll find the
multi-million-pound Sea Life Centre (see page 144) with its
sea star viewing tunnel and shark encounter, along with the
Pirate's Cove Adventure Golf and Amazonia World of Reptiles.
Opposite is the Hippodrome (see page 145), which has been
thrilling audiences with its circus and water shows for decades.
The building dates from 1903 and is one of only a handful of
surviving purpose-built circus venues in the world, and the only
one in England.

Market Gates shopping mall, off Temple Road, and Victoria
Arcade near the Town Hall, provide a vast selection of shops
between them. High street names sit next to tiny specialist

shops selling designer
goodies. In the centre of town,
the Market Place, which is
thought to have been a centre
of trading since before the
town was granted a charter
in 1208, is a wide open space
full of trees and benches
– plus stalls six days a week.
Here, and throughout the
town, you will find stylish
restaurants, pubs and
pavement cafes to make your
visit to Yarmouth complete.

◀ The Pleasure Beach

VISIT THE MUSEUMS

Elizabethan House Museum

nationaltrust.org.uk/
elizabethanhousemuseum
4 South Quay, NR30 2QH
01493 855746 | Open Apr–Oct
Sun–Fri 10–4

This super museum, housed in a 16th-century quayside building, tells the story of everyday folk who lived from Tudor through to Victorian times. You can see room sets, including the wood-panelled Conspiracy Room (was this where Charles I's fate was sealed?) and the kitchen, which give you a glimpse of how people lived. You can dress the family in Tudor costumes too and discover Victorian life, upstairs and downstairs. Children can play in the toy room while the adults relax in the delightful walled garden.

The Rows and Greyfriars' Cloister

english-heritage.org.uk
South Quay, NR30 2RG
01493 857900 | Open Apr–Sep
Mon–Fri 11–4

Known as the Rows, these narrow passageways ran inland from the quayside and were lined with the homes of fishermen. Today, few of the 17th-century houses remain, but the Old Merchant's House, owned by English Heritage, has been converted into a museum, and is open to the public. These houses are unique to Great Yarmouth. Guided walking tours explain how the rich and poor lived in these properties through history. The tours also visit the remains of a Franciscan friary, Greyfriars' Cloister, which has some rare early wall-paintings.

Time and Tide Museum

museums.norfolk.gov.uk
Tower Curing Works, Blackfriars' Road, NR30 3BX | 01493 743930
Open Apr–Oct daily 10–4.30,
Nov–Mar Mon–Fri 10–4,
Sat–Sun 12–4

Full of interactive technology that will keep the whole family occupied for hours, the Time and Tide is an award-winning museum housed in a restored Grade II listed Victorian herring-curing factory. It's one of the best preserved such factories from the period. The museum tells Great Yarmouth's fascinating story, from prehistoric times right through to the present day. You can visit the original smokehouse and see displays about fishing, wrecks and rescue, seaside holidays, port and trade, and the world wars. It also brings to life the herring-curing industry and the lives of the people who worked along the coast.

The Tolhouse Gaol

museums.norfolk.gov.uk
Tolhouse Street, NR30 2SH
01493 858900 | Dates and times vary – see website for details

You can discover the fate of convicted thieves, smugglers, witches, pirates and murderers at a time when punishments included transportation or execution in this gruesome but fascinating museum. It's housed in one of the oldest prisons in the country, and tells the story of Great Yarmouth's criminals and punishment. With the free audio guide you can hear the gaoler and his prisoners describe their experiences. Other exhibits detail the history of this former 12th-century merchant's house that went on to become one of the town's most important civic buildings.

David Howkins Museum of Memories

davidhowkinscharitymuseum.co.uk
39–40 King Street, NR30 2PN
01493 852637 | Open Apr–Sep
Mon, Wed, Fri 10–4

Housed in the former 1912 showrooms of the Great Yarmouth Gas Company, with art nouveau stained glass windows and a grand staircase, this museum is packed with nostalgia. Visit the toy room with its dolls' houses and miniatures, teddy bears' picnic and dolls' tea parties, and marvel at the 19 Yarmouth needlework tapestries depicting 800 years of the town's history. The Stamp Room has an extraordinary collection of postage stamp-encrusted furnishings from a Victoria parlour. The true story of Joseph Merrick, the Elephant Man, is told here; there's also a host of commemorative objects and a collection of iconic holiday posters as well as souvenir collector's items.

Nelson Museum

nelson-museum.co.uk
26 South Quay, NR30 2RG
01493 850698 | Open Feb–mid-Nov
Mon–Thu 10–4, Fri, Sun 1–4
(subject to change)

The only museum dedicated solely to the life and times of Norfolk man and national hero Admiral Horatio Lord Nelson, it is fascinating for adults and fun for children. From Nelson's childhood to his notorious love life, through his naval career to his famous battles and tragic death, there's much to discover among the memorabilia, which includes original letters, paintings, portraits and prints. Medals, coins, ceramics, badges and models are among the commemorative ephemera on display. A maritime play area, complete with wobbly plank, games and dressing up opportunities, keeps youngsters involved; there's a cafe, a picnic area and Georgian herb garden in the courtyard.

MEET THE SEALIFE
Sea Life

visitsealife.com/great-yarmouth
Marine Parade, NR30 3AH
01493 330631 | Open Mon–Fri
from 11, Sat–Sun from 10 (closing
times vary)

See sharks and clownfish, jellyfish, lobsters, penguins and dwarf crocodiles at Sea Life, located right on the seafront. Many of the specimens are endangered species and have been rescued or bred as part of a conservation project. The centre supports conservation around the world, and is actively involved with seahorse breeding programmes and rescuing seals and other creatures. There's an adoption scheme if you want to become more involved.

ENTERTAIN THE FAMILY

Hippodrome

hippodromecircus.co.uk
St George's Road, NR30 2EU
01493 844172
Box office open daily 10–8 during performance seasons, otherwise Sat 11–3. Show times vary; see website
Yarmouth's Hippodrome, which first opened its doors in 1903, is an institution. Housed in the last remaining purpose-built circus building in England, and one of only a few left in the world, it has a programme of summer and Christmas circus and water shows that are simply spectacular. Halloween gets a special half term Spooktacular. In winter you may catch an opera or concert. There's a small museum, the Hippodrome Circus Museum, where you can see props and old photographs and which you can visit after the show.

Britannia Pier

britannia-pier.co.uk
Marine Parade, NR30 2EH
01493 842914 | Open daily
Two amusement arcades can be found along Britannia Pier, with a host of traditional slot machines and more futuristic interactive attractions. You can try your hand at bowling, bingo and mini-karting, or hop aboard the ghost train, dodgems or

10 famous people from Norfolk

- **Henry Blogg**, UK's most celebrated lifeboatman
- **James Blunt**, singer
- **Howard Carter**, archaeologist
- **Diana, Princess of Wales**
- **Stephen Fry**, comedian
- **Myleene Klass**, singer and model
- **Sir Matthew Pinsent**, Olympic rowing champion
- **Admiral Horatio Lord Nelson**
- **Roger Taylor**, musician
- **Robert Walpole**, first British prime minister

carousel. There are plenty of places to eat; you can nibble on everything from burgers and doughnuts to shellfish. At the end of the pier, the historic theatre offers comedy and musical shows year round.

Wellington Pier

wellington-pier.co.uk
Marine Parade, NR30 3JF
01493 845947 | Open daily
Along with the Britannia, the Wellington Pier is a landmark in Great Yarmouth and is a magnet for families looking for traditional seaside fun. There are amusements and simulator rides, slot machines and a family 10-lane 10-pin bowling alley. Shops, an ice cream parlour, cafe and bar, among many other things, can be found along its length.

Merrivale Model Village

merrivalemodelvillage. co.uk

Marine Parade, NR30 3JG

01493 842097 | Open end-Mar–Dec daily from 10 (closing times vary)

Merrivale Model Village offers an altogether different experience. Set in more than an acre of attractive landscaped gardens, complete with winding pathways, streams and waterfalls, and even a lake full of koi carp, this mini village is delightful. As you wander leisurely among its tiny houses it's hard to believe you are so close to the bustle of central Yarmouth. The village is built on a scale of 1:12. Among the models are a working fairground, a stone quarry, houses, shops and a garden railway. The Penny Arcade gives you the chance to play old amusements, while a traditional tea room provides a welcome break.

TAKE TO THE WATER

Lydia Eva

lydiaeva.org.uk

South Quay, NR30 2QJ

078894 12333 | Open Mar–Oct daily 10–4

The world's last surviving steam-powered herring drifter was built in 1930 and became a floating museum dedicated to fishing when its working days were up. A heritage lottery grant meant that it could be restored. In recent times, it has been MCA-coded, which means that it can now go to sea with up to eight passengers on board.

PLAY A ROUND

Great Yarmouth and Caister Golf Club

club-noticeboard.co.uk/ greatyarmouth

Beach House, Caister-on-Sea, NR30 5TD | 01493 728699

Open daily all year

This traditional, classic links-style course with a history that goes back to 1882 offers play over tight and undulating fairways partly set among sand dunes, with gorse and marram grass to negotiate. The greens are well drained and a challenge for all golfers, especially where they cross the racecourse.

EAT AND DRINK

Andover House ◉◉

andoverhouse.co.uk

28–30 Camperdown, NR30 3JB

01493 843490

A touch of boutique styling has been sprinkled over the

white-painted Victorian terrace that is Andover House, and these days it's a rather cool hotel, restaurant and bar, with muted pastel tones and a distinct lack of chintz. There's a daily specials board in support of the à la carte menu. The cooking treads a modish path and there are plenty of global flavours on show.

Imperial Hotel ❀
imperialhotel.co.uk
North Drive, NR30 1EQ
01493 842000
The grand old Imperial Hotel on Great Yarmouth's seafront has been providing generations of visitors with what they want, and in the 21st century that means the contemporary style of the made-over Cafe Cru Restaurant. Daily-changing blackboard specials bolster a repertoire of unpretentious modern British dishes wrought from splendid local materials, while smart staff in black aprons lend a buzzy bistro vibe to proceedings. Plump Morston mussels are a perennial favourite.

▶ PLACES NEARBY
The Roman remains of Burgh Castle, one of a chain of castles built to protect East Anglia from invasion, along with the ruins of St Olave's Priory, are just a few miles away as are the seaside towns of Caister-on-Sea (see page 83) and Lowestoft (see page 189). There are golf courses at Caldecott Hall in Fritton and the Gorleston Golf Club in Gorleston-on-Sea. For refreshments try the Fisherman's Return in Winterton-on-Sea.

▼ Burgh Castle

Burgh Castle

english-heritage.org.uk
NR31 9PZ | 0370 331 1181
Open at any reasonable time

This once imposing castle is one of the best preserved Roman structures in the country. Sections of its massive walls still stand and make an impressive sight overlooking the inland waterway known as Breydon Water (into which part of the castle collapsed long ago). The castle was built in the third century AD by the Romans, and would have dominated this part of the Saxon Shore, a stretch of coast that extends from the Solent to the Wash. It was one of a chain of forts built of mortared flint covered with cut flint and tile.

St Olave's Priory

english-heritage.org.uk
0370 333 1181 | Open at any reasonable time in daylight

The remains of an Augustinian priory, St Olave's is best known for its intricately carved, and virtually complete, brick-vaulted undercroft dated to the 14th century. It was founded nearly 2,000 years after the death in 1030 of St Olave, the patron saint of Norway.

Caldecott Hall Golf and Leisure

caldecotthall.co.uk
Caldecott Hall, Beccles Road, Fritton, NR31 9EY | 01493 488488
Open daily all year

The sprawling complex of Caldecott Hall has a parkland links-style course with testing dog-leg fairways. Facilities include a driving range and practice green.

Gorleston Golf Club

gorlestongolfclub.co.uk
Warren Road, Gorleston-on-Sea, NR31 6JT | 01493 661911
Open daily all year

The Gorleston Golf Club has a clifftop course, the most easterly in the British Isles. One of the outstanding features of the course is the 7th hole, which was rescued from cliff erosion about 20 years ago. The green, only 8 yards from the cliff edge, is at the mercy of the prevailing winds so club selection is critical. A well-stocked bar offers refreshment back at the clubhouse.

Fishermans Return

fishermansreturn.com
The Lane, Winterton-on-Sea, NR29 4BN | 01493 393305

This dog-friendly, 350-year-old brick-and-flint free house stands close to long beaches and National Trust land, making it the ideal spot to finish a walk. Guest ales support Woodforde's Norfolk Nog and Wherry behind the bar, while the menus range from popular favourites such as omelettes and filled jacket potatoes to sirloin steak and three-bean chilli. Look out for fish and seafood specials on the daily-changing blackboard, where freshly caught mackerel or sea bass may be on offer. Don't miss the beer festival on August bank holiday.

> ## Gressenhall
se Dereham, page 117

> ## Hadleigh MAP REF 290 A5

While Hadleigh cannot boast a great castle or manor house, it does have a high street lined with some of the most beautiful buildings imaginable. There are not many towns of such character left in England today, and its medieval charm and architectural styles, ranging from timber-framed to Georgian – some painted in Suffolk pink and others with ornamental plasterwork known as pargeting – are a great attraction for tourists. The town's historic assets are bolstered by its thriving business and community spirit, so spend some time exploring its wide range of interesting shops, pubs and restaurants.

Hadleigh was once the royal town for the ninth-century Danish King Guthrum, who took a liking to it and is said to be buried in St Mary the Virgin church. Later it became one of the most important wool and market towns in England. By the 16th century, in Suffolk, only Ipswich and Bury St Edmunds were more prosperous than Hadleigh. This prosperous past has left a legacy of more than 240 listed buildings.

SEE A LOCAL CHURCH
Church of St Mary
stmaryshadleigh.co.uk
Church Street, IP7 5DT
01473 527499 | Open daily
A grand Suffolk church, large and long, with a medieval spire and the oldest inscribed bell in the county, the Church of St Mary was built in the 14th century and much rebuilt by cloth merchants' wealth in the 15th. The broad arcades date from that era and the magnificent south doorway retains its 15th-century doors. Windows hold stained glass, ancient and modern – one remembers the Puritan preacher and rector of the church, Rowland Taylor, who was burned at the stake on nearby Aldham Common during the reign of Mary I. Behind the church is the grand red-brick Deanery Tower, built in 1495 and all that remains of a 15th-century Archdeacon's Palace. Look out for the 15th-century timber-framed Guildhall, also nearby.

> ### PLACES NEARBY
Just a couple of miles outside Hadleigh is the Brett Vale Golf Club in the village of Raydon. To the east of Hadleigh is Wolves Wood RSPB nature reserve, while all around are scenic hamlets, often with venerable country pubs. Kersey, an impossibly picturesque country village less than 3 miles northwest of Hadleigh, has a main street lined with medieval houses and cottages, a church

dating from the 12th century crowning the hill and ducks crossing 'the splash', a ford that crosses a stream, it captures the essence of rural Suffolk.

Brett Vale Golf Club

brettvalegolf.co.uk
Noakes Road, Raydon, IP7 5LR
01473 310718 | Open daily all year
The Brett Vale course takes you through a nature reserve and lakeside walks, affording views over Dedham Vale. The excellent fairways demand an accurate tee and good approach shots. Some of the holes are affected by crosswinds, but once in the valley it is much more sheltered. Although short, the course is testing and interesting for all levels of golfer.

RSPB Nature Reserve Wolves Wood

rspb.org.uk
near Hadleigh, IP7 6QJ
01206 391153 | Trails open at all times; car park locked from 6pm (or dusk if earlier) to 9am
This RSPB reserve is one of the few remnants of the ancient woodland that once covered East Anglia. It attracts a wide variety of birds, including nightingales, warblers and woodpeckers; in winter,

sparrowhawks display high above the trees. The circular nature trail of about a mile is often wet and muddy, so come prepared.

The Bell Inn

kerseybell.co.uk
Kersey, IP7 6DY | 01473 823229
Laden with history and charm, oak beams and flagstone floors, the timber-framed Bell Inn dates back to the 14th century. A great place to relax after a country walk, the bar serves real ales (by a cosy log fire in winter), and the tasty home-cooked pub food is good value.

The Bildeston Crown

thebildestoncrown.com
High Street, Bildeston, IP7 7EB
01449 740510
A former coaching inn dating from the 15th century, this cosy hostelry with its 12 individually designed rooms serves notable food in its restaurant. Chef and co-owner Chris Lee brings his innovative style to both the 'Classics' and the more adventurous 'Select' menus. The desserts are glorious and the Sunday lunch memorable. Using quality produce in season, the eclectic dishes should please all tastes.

▶ Haverhill MAP REF 288 C5

Haverhill lies almost on the Suffolk border where Essex meets Cambridgeshire, and although it can trace its roots back to Saxon times and was even mentioned in the Domesday Book of 1086, it has few historic monuments today. A fire swept through the town in 1667. In fact, it is now a sprawling town with a number of industrial areas that provide work for its

large and growing population. It has plenty of amenities –
everything from community halls to gyms, schools to
eateries – including a particularly good golf club that
welcomes visitors. Haverhill's original expansion was largely
the result of families moving here from London when their
homes were destroyed in World War II.

PLAY A ROUND
Haverhill Golf Club
haverhillgc.co.uk
Coupals Road, CB9 7UW
01440 761951 | Open daily all year
An 18-hole course lying across
two valleys in pleasant parkland
sets the Haverhill Golf Club
apart. The front nine with
undulating fairways is
complemented by a saucer-
shaped back nine, bisected by
the River Stour, presenting a
challenge to all golfers. The
friendly clubhouse offers a wide
range of refreshments.

▶ Heacham MAP REF 292 C2

Just a 10-minute drive away along the Wash estuary from
Hunstanton is the quiet Norfolk village of Heacham. It's an
unassuming place so it might come as a surprise to learn that
one of its most famous residents was John Smith who, in 1614,
married Pocahontas, the Native American best known for
protecting English settlers in Jamestown, Virginia. Her image
is depicted on road signs throughout the village. Heacham is
known for its huge skies, brilliant sunsets, peaceful beach and
fields of lavender.

ENTERTAIN THE FAMILY
Norfolk Lavender
norfolk-lavender.co.uk
Caley Mill, PE31 7JE | 01485 570384
Open daily 9–5; lavender is in bloom
mid-Jun to Aug
Norfolk Lavender is England's
premier lavender farm, and
home to the National Collection
of Lavender. There are plants
for sale and tours are available,
including a tour of the distillery,
from May to August. A lavender
festival is held here every July.
Facilities include an animal rare
breeds centre, a play barn and
farm shop, along with the
Lavender Kitchen, where the
menu features locally sourced
Norfolk ingredients and freshly
baked lavender scones.

PLAY A ROUND
Heacham Manor Golf
heacham-manor.co.uk
Hunstanton Rd, PE31 7JX
01485 536030 | Open daily all year
The championship-length
course at Heacham Manor has
been designed to incorporate
the natural features of the
surrounding landscape. With
two rivers – an integral part of
several holes – and four lakes
to negotiate, it varies between
links and parkland styles with

views of the Wash. It's a long course, but with a number of teeing areas on each hole it is playable for all handicaps.

EAT AND DRINK

Heacham Manor Hotel ⊛

heacham-manor.co.uk

Hunstanton Road, PE31 7JX

01485 536030

Originally built as an Elizabethan manor, the Heacham Manor has been brought smartly up to date and its airy conservatory-style Mulberry restaurant is reason enough to pay a visit. The kitchen's output is simple, staunchly seasonal and driven by a sincere belief in local sourcing – salt marsh lamb comes from Wells-next-the-Sea, and the locally landed fish and seafood rack up very few food miles on their way to the table.

▶ Holkham MAP REF 293 E1

Holkham is a quiet village on the Norfolk coast in the heart of the Holkham National Nature Reserve. Around 9,600 acres of pine-covered sand dunes, salt marshes and marshland provide habitats for a wide variety of flora and fauna. This area is North Norfolk's largest and most diverse nature reserve, and one of its most tranquil.

The reserve is known for its wildfowl and migrant birds, including thousands of pink-footed geese, and salt marsh plants such as sea lavender and sea aster. The sand dunes here were planted with Corsican pines in the late 19th century in an attempt to protect reclaimed farmland from wind-blown sand, and the trees have integrated into a landscape of wide windswept sands backed by a bank of dark green foliage.

The village is home to Holkham Hall, one of the country's finest estates, where you can easily spend a day looking around the hall, its walled gardens and tranquil parkland. A superb Palladian mansion, Holkham Hall is the home of the Coke family and the earls of Leicester. It was built by Thomas Coke, first Earl of Leicester, between 1734 and 1764. It is said he was so inspired by Italian Renaissance architecture that he had the mansion built in a similar style. It remains largely unchanged today, a striking sight in rural North Norfolk.

Two local craftsmen spent 20 years sculpting the alabaster interior of the Marble Hall, copying classical Roman interiors. 'Capability' Brown landscaped some of the 3,000 acres of grounds, home to a large herd of fallow deer, and created the mile-long lake. The evergreen oaks that flourish here were originally brought from Italy. There is free daytime access to the walking and cycling routes in the park. Thomas William Coke (1754–1842), nephew of the hall's creator, devoted his

▲ Holkham beach

efforts to improving the estate and is renowned in agricultural circles as 'Coke of Norfolk'. He is credited along with Charles 'Turnip' Townshend of nearby Raynham Hall with devising the four-crop rotation system, which vastly improved farming productivity. He also served as a Norfolk MP for 50 years.

Holkham village serves mainly as an access point to the park and hall, and for Lady Anne's Drive, the estate road crossing the salt marshes to Holkham Beach.

▶ Holkham Hall   MAP REF 293 E1

holkham.co.uk

NR23 1AB | 01328 713111 | Hall open Mar–Oct Sun–Mon, Thu 12–4; walled
gardens and children's adventure play area Mar–Oct daily 10–5

Holkham Hall is a testament to Thomas Coke's ambition and style.
At the turn of the 17th century, the land on which the hall now
stands was little more than desolate heathland. When Coke told
his friends where he planned to build his home, many reacted with
horror. That the designs for Coke's new house were inspired by
buildings he had admired in the warm and gentle climate of Italy
made his choice of location even stranger.

Today, as you enjoy the lawns and shade of abundant oaks and
beeches, it is difficult to imagine that it was once an uncultivated
heath. Some of the trees were planted as early as 1712 in
anticipation of the splendid park that was to follow. You may picnic
next to the lake or wander through acres of landscaped gardens
and parklands. Don't miss the walled garden with its seven 'rooms'
and large Victorian glasshouses. Bright with spring and summer
colour, it is being restored to its 18th-century grandeur.

At the centre of all this is the resplendent hall itself, offering
you the chance to see 2,000 years of fine art amassed by Coke.
Holkham is one of the finest examples of Palladian revival
architecture in England, with room after room of glittering
splendour. Everywhere you'll see evidence of William Kent's
outstanding talent, especially in the carved scrolls, shells, cherubs
and flowers on the ceilings, the walls and the furnishings.

Visit the redeveloped courtyard, where the cafe serves coffee,
cakes and lunches, to see the Field to Fork exhibition that
engagingly tells the story of Holkham's farming history.

Look out for the flint church of St Withburga standing about half
a mile from the hall towards the coast. It dates, in part, from the
13th century.

▶ **Holt** MAP REF 294 B2

The historic Anglo-Saxon town of Holt is the thriving hub of
North Norfolk and effortlessly manages to retain the charming
atmosphere of a small country town. If you stroll down its main
street you will see one elegant Georgian house after another.
That's because in 1708 the town was all but obliterated in a
massive fire that saw its fine medieval homes burned to the
ground. The townsfolk received donations from all over
England to help with its reconstruction.

Today, Holt is bordered by the parkland of the Holt Country
Park where once a racecourse brought members of the nobility
to compete at race meetings for the 'Town Plate'. Now the 104
acres are covered in mature woodlands. There are more than
30 different species of tree here, including Scots pine, silver
birch and oak. It is a sustainable working woodland.

The visitor centre provides lists of the flora and fauna you
can see in the park. If you are lucky you might catch glimpses
of red deer, muntjac deer or red fox at dawn or dusk, grey
squirrels and large numbers of butterflies, including the red
and white admiral, painted lady and purple hairstreak.

EAT AND DRINK

The Lawns ◉
lawnshotelholt.co.uk
26 Station Road, NR25 6BS
01263 713390
Fresh, seasonal local produce
and a relaxed modern brasserie
are at the heart of the appeal of
this smart Georgian town house
restaurant in the centre of town.
The fashionably decked-out
restaurant – dark wood tables
and leather high-backed chairs
– smart bar area, bright
conservatory and terrace
overlooking the garden, provide
plenty of choice.

The Pheasant Hotel
and Restaurant ◉
pheasanthotelnorfolk.co.uk
Coast Road, Kelling, NR25 7EG
01263 588382
With the stretching beaches
and marshland of the North
Norfolk coast on hand, The
Pheasant is plumb in one of
the county's most fashionable
resort areas. In the Orangery
restaurant, the menus feature
classic British favourites with
the emphasis on the region's
abundant larder, from seasonal
vegetables to fish, seafood and
Norfolk cheeses. Afternoon
teas, with scones and crustless
sandwiches piled on cake
stands, are an abiding part of
The Pheasant's appeal.

Wiveton Bell ◉◉
wivetonbell.com
The Green, Blakeney Road,
NR25 7TL | 01263 740101
Immaculately spruced-up
though it is, and while
renowned for its cuisine, the
Bell remains faithful to its roots
as a traditional village pub.
Even in full walking gear (dog in

tow) you are welcome to drift in for just a pint of Woodforde's Wherry or Norfolk Moon Gazer. In a village pub so close to the unspoilt salt marshes of the North Norfolk coast – an Area of Outstanding Natural Beauty – and just 10 minutes' walk from Blakeney nature reserve, that's a wise approach. Built in the 18th century, the pub has earthy, heritage-coloured walls, stripped beams, chunky tables and oak-planked floors. On a winter's evening head for the tables close to the inglenook fireplace. On Sunday there's an excellent choice of roasts, but booking is essential.

Byfords
byfords.org.uk
1–3 Shirehall Plain, NR25 6BG
01263 711400
Transformed into a cafe, restaurant, store and stylish B&B, this Grade II listed building is reputed to be the oldest in Holt and it's full of character. Indulge in a full breakfast or afternoon tea, a friendly lunch or relaxed dinner.

▶ PLACES NEARBY
Saxthorpe is just 6 miles or so from Holt and signposted from its main crossroads you can find Mannington Hall. It's open by appointment only, but you can visit the garden during the summer. For country inn dining, you could head to The Kings Head in Letheringsett, or The Pigs in Edgefield.

Mannington Hall and Gardens
manningtongardens.co.uk
Saxthorpe, NR11 7BB
01263 584175 | Gardens and tea room open Jun–Aug Wed–Fri 11–5, also Sun 12–5; hall open by prior appointment only

▼ Flint buildings at Holt

Mannington Hall is a handsome 18th-century moated manor house that belonged to Horatio Nelson, the British Admiral best known for his part in the Napoleonic Wars, in particular the Battle of Trafalgar, where he died in 1805. It is the focal point in an extraordinary garden, which contains a beautiful heritage rose garden, divided into several areas, each representing a period of the rose's historical development. In all there are more than 1,000 different varieties of rose here.

Around the corner of the house, a yellow rose climbs vigorously near a mauve wistaria, while other low-growing shrubs brighten up the gravel with their pink and white flowers in early summer. Within the moat, sweetly scented herbs are planted to mirror the intricate pattern of the hall's dining-room ceiling.

The medieval garden has turf seats and some very old roses. Other formal areas of Mannington Hall include a tranquil 17th-century knot garden. You can also see lakes and a ruined church, which stands among unusual trees, including specimens of *Acer palmatum*, which are well over 100 years old. Music and theatre events are a regular feature at Mannington Hall.

The Kings Head
kingsheadnorfolk.co.uk
Holt Road, Letheringsett,
NR25 7AR | 01263 712691

From the outside this looks to be a grand, manor-like building, but step through the door to find elegant, rustic-chic decor throughout the rambling dining areas that radiate from the central bar, with warm heritage hues, rugs on terracotta tiles, feature bookcases and squashy sofas and leather chairs fronting blazing winter log fires. The atmosphere is informal, the beer on tap is Woodforde's Wherry, and the modern British food is prepared from top-notch ingredients supplied by local producers. This gastropub has superb alfresco areas including an excellent children's garden and a gravelled front terrace with benches and brollies.

The Pigs
thepigs.org.uk
Norwich Road, Edgefield,
NR24 2RL | 01263 587634
This 17th-century country inn on the edge of a lovely village has been transformed into a thriving local that celebrates all things Norfolk, both on the plate and in the glass. The lovely tranquil setting at the fringe of the village allows for a peaceful garden. An impressively versatile menu emerges from the kitchen, utilising forgotten cuts of locally sourced meat and produce from the pub's adjoining allotment. Should you decide to stay, there are 19 country-style rooms and a spa, with seven luxurious spa rooms.

▶ Horsey MAP REF 295 E3

In 1938 a devastating combination of high tides and storms hit Horsey. The sea surged inland, flooding buildings and fields, and forcing people to evacuate their homes. It was four months before the water subsided and the villagers were able to resume normal life, although it took another five years before the damaging effects of salt water on the fields was finally overcome and crops could be grown again.

Horsey is barely 3 feet above sea level and, as you walk around the reed-fringed mere and stroll along its many drainage channels, you will appreciate the wildness of this part of Norfolk and how vulnerable it is to the sea. The village and surrounding area are now in the care of the National Trust.

The village's most famous feature is the Horsey windpump, built to pump water from the surrounding farmland. It dates from the middle of the 19th century. Today, it is fully restored and you can go inside to the top.

Nearby, All Saints' Church dates from the 13th century and has an attractive thatched nave. Go inside and look for the stained-glass window in the south chancel commemorating Catherine Ursula Rising, who died in 1890. She is shown painting in her drawing room at nearby Horsey Hall.

▼ Horsey Gap

GET INDUSTRIAL
Horsey Windpump

nationaltrust.org.uk/horsey-windpump

Horsey Mere, NR29 4EF

01263 740241 | Open end-Mar–Oct daily 10–4.30

In 1912 the main structure of the present pump was built on the foundations of an 18th-century mill by noted Norfolk millwright Dan England, using bricks from the nearby village of Martham. It was in full working order when it was struck by lightning in 1940 and has since been fully restored – it is now owned by the National Trust.

You can climb the five floors of this lovely old traditional windmill-like windpump, whose predecessor was built 200 years ago to drain the area, and see its inner workings, such as the drive shaft and giant cogs. From the top, there are panoramic views over Horsey Mere and the surrounding countryside. Grade II listed, the building features red-brick walls and a handsome weatherboarded cap in the shape of a boat.

The windpump stands in an idyllic and remote spot on the edge of the Norfolk Broads overlooking Horsey Mere and marshes, noted for their wild birds and insects. The whole area is regarded as being internationally important for the conservation of a number of natural habitats found here. Wait long enough and you'll see hundreds of wigeon in winter, along with teal, shoveler, pochard, gadwall, goldeneye and tufted duck.

Bitterns may be seen at any time of year. Look out for stonechats, yellow wagtails and grasshopper warblers if you head towards the dunes. You might also spot two rare warblers – Cetti's and Savi's.

The former is a newcomer, and the latter is returning to areas where it was once common. A great way to appreciate the pump's setting is to take a walk around Horsey Mere along the signposted footpath.

▷ Hoveton MAP REF 295 D3

The Norfolk village of Hoveton lies immediately opposite Wroxham on the River Bure and is a popular sailing and boating centre, buzzing with nautical activity. Hoveton is dominated by two churches, St Peter and St John, and has many upmarket houses, including the elegant 19th-century Hoveton Hall which, although not open to the public, stands in gardens where visitors are welcome (opening times can vary). See also the Norfolk Broads, page 203.

ENTERTAIN THE FAMILY
BeWILDerwood
see highlight panel opposite

VISIT A MUSEUM
RAF Air Defence Radar Museum
radarmuseum.co.uk
RRH Neatishead, NR12 8YB
01692 631485 | Open Apr–Oct Tue–Thu, Sat and Bank Holiday Mon 10–5
This multi-award-winning museum is run by volunteers, most of whom worked at RAF Neatishead. It is housed in an original 1942 Radar Operations building and features themed exhibits, including the Battle of Britain Room, 1942 Ground Controlled Interception Room, Radar Engineering, Military Communications Systems and the Cold War Operations Room. You can see a display dedicated to the Royal Observer Corps, to space defence,

bloodhound missiles and original mobile radar vehicles. The museum's newest addition is a Victor K2 Cockpit, previously used as a training simulator at RAF Marham.

EAT AND DRINK
The Old Barn Restaurant
wroxhambarns.co.uk
Wroxham Barns, Tunstead Road, NR12 8QU | 01603 777106
The comfortable Old Barn Restaurant is set in extensive parkland within a complex known as Wroxham Barns. Here you can see a collection of 18th-century barns that have been reborn as small shops and working craft galleries – the sort of place where you'll want to wander, shop, sit and drink in the scenery. Children love the Junior Farm. The restaurant serves breakfast, as well as lovely light lunches, sandwiches, scones and cakes.

▶ BeWILDerwood   MAP REF 295 D4

bewilderwood.co.uk
Horning Road, NR12 8JW | 01692 633033 | Open Feb half term to
Oct half term 10–5.30; dates and times vary – check website
BeWILDerwood is an award-winning wild and imaginative
adventure park with magical treehouses, zip wires, jungle bridges,
boat trips and storytelling. The setting for the book *A Boggle at
BeWILDerwood* by local children's author Tom Blofeld, it's a
wonderful, mystical land of brave adventurous creatures you may
never see anywhere else in the world. Parents are encouraged to
play alongside their children, which makes for an exciting day out
for the whole family.

▶ Hunstanton   MAP REF 292 C1

Lying on the North Norfolk coast, Hunstanton is the only East Anglian seaside resort to face west. As such, it is known for its dramatic sunsets. The town is one of two halves: the old part where ancient red and white chalk limestone rocks offer a fabulously colourful backdrop to its beach, and a village steeped in history and legend; and the newer area of Hunstanton that dates from its life as a fashionable Victorian seaside resort.

You can see the ruins of a chapel and a lighthouse in Old Hunstanton. It is said that St Edmund, who went on to become King of East Anglia (see page 75), was shipwrecked in AD 855, and was so grateful for being spared a watery death in the Wash that he built a chapel in thanks. The 13th-century ruins still stand today, looking out across grey stormy seas. A later lighthouse, now privately owned, has become a symbol of Hunstanton, although it is no longer used as a beacon. The light was extinguished and was never lit again following its decommission in the 1920s. The newer part of the town dates from the mid-1840s and has an essentially Victorian atmosphere, with handsome hotels built in mock-Tudor style using the warm-coloured local limestone known as carrstone. They line the well-tended esplanade gardens next to the sea.

The resort was developed by Henry Styleman Le Strange of Hunstanton Hall, who promoted the idea of a railway line between the town and King's Lynn to attract visitors. Members of the Le Strange family have been squires and landlords here for more than 800 years. They laid claim to the beach and all that is in the sea for as far as a horseman can hurl a spear at low tide. The family still holds the title of Lord High Admiral of the Wash.

Today, the town offers a range of attractions including a Sea Life Sanctuary and a 400-seater theatre, along with vast expanses of white sandy beaches, walks along Peddars Way and birding aplenty.

MEET THE SEALIFE
Hunstanton Sea Life Sanctuary
visitsealife.com/hunstanton
Southern Promenade, PE36 5BH
01485 533576 | Open Mon–Fri 11–4, Sat–Sun 10–4
A £3 million refurbishment following the devastating tidal surge of December 2013 has resulted in a state-of-the-art sanctuary with underwater seal viewing and a new seal hospital, close encounters with rays and sharks, dive pools for the otters and an exciting domed tank of Amazonian piranha fish.

▶ Hunstanton beach and cliffs

10 top attractions for kids

MEET THE SEALIFE
Sea Tours
seatours.co.uk

Sea Tours kiosk, Central Promenade, PE36 5BH | 01485 534444

The Wash Monsters, two historic amphibious vessels, take passengers on seal safaris to the sandbanks where large colonies of common seals haul themselves up to sleep for much of the day. Learn about local history on guided coastal cruises or take in panoramic views of the striped cliffs, one of the top geological sites in the UK, on a shorter shoreline trip.

GO SHOPPING
Le Strange Old Barns
lestrangeoldbarns.com

Golf Course Road, PE36 6JG

01485 533402 | Open daily from 10

With antiques and collectables, original art, local crafts, workshops and demonstrations, this is a popular place to root around for gifts and mementoes.

PLAY A ROUND
Hunstanton Golf Club
hunstantongolfclub.com

Golf Course Road, PE36 6JQ

01485 532811 | Open daily all year

A championship links course established in 1891, Hunstanton Golf Club is set among some of the best natural golfing country in East Anglia. Keep out of the numerous bunkers and master the fast greens to play to your handicap – then you only have the strong wind to contend with. Good playing conditions all year round.

Searles Resort Golf Course
searles.co.uk

South Beach Road, PE36 5BB

01485 536010 | Open daily all year

The nine-hole par 34 course of the Searles Resort Golf Club is designed in a links style and provides generous fairways with good greens. A river runs through the 3rd and 4th holes. There are good views of Hunstanton and the surrounding countryside. The course offers a challenge for all standards of golfers. The resort also includes plenty of activities for the whole family.

EAT AND DRINK
The Ancient Mariner Inn
traditionalinns.co.uk
Golf Course Road, Old Hunstanton,
PE36 6JJ | 01485 534411
Summer evenings can be spectacular here when the sun sets across the sands of the Wash, and the light matches the colour of the real ales enjoyed by drinkers in the peaceful gardens of the Ancient Mariner Inn. Up to seven beers may be on tap at any one time. Equally enticing is the menu of modern pub classics such as fish pie, Cumberland sausage or vegetarian Wellington. Daily specials boost the choice. The appealing flint-and-brick inn is creatively incorporated into the stable block of a Victorian hotel, the stylish rooms of which are popular with visitors to the beautiful Norfolk Coast Area of Outstanding Natural Beauty.

Caley Hall Hotel ◉
caleyhallhotel.co.uk
Old Hunstanton Road,
PE36 6HH | 01485 533486
At the core of Caley Hall, a 10-minute walk from

▼ Beach huts at Old Hunstanton

Hunstanton's unspoiled beach, is a 17th-century manor, with the restaurant in an attractive, spacious former stable block. Decor includes high-backed leather-look seats at wooden tables, a tartan-patterned carpet and a vaulted ceiling. The kitchen goes out of its way to find fresh local produce and puts together a short, mainstream menu with more adventurous specials.

The Lodge

thelodgehunstanton.co.uk
46 Old Hunstanton Road, PE36 6HX
01485 532896

The Lodge can trace its history back to the 16th century, when it was a farmhouse. Many transformations later and this red-brick pub with rooms is gaining a good reputation for its food. Vegan and vegetarian options may appear on the menu alongside Mediterranean favourites. The puddings are tempting and the specials board, with its emphasis on fresh fish and locally sourced produce, changes daily. For sports fans, the open bar has a big TV screen.

The Neptune Restaurant with Rooms ❀❀❀

theneptune.co.uk
85 Old Hunstanton Road,
PE36 6HZ | 01485 532122

A creeper-covered 18th-century coaching inn not far from the sea has been updated into the Mangeolles' restaurant with rooms. The modern look of the pint-sized restaurant contrasts nicely with the period features, with a plain boarded floor, original artwork hung above the half-panelled walls and high-backed wicker chairs at white-clothed tables with flowers. The menus run to just a handful of choices per course, all built on local and seasonal produce, and there's nothing pretentious or gimmicky. Breads are made in-house, canapés are stars in their own right and a pre-dessert arrives before the real McCoy.

▶ PLACES NEARBY

Snettisham Park, where you can enjoy a deer safari, is within easy reach of Hunstanton, as is the RSPB's reserve. Stop for a while at the nearby King William IV Country Inn and Restaurant or The Rose and Crown for a spot of refreshment, or pop into Thornham for the Orange Tree.

Snettisham Park

snettishampark.co.uk
PE31 7NG | 01485 542425
Open daily 10–4, half-term 9–4

Along with its hugely popular deer safari, which takes you on a 45-minute ride to see its herd of red deer, Snettisham Park offers farming activities such as bottle-feeding the lambs, collecting eggs and feeding the calves. Children can enjoy pony rides and meeting the baby animals on this busy working farm. There are special seasonal shows and walking trails, a picnic area, plus a visitor centre selling local produce, and a tea room. Evening safaris also take place during the summer months.

RSPB Nature Reserve Snettisham

rspb.org.uk
Snettisham, PE31 7PD
01485 210779 | Open at any reasonable time

Two great bird spectacles are witnessed here: massive clouds of whirling wading birds when high tides push them off the vast expanses of mudflats, and huge flocks of pink-footed geese in V formation at dawn and dusk in winter. Suggested visiting dates and times are on the RSPB website.

The King William IV Country Inn and Restaurant

thekingwilliamsedgeford.co.uk
Heacham Road, Sedgeford,
PE36 5LU | 01485 571765

This free house has been an inn for 175 years. Made cosy by log fires in winter, it has four dining areas plus a covered alfresco terrace where you can enjoy a local crab salad in the summer. You'll find five real ales on tap, and extensive menus, including gluten-free and vegetarian. Events include quiz Mondays, curry Tuesdays and piano Fridays.

The Rose and Crown ◉

roseandcrownsnettisham.co.uk
Old Church Road, Snettisham,
PE31 7LX | 01485 541382

The Rose and Crown was built in the 14th century for craftsmen working on the beautiful village church. Its rose-hung facade conceals twisting passages and hidden corners, low-beamed ceilings, uneven red-tiled floors and inglenooks, Locally supplied produce includes shellfish and samphire from Brancaster, beef from salt marsh-raised cattle, game shot by men in wellies who drink in the back bar, asparagus and strawberries from farmers, and herbs from village allotments.

The Orange Tree

theorangetreethornham.co.uk
High Street, Thornham, PE36 6LY
01485 512213

Standing in the centre of the village opposite the church, this family-run pub makes a useful stop for walkers on the Peddars Way. Formerly a smugglers' haunt, the 400-year-old whitewashed inn has evolved over the years into the stylish country pub it is today. Develop an appetite with a stroll to the local staithe, where working fishing boats still come and go through the creeks of Brancaster Bay, before returning for meal and a pint of East Anglian ale. The chef makes the most of freshly landed local seafood, while most of the meat is sourced from the Sandringham Estate. Look to the board for the daily sandwich selection. Leave space to sample the appetising selection of desserts. Dogs get their own beer and menu, while children will love the climbing frame in the pub's garden.

▶ Ipswich   MAP REF 290 C5

Suffolk's county town covers a large area and has masses of historic charm in its pedestrianised centre not far from its harbour on the River Orwell. One of England's oldest towns, Ipswich was originally founded as the Anglo-Saxon trading port of Gippeswic in the Kingdom of East Anglia around AD 600, and retains much of its original street plan.

You'll find the centre easy to navigate, and do take a walk to the attractive harbour area, Neptune Marina Quay, which now has swish apartments and wine bars.

In the town centre, you'll see some fine examples of period houses and churches surrounded by modern offices and shops. Ancient House is one of the most beautiful. A Grade I listed mansion in one of Ipswich's main shopping streets, the Buttermarket, the Ancient House was built in the 15th century and has a facade decorated with elaborate pargeting (decorative plasterwork) and wood carvings. Four panels depict Europe, Asia, America and Africa, giving a glimpse of social history since Australia hadn't been 'discovered' when the house was built.

Other impressive places to look out for include the Cornhill, which is surrounded by Victorian buildings, including the Town

▼ Ipswich waterfront

Hall, and which was once the setting for markets, fairs and executions. In 1555, the so-called Ipswich Martyrs were burned at the stake here for their Protestant beliefs.

There are ruins of Ipswich's 13th-century Blackfriars friary, and many churches, the finest of which is St Mary le Tower, and a 16th-century college founded by Cardinal Thomas Wolsey. Look out for the beautiful timber-framed house on the corner of Silent Street. There's a plaque on the wall to Wolsey (c.1471–1530), the son of an Ipswich butcher, who became Lord Chancellor of England under Henry VIII but who was eventually charged with high treason and executed. Two doors along, another plaque marks the birthplace of the author V S Pritchett (1900–97).

A building in stark contrast is the Willis Faber and Dumas headquarters. A remarkable black-glass structure, it was designed by Norman Foster in 1975. Not far from here is the Wolsey Theatre, one of the finest drama venues in the region.

Ipswich is a bustling place of modern offices, shops and homes, sports centres, chic restaurants and gastro-pubs, riverside walks and gardens, and while it celebrates 21st-century living in its own distinct style, reminders of its great past are everywhere.

TAKE IN SOME HISTORY
Christchurch Mansion
cimuseums.org.uk
Soane Street, IP4 2BE
01473 433554 | Open Mar–Oct
Tue–Sat 10–5, Sun 11–5; Nov–Feb
Tue–Sat 10–4, Sun 11–4
Christchurch Mansion is a beautiful Tudor property built in 1548 on the site of an Augustinian priory and set in a park. You can see period rooms, including a Tudor kitchen, Georgian saloon and Victorian chambers. An art gallery has changing exhibitions, and is the venue for the Suffolk Artists' Gallery with its collection of paintings by John Constable (see page 110) – the largest collection outside London – and works by Thomas Gainsborough who was born in Sudbury in 1727 (see page 256).

VISIT A MUSEUM
Ipswich Museum
cimuseums.org.uk
High St, IP1 3QH | 01473 433551
Open Tue–Sat 10–5, Sun 11–5
The Ipswich Museum is a fascinating place and includes a full-sized reproduction of a woolly mammoth, based on a skeleton discovered in Suffolk, in its natural history gallery. It's accompanied by a giraffe, a rhino and a group of gorillas, all mounted in their original Victorian cases. The museum has sections on Suffolk wildlife, Suffolk geology, Roman Suffolk and Anglo-Saxon Ipswich, plus one of the best bird collections in the country.

▲ Ipswich town centre

See work by local and international artists in a range of media in the art gallery.

Ipswich Transport Museum
ipswichtransportmuseum.co.uk
Old Trolleybus Depot, Cobham Road, IP3 9JD | 01473 715666
Open Mon–Fri 1–4, Mar–Dec Sun 11–4, check website for special events and themed open days
All the transport and engineering objects displayed in this museum were made or used in the Ipswich area. Here are buses and bicycles, trams, trolleybuses, fire engines, lorries, forklifts and compressors – all lovingly restored and cared for by volunteers.

LOOK OUT FOR GRANDMA
On the corner of Princes Street and Queen Street, close to the Buttermarket, is a gorgeous statue of 'Grandma', one of the best-known cartoon characters of Carl Giles (1916–95) who drew cartoons for the *Daily Express* for decades, starting in the 1940s. Carl Giles worked in Ipswich and lived to see his creation unveiled as a statue.

CATCH A PERFORMANCE
New Wolsey Theatre
wolseytheatre.co.uk
Civic Drive, IP1 2AS | 01473 295900
The Wolsey Theatre has a whole host of performances, from cheeky comedies and musicals to thought-provoking dramas, opera and dance. A popular highlight is its 'An audience with…' series, and its Christmas panto. Top names in television and film have appeared at the Wolsey.

Ipswich Regent Theatre
apps.ipswich.gov.uk
3 St Helen's Street, IP4 1HE

10 top performance venues

01473 433100 | Box office open Mon–Sat 9.30–5.30
Seating over 1,500 people, East Anglia's largest theatre presents musicals, tribute bands, plays, pantomimes, ballet, comedy and concerts. Some of the biggest names in music, including the likes of The Beatles and Jimi Hendrix, have played here.

PLAY A ROUND
If you are a golfer you will be spoilt for choice in Ipswich.

Alnesbourne Priory Golf Course
priory-park.com
Priory Park, IP10 0JT
01473 727393 | Open daily all year

A fabulous outlook facing due south across the River Orwell is one of the many features of this course set in woodland. It has holes running among trees with some fairways requiring straight shots. The 8th green is on saltings by the river.

Ipswich Golf Club
ipswichgolfclub.com
Purdis Heath, Bucklesham Road, IP3 8UQ | 01473 728941
Open daily all year
Many golfers are surprised when they hear that Ipswich has, at Purdis Heath, a first-class course. In some ways it resembles some of Surrey's better courses; it has beautiful heathland with two lakes and easy walking. The nine-hole course is available on a pay-and-play basis.

Rushmere Golf Club
club-noticeboard.co.uk
Rushmere Heath, IP4 5QQ
01473 725648 | Open daily all year
The heathland course of the Rushmere Golf Club has gorse and prevailing winds. It is challenging and a good test of golf. The clubhouse features a large bar area and a lounge that overlooks the putting green.

EAT AND DRINK
Best Western Claydon Country House Hotel
hotelsipswich.com
16–18 Ipswich Road, Claydon
IP6 0AR | 01473 830382
Two old village houses were joined seamlessly together to form this friendly, small-scale

hotel to the northwest of Ipswich. The Victorian-style restaurant overlooks the gardens through a conservatory extension, although the classic look has been given a gentle update by ditching the cloths on its darkwood tables and adding high-backed leather chairs. Staff are smartly turned out, and the kitchen draws on splendid, locally sourced produce as the bedrock of its unfussy European-accented modern British dishes.

The Fat Cat

fatcatipswich.co.uk
288 Spring Road, IP4 5NL
01473 726524

Good beer and conversation are the two main ingredients in this no-frills free house. The Fat Cat is a top spot for beer aficionados, with a friendly atmosphere in two homely bars and a raft of real ales served in tip-top condition from the taproom behind the bar. The head-scratching choice – up to 20 beers every day – come from Adnam's, Skinner's, Hop Back and a host of local microbreweries. Soak up the beer with a range of simple bar snacks such as homemade Scotch eggs, sausage rolls, pork pies and filled rolls.

Mariners ◉◉

marinersipswich.co.uk
Neptune Quay, IP4 1AX
01473 289748

Moored alongside Neptune Quay, close to the town centre, this floating French brasserie on an old gunboat is a quirky destination in which to enjoy some good Gallic cuisine. The vessel might date back to 1899, when it was launched in Belgium, but inside it's still shipshape and has its original brass and woodwork. Go up on deck for an alfresco lunch in the sun but, wherever you choose to eat, look forward to good, honest French food confidently presented.

milsoms Kesgrave Hall ◉

milsomhotels.com
Hall Road, Kesgrave, IP5 2PU
01473 333741

Hiding in woodland near a little village to the east of Ipswich, Kesgrave Hall is no monument to twee rusticity, but a sparkling-white boutique hotel with a portico and veranda seating out front. The Brasserie dining room is fitted with an up-to-the-minute open kitchen and plain wooden tables. A quirk of the system is that you write down your food order and take it to the bar for service, which seems to run smoothly. An extensive menu of global modernism kicks off with starters in two sizes – 'ample' or 'generous'.

Salthouse Harbour Hotel ◉◉

salthouseharbour.co.uk
1 Neptune Quay, IP4 1AX
01473 226789

A harbourside warehouse makeover in sea-salted red brick with eye-popping interior collisions of lime-green and violet, the Salthouse is a hotel for the style-hungry of the 21st century. Sub-Pollock abstracts and inscriptions of italic food terminology on matt black walls are only the half of it; the brick-walled Eaterie is adorned with art objects, waterfront views and relaxed service. They serve stylish brasserie food with look-at-me flavours.

▶ PLACES NEARBY

Heading out of Ipswich on the road to Hadleigh you will come to one of the prettiest villages in this part of Suffolk. Hintlesham is quiet, leafy and probably best known locally for its superb 16th-century Grade I listed mansion, Hintlesham Hall, now a country house hotel and restaurant with a championship golf course in its parkland. Other eateries worth checking out are the riverside Butt and Oyster at Pin Mill and the nearby Compasses at Holbrook, also the Moon and Mushroom Inn at Swilland. In the hamlet of Lindsey take a look at the tiny St James's Chapel, while in Witnesham you could enjoy a round of golf at the Fynn Valley Golf Club.

The Butt and Oyster

debeninns.co.uk/buttandoyster
Pin Mill, IP9 1JW | 01473 780764
First recorded as a public house in 1553, this waterfront pub on the River Orwell was frequented by author Arthur Ransome, who featured it in his 1937 children's book *We Didn't Mean to Go to Sea*. The large open fireplace keeps it cosy in winter and the river views make it popular for drinks and alfresco meals in summer. It serves traditional pub food, has daily specials and the bar is racked with kegs of ale.

The Compasses

compassesholbrook.com
Ipswich Road, Holbrook,
IP9 2QR | 01473 328332
On the spectacular Shotley peninsula, bordered by the rivers Orwell and Stour, this traditional 17th-century country pub offers a simple, good-value menu. There's nothing self-consciously primped and styled about its interior or its food offerings; it prides itself on not being a gastro-pub but offering good value and plenty of choice. There's a separate children's menu and some good vegetarian choices.

Fynn Valley Golf Club

fynn-valley.co.uk
Witnesham, IP6 9JA | 01473 785267
Open daily all year
An undulating and mature parkland course overlooking the Fynn Valley, the 18 holes here are an excellent test of golf, enhanced by more than 100 bunkers, tree-lined fairways and protected, immaculately kept greens that have tricky slopes and contours. In addition to the 18-hole course there is a nine-hole one plus various practice greens, a 22-bay floodlit golf range, two golf shops and a clubhouse.

Hintlesham Hall Hotel 🏵🏵

hintleshamhall.com

George Street, Hintlesham,
IP8 3NS | 01473 652334

Hintlesham Hall is a beautifully proportioned building of three wings, the facade a 1720 addition to the 16th-century core. The interior is equally impressive, with all the elements expected in a grand country-house hotel, from oil paintings to antiques. The Salon dining room is truly stunning, with ruched drapes at the windows, an ornate fireplace, and portraits on white walls contrasting with a red carpet. The kitchen works around a slate of contemporary ideas and displays a level of originality not commonly seen in such surroundings.

Hintlesham Golf Club

hintleshamgolfclub.com

IP8 3JG | 01473 652761

Open daily all year

The magnificent championship course of the Hintlesham Golf Club blends harmoniously with the ancient parkland surrounding it. Opened in 1991 but seeded two years beforehand, this parkland course has reached a level maturity that is rivalled in the area only by a few ancient courses. Both the 17th and 18th have water as a challenge at a very inconvenient interlude; at the latter an eagle is possible if you're brave. The 4th hole, measuring well over 200 yards, has been described as the hardest par 3 in Suffolk.

There are superb practice facilities and a clubhouse with a bar function room and large decking area that overlooks the course.

St James's Chapel

english-heritage.org.uk

Rose Green, Lindsey, IP7 6QA

0370 333 1181 | Open daily 10–4

Built mainly in the 13th century, this tiny thatched, flint-and-stone chapel incorporates some earlier work. Although little documentation survives, it is thought the chapel served a castle that once stood in Lindsey, the remains of which are located nearby.

Moon and Mushroom Inn

themoonandmushroom.co.uk

High Road, Swilland, IP6 9LR

01473 785320

The delightful sight of several firkins of East Anglian beer behind the bar welcomes drinkers to this 400-year-old free house in the Suffolk countryside. Diners, too, relish the prospect of indulging in home-cooked specials such as wild rabbit pie or mushroom steamed pudding. The pub was reputedly a staging post for the despatch of convicts to Australia, and the records at Ipswich Assizes do indeed show that a previous landlord was deportedfor stealing two ducks and a pig. Today's guests are able to linger longer in the colourful cottagey interior or the fragrant rose garden.

▲ The Custom House, King's Lynn

▶ King's Lynn MAP REF 292 C3

Known to locals simply as Lynn, its original name, King's Lynn is an architectural dream, with almost every period represented, ranging from St Nicholas' Chapel – built between 1145 and 1420 – to picturesque Burkitt Court almshouses, built in 1909 in memory of a Lynn corn merchant. You can take a stroll to see this living heritage – it makes for a great day out.

King's Lynn was an unassuming little place until it caught the eye of the Bishop of Norwich and then Henry VIII. Strategically placed on one of the most important waterways in medieval England, the town had a huge amount of trade passing through it. It exported corn from Lincolnshire, lead from Derbyshire, salt from Norfolk and Lincolnshire and, most importantly, wool from the East Midlands.

On top of this, it imported dried cod from Iceland and timber, pitch and resin from the Baltic, as well as Flemish and Italian cloths. With all these revenues, Lynn became a wealthy place, and Herbert de Losinga, the first Bishop of Norwich, decided he

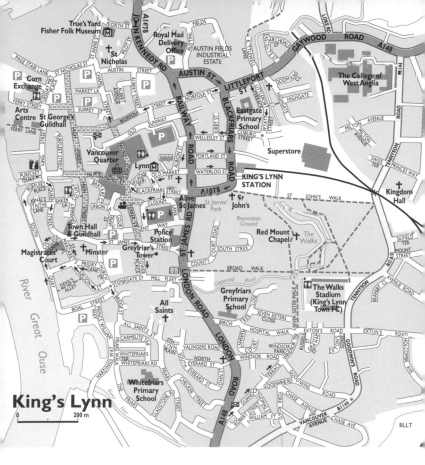

King's Lynn

0   200 m

wanted it for himself. It became known as Bishop's Lynn, and so it remained until the 1530s, when Henry VIII quashed its ecclesiastical association and named it King's Lynn. The change in name meant little to Lynn's merchants, who remained prosperous and continued to build their grand houses and churches, many of which can still be seen today.

Look out for the 14th-century Greyfriars Tower, once part of a Franciscan friary, and the churches and guildhalls of the market places. Despite the attentions of postwar planners, Lynn retains great character. It grew around not one but two market places, each close to the river and each with a noble medieval church and guildhall. Saturday Market Place's church, King's Lynn Minster, is famous for its elaborate 14th-century brasses, baroque pulpit and 18th-century organ case, while the square's Trinity Guildhall has 15th-century chequered flintwork, extended in 1624 and 1895 in the same style. To the north is Tuesday Market Place with St Nicholas' Chapel and St George's Guildhall, another 15th-century edifice and the largest surviving medieval guildhall in England – now used as a theatre and arts centre. Between the two, on the quay, is the graceful old Custom House, containing the tourist information centre. King's Lynn's Town Hall, with its distinctive chequerboard facade and majestic interior, dates from 1421 and hosts a multimedia Stories of Lynn exhibition.

The refurbished warehouses along South Quay make for pleasant waterside strolling. Of the museums, True's Yard Fisherfolk Museum, at the heart of the old fishing quarter in the North End, tells of the people and their livelihood that once made the town famous. Foremost among the exhibits at the award-winning Lynn Museum is the enigmatic 4,000-year-old timber circle surrounding an upturned tree stump discovered preserved in shifting sands near Holme Beach in 1998, still with portions of the honeysuckle-stem rope used to haul it into place. Quickly dubbed Seahenge, the endangered Bronze Age relic was excavated amid huge controversy, but many of the protestors may be relieved that it has at least stayed in Norfolk.

Across the Ouse at West Lynn, a dramatic change in scenery occurs, with flat arable fields, straight drainage ditches and scattered, isolated villages. This is the reclaimed landscape of the Fens bordering the Wash, a vast square-mouthed estuary between Norfolk and Lincolnshire. The coast here is mainly inaccessible, but the 13.5-mile Peter Scott Walk, named after the naturalist and wildlife painter who lived in the area, takes you along the old sea bank from West Lynn to his former lighthouse home near Sutton Bridge in Lincolnshire.

VISIT THE MUSEUMS AND CHURCHES

King's Lynn Minster

kingslynnminster.org
St Margaret's Place, PE30 5DL
01553 767090

The Norman towers of this great church, which is almost of cathedral size and impact, dominate the west end of the building and, indeed, the skyline of King's Lynn. Between the two towers are a huge west window and a grand porch. Set into the southwest tower is an unusual 17th-century clock that tells the phases of the moon and the state of the tides on the Great Ouse. Look out for the words written round its face, 'Lynn High Tide'. The Minster was enlarged in the 13th century. Disaster struck on 8 September 1741 when a gale brought the spire of the southwest tower crashing down, destroying the lantern of a central tower and doing huge damage to the body of the church. The rebuilding work was completed in 1744, in the Gothic style, an unusual form to use at this time.

Inside, there are differing architectural features from its eventful history. And you can see two of the largest and most impressive brasses in Britain – the earliest is to Adam de Walsoken, who died in 1349, and the other is to Robert Braunche, who died in 1364. Both men were town mayors.

Take a look at the stalls and their misericords; they date from the late 14th century, as does the screenwork behind them. There are also screens with excellent woodwork from the 15th and 16th centuries. The beautiful wooden pulpit is Georgian and the eagle lectern is a rare brass example from the 16th century. The sumptuous reredos dates from 1899. It's well worth dedicating at least an hour to the Minster while you are in Lynn.

St Nicholas' Chapel

stnicholaskingslynn.org.uk
St Ann's Street, PE30 1NH

Although St Nicholas' is a large and imposing building, it served as a chapel for the nearby Minster for decades. It was rebuilt in grand style in the 15th century, and its south porch is an outstanding example of Perpendicular architecture. This is covered in a wealth of rich and complex carving, including a row of statue niches. Look out for the elegant spire built in the late 1800s to the designs of Sir George Gilbert Scott. Also striking from the outside is the enormous west window. The spacious interior is dominated by its superb wooden roof, lined with angels. The font was presented to the church in 1627 by Bishop Harsnett. The church has many tombs and memorials, one of the most noticeable being that

to Benjamin Keene, made in 1757 by Scottish architect Robert Adam. It resembles a huge stone sugar bowl on top of an even larger stone cube.

True's Yard Fisherfolk Museum

truesyard.co.uk
North Street, PE30 1QW
01553 770479 | Open Tue–Sat 10–4

Lynn's Old North End, with its yards, courts and passages, once teemed with the fisher families who lived in a close-knit community in the shadow of St Nicholas' Chapel. This fascinating little heritage museum is built around the last surviving cottages and the tiny, re-created rooms capture the harsh realities of fishing life. There's a local and family history research centre and spoken memories on MP3 and audio files.

▼ The Guildhall, King's Lynn

Lynn Museum

museums.norfolk.gov.uk
Market Street, PE30 1NL
01553 775001 | Open Tue–Sat 10–5

Following a £1.2 million redevelopment, this charming museum tells the story of west Norfolk, and is home to Seahenge, the astonishing Bronze Age timber circle. A whole gallery is devoted to these unique 4,000-year-old timbers, and includes a life-sized replica of the circle, which was discovered off the coast of Hunstanton in the late 1990s. Original timbers are also displayed. The main gallery narrates the history of the area from the Iron Age to the 20th century. The museum also features the Iron Age gold coin hoard from Sedgeford, a display of pilgrims' badges and the beautiful 19th-century fairground gallopers made by Savages of Lynn.

ENJOY THE ARTS

King's Lynn Arts Centre

kingslynnarts.co.uk
29 King Street, PE30 1HA
01553 766834 | Open Jan–Oct Tue–Sat 11–5, Nov–Dec 11–4

St George's Guildhall is considered the largest and most complete medieval guildhall in England and today is home to the innovative King's Lynn Arts Centre. There are four art galleries within the complex, all with changing exhibitions, a craft shop, and a theatre hosting live events that include drama, comedy, music, dance and shows for children.

PLAY A ROUND

Eagles Golf Centre

eaglesgolfonline.co.uk
39 School Road, Tilney All Saints, PE34 4RS | 01553 827147
Open daily all year

The parkland course of the Eagles has a variety of trees and shrubs lining the fairways. A large water area comes into play on several of the holes.

King's Lynn Golf Club

kingslynngolfclub.co.uk
Castle Rising, PE31 6BD
01553 631654 | Open daily all year

The course is set among silver birch and fir woodland and benefits from well-drained sandy soil.

EAT AND DRINK

Bank House ◉

thebankhouse.co.uk
King's Staithe Square, PE30 1RD
01553 660492

The Georgian townhouse hotel on the south quayside amid the town's cultural district (the Corn Exchange Theatre and Arts Centre are close by) is a far jollier prospect as a hotel than when it was a bank. Post conversion, what was the bank manager's office is now the bar. Three smart dining rooms have polished tables, candlelight and music, and trade in gently modernised traditional British fare.

The Stuart House Hotel, Bar and Restaurant

stuarthousehotel.co.uk
35 Goodwins Road, PE30 5QX
01553 772169

In a central but nevertheless quiet location, this hotel and bar is one of the town's favoured eating and drinking places. Top-notch East Anglian ales and traditional snacks are served in the bar, and there's a separate restaurant menu. Daily specials, like everything else, are home cooked from fresh local produce. Events include regular live music, murder mystery dinners and a July beer festival.

▶ PLACES NEARBY

The historic village of Castle Rising is about a five-minute drive from the outskirts of King's Lynn and is well worth a visit. It is famous for having been a 'rotten' parliamentary borough because of its small population, though it had a notable MP in Robert Walpole, Britain's first prime minister from 1721 to 1742; the Reform Act of 1832 put an end to its status. But the village is best known for its dramatic castle, one of the finest 12th-century hall-keep castle ruins in the country. Walpole's home, Houghton Hall, is close by, too.

If you fancy a round of golf, you could head for Middleton Hall Golf Club in the nearby village of Middleton, while for refreshment you could try the Hare Arms at Stow Bardolph or Congham Hall Country House Hotel in Grimston.

Castle Rising
english-heritage.org.uk
PE31 6AH | 01553 631330
Open Apr–Nov daily 10–6, Nov–Mar
Wed–Sun 10–4

▼ Castle Rising

This castle has seen battles and a royal resident. Edward II was horribly murdered in 1327, on the orders of his wife, Queen Isabella, and her lover, Roger Mortimer. At this time, Edward's heir, Edward III, was only 15 years old, and Mortimer and Isabella were able to rule England together by manipulating the young king. This state of affairs continued for three years until Edward III began to take matters into his own hands. Learning of the roles of his mother and Mortimer in the death of his father, Edward had Mortimer tried for treason and hanged in 1330. Isabella was spared trial but banished to live in the wilds of Norfolk in Castle Rising.

The village is inland but at one time it was on the coast. As late as the 18th century, paintings of the castle show ships in the background. Look out for the massive Norman earthworks that surround the castle, and the mighty, square keep built between 1138 and 1140. Several rooms remain in excellent condition.

Houghton Hall
houghtonhall.com
King's Lynn, PE31 6UE
01485 528569 | Open Jun–Aug Oct Wed–Thu, Sun 11.30–5, Fri–Sat 11.30–9, Sep–Oct Wed–Sun 11.30–5
Robert Walpole, first Earl of Orford, was born in 1676. While he was First Lord of the Treasury and Chancellor, his brother-in-law and ally, Charles, Second Viscount Townshend, was Secretary of State, and between them they wielded a formidable amount of power. When the relationship between these powerful men began to break down, Townshend was infuriated by Walpole's decision to build himself a glittering new palace at Houghton, a mere 10 miles from Townshend's ancestral seat of Raynham Hall. By the time Walpole became prime minister, he had managed to engineer Townshend's resignation from the government, and Townshend retired to Raynham in bitter defeat. When Walpole began lavishly entertaining his influential friends, Townshend left the area altogether.

Walpole built up a fine collection of Old Masters, as well as vast collections of furniture and sculpture. After his death in 1745, his feckless grandson sold most of the pictures to Catherine the Great, and they now grace the walls of the Hermitage Museum in St Petersburg. In 1797, Houghton passed to the Cholmondeley family, but it was not until 1913 that this magnificent palace became their permanent home.

Building at Houghton Hall was started in 1721 on the site of two earlier houses. The village of Houghton was demolished, and its inhabitants relocated outside the park gates; it then became known as New Houghton. It was not unusual in the 18th century for villages to be moved to suit their landlords. Walpole's house was originally designed by Colen Campbell, but James Gibbs added the cupola-like domes at each corner, and suggested that the main building material should be hard-wearing yellow sandstone brought by sea from Whitby.

Walpole left the entire interior design to William Kent, who added marble fireplaces, carved woodwork, many of the murals and much of the furniture. Kent's masterpiece is the cube-shaped 'stone hall', which has a plaster ceiling frieze and reliefs over the fireplace and door.

Middleton Hall Golf Club

middletonhallgolfclub.com
Hall Orchards, Middleton, PE32 1RY
01553 841800 | Open daily all year
The natural undulations and mature specimen trees at the Middleton Hall Golf Club offer a most attractive environment. The architecturally designed course provides a challenge for the competent golfer. There is also a covered floodlit driving range and short game facilities.

Congham Hall Country House Hotel 🏵🏵

conghamhallhotel.co.uk
Lynn Road, Grimston, PE32 1AH
01485 600250
The Georgian house was built in the 1780s by a wealthy merchant from King's Lynn, which is about the time that the nearby royal residence of Sandringham House was

constructed. If an invite to the latter is not forthcoming, fear not, for Congham Hall can provide plenty of cossetting luxury, with gorgeous gardens, a swish spa and a restaurant that has genuine Georgian charm. The dining room has French windows looking on to the garden and pristine, linen-clad tables. There's a herb garden in the grounds with an amazing 400 varieties finding their way to the table, plus a kitchen garden and orchards, and ingredients that don't hail from the grounds are sourced with care from the local environs. The cooking is gently modern and shows allegiance to both the crown and our European partners.

The Hare Arms

theharearms.co.uk
Lynn Road, Stow Bardolph,
PE34 3HT | 01366 382229
Peacocks and hens roam the garden of this ivy-clad pub. It was named after the Hare family, who purchased Stow Bardolph estate in 1553 and still play an important part locally. Memorabilia are on display throughout the music-free, L-shaped bar, where two guest ales partner those of Greene King. There's plenty to contemplate on the menu and the daily specials board. There's an especially good vegetarian section. The Hare Bar is convivial but for a quieter vibe there's the Tortoise Room. Booking ahead is recommended.

▶ Lavenham   MAP REF 289 F4

Don't be a bit surprised to find a film crew at work when you visit Lavenham. This impossibly gorgeous Suffolk town is one of the best-preserved medieval towns in England and regularly provides the backdrop to historical dramas on television and in films. During the 15th and 16th centuries it grew rich on the wool trade, exporting cloth to Europe and Asia. At one time its people paid more in taxes than the people of Lincoln and York.

Merchants and clothiers built the half-timbered houses that still attract visitors today. Many tea rooms, restaurants and souvenir shops have opened to meet the demands of tourists. At times, when coaches clog the High Street, you can't help but think that Lavenham is just too pretty for its own good. It's like an open-air museum of medieval architecture.

When the wool trade declined, nothing took its place, with the result that the town centre retains its medieval street plan, a network of lanes fanning out from the market square, dominated by the spectacular 16th-century Guildhall of Corpus Christi. Entire streets, such as Water Street, are lined with crooked, half-timbered houses, delicately colour-washed in ochre, mustard and Suffolk pink. Look out, too, for the pargeting (decorative plasterwork) such as the Tudor rose and fleur-de-lis on the facade of the Swan Inn. Lavenham has had a few famous residents. The artist John Constable attended the

▼ Little Hall, Lavenham

Old Grammar School in Barn Street. One of his friends was Jane Taylor, who wrote the nursery rhyme 'Twinkle, Twinkle Little Star' (1806) and who lived at nearby Shilling Grange. But the biggest name in Lavenham's history has been that of the de Vere family. Aubrey de Vere was granted the manor by his brother-in-law William the Conqueror. Four centuries later, John de Vere, 13th Earl of Oxford, led Henry VII's victorious army at the Battle of Bosworth in 1485. This was the final battle of the Wars of the Roses and it was in thanks for his safe return that local merchants built the parish church of St Peter and St Paul. One of the largest parish churches in England, its 141-foot flint tower dominates the skyline. With its rich Gothic tracery, coffered roof, graceful arches, columns and aisles, it is also one of the finest examples of the Perpendicular style.

VISIT THE MUSEUM
The Guildhall of Corpus Christi

nationaltrust.org.uk/lavenham
Market Place, CO10 9QZ
01787 247646 | Open Jan–Feb
Fri–Sun 11–4, Mar–Oct daily 11–5,
Nov–Dec Thu–Sun 11–4

The Guildhall of Corpus Christi is one of the finest timber-framed buildings in Britain. It was built around 1530 by the prosperous Corpus Christi Guild, for religious rather than commercial reasons. The hall now houses a local history museum telling the story of Lavenham's cloth trade riches in the 15th and 16th centuries. You can also see the walled garden with its 19th-century lock-up and mortuary.

EAT AND DRINK
Lavenham Great House ◉◉◉

greathouse.co.uk
Market Place, CO10 9QZ
01787 247431

Opposite the 16th-century timber-framed Guildhall, owned by the National Trust, the Great House is itself pretty ancient behind its Georgian facade, though its dining room has been given a thoroughly modern look. It's a calm and soothing room, decorated in soft tones, with a dark wood floor and comfortable upholstered chairs at white-clothed tables set with flowers and sparkling glasses. The cooking has its roots in the great French repertoire, but that's not to say there aren't some more global influences at play as well. There's a patio for warm days.

The Swan at Lavenham ◉◉

theswanatlavenham.co.uk
High Street, CO10 9QA
01787 247477

The asymmetrical timbered white building on Lavenham's main street gives evidence of its own great age. Dating back to the 15th century, it's an endearing maze of crannies and beams within, beautifully maintained and bursting with character. The Airmen's Bar is

▲ The Swan at Lavenham

restaurant is the Gallery. Here the handsome, high-vaulted timbered ceiling and minstrels' gallery, and polished and attentive service from smartly uniformed staff, add to the sense of occasion. The modernism of the cooking is productively at odds with the venerability of its surroundings.

named for its World War II memorabilia left by the airmen stationed here who would come in for many a boozy session. There's informal dining in the Brasserie, which serves a repertoire of crowd-pleasing pub classics; but the main

▸ **PLACES NEARBY**

The equally gorgeous architecture found in the village of Kersey (see page 149), and at Melford Hall and Kentwell Hall in Long Melford (see below), is worth adding to your schedule when exploring this part of Suffolk. Both villages are little more than a 10-minute drive from beautiful Lavenham on scenic rural roads.

▸ **Long Melford** MAP REF 289 E5

Long Melford takes its name from its layout: lots of gorgeous pink- and yellow-washed period country houses and shops dotted along a long, straight, three-mile stretch of road, and a mill ford crossing. You can wander along this road, Hall Street, where you'll find chic tea emporia, designer fashion studios, art and fine food galleries and showrooms full to bursting with antiques. Long Melford is big on antiques, and featured prominently in the television series *Lovejoy*. Holy Trinity church, long, large and built almost entirely in the 15th century, is one of the great Suffolk wool churches.

Two of the country's most magnificent country estates can be found in Long Melford, just a couple of miles apart. You could easily spend a day or more in Long Melford, visiting not only Hall Street, but also the delightfully romantic moated Kentwell Hall and the impressive red-brick pile of the Hyde Parker family, Melford Hall. The estates are easy to find – at the end of Hall Street is an expansive village green and their entrances can be found ahead and to the right.

TAKE IN SOME HISTORY
Kentwell Hall
kentwell.co.uk
CO10 9BA | 01787 310207
Open Mar–Sep (check website)

Kentwell Hall is a moated red-brick Tudor country house with stunning gardens, woodland walks and a rare breeds farm. You approach the house along a mile-long lime tree-lined driveway that culminates in a spectacular view of the property and its front courtyard.

Restoration started here in 1971 and still continues today, with new features being added all the time. You can see the living areas of the house, such as the drawing room and the great hall, the kitchens, bakery and dairy.

In the Domesday Book, the manor of Kentwell was valued at £4 and owned by Frodo, brother of the first Abbot of Bury St Edmund's. The manor of Kentwell has been sold several times during its long history. It remained in Frodo's family until it passed to a family that took the name of the manor itself – the de Kentwells.

By 1250, it was in the hands of Henry III, who granted it to his half-brother, Sir William de Valence. The Hall was owned briefly by the 14th-century poet John Gower, and eventually came to Sir William Clopton through his mother Katharine Mylde in 1403. William's son, John (1423–97), seems to have been responsible for the earliest parts of the existing complex.

One of the highlights of Kentwell Hall is its now legendary re-creations of

▼ Kentwell Hall

everyday life in Tudor times. Actors and members of the public – you can apply to take part – dress in Tudor costumes and tell of their lives as members of the noble family, musicians, farm workers, dairymaids, blacksmiths, bakers or cooks. The hall also hosts 1940s Britain days. No visit to Kentwell would be complete without admiring the grounds. The rare breeds farm is well worth a visit too.

Melford Hall

nationaltrust.org.uk/melfordhall
CO10 9AA | 01787 379228
Open end-Mar–Oct Wed–Sun 12–5
(house fully open 1–4.30)
Melford Hall has changed little externally since 1578 when Elizabeth I was entertained here, and retains its original panelled banqueting hall. It was first the home of monks, and then the Hyde Parker family from 1786 to the present day. It is run on a day-to-day basis by the National Trust.

You can see the Regency library, Victorian bedrooms, extensive collections of furniture and porcelain, and a small display of items connected with Beatrix Potter, who was related to the family, including the original Jemima Puddleduck given to a child of the family by Beatrix herself.

The garden contains some spectacular specimen trees, rare orchids and a banqueting house and there is an attractive mile-long walk through the park. Special events are held throughout the year, including the annual Beatrix Potter Fun Day in July.

EAT AND DRINK
Long Melford Swan 😊😊
longmelfordswan.co.uk
Hall Street, CO10 9JQ
01787 464545
Slap bang in the middle of the high street in Long Melford, this elegant restaurant with rooms has undergone a complete refurbishment. With feature wallpaper, pastel colours and a large patio offering alfresco dining opportunities, quality oozes from every corner of this friendly, family-run operation, where service is cheerful and efficient. In the kitchen, the ambitious young team conjure some innovative combinations from tip-top ingredients and although the style is broadly modern British, influences look far beyond the doorstep.

▶ PLACES NEARBY
The George 😊😊
thecavendishgeorge.co.uk
The Green, Cavendish, CO10 8BA
01787 280248
This 16th-century whitewashed inn is Grade II listed, and better described as a restaurant. The George's interior is dominated by wood, from the bare tables to the heavy beams that lend the place its character. The reassuring buzz of kitchen activity in the background reminds you what the main priority is. A Mediterranean-inflected repertoire of modern British dishes is on offer.

▶ **Lowestoft** MAP REF 295 F6

The busy seaside resort of Lowestoft is Britain's most easterly town, and as such the first place in the country to catch the morning sun. You'll find it has a very different vibe to Great Yarmouth to its north, with a more stately feel about it.

The main street is a pretty enough place, lined with merchants' houses dating from the time when Lowestoft was a busy, although less frenetic than some, fishing harbour. There are major shop chains, schools and more informal eateries too. Away from the centre, the town's streets were once flanked by breweries, small industries and cottages, many occupied by labourers who worked on the farms that surrounded the town before development took over and farmland became covered in shiny new housing estates.

Evidence suggests that Lowestoft has been inhabited for around 700,000 years, and saw communities evolve during the Neolithic, Bronze and Iron Ages right through to Roman and Saxon times. Since the 14th century, when this small harbourside village began its expansion, Lowestoft has evolved into a major fishing port, which was later steadily replaced by light industry and North Sea oil and gas exploitation as its fisheries saw a decline. One of its major industries was the production of soft-paste porcelain, which became highly desirable and which, today, is extremely rare and valuable. Ahead of the tourist-industry curve, the Lowestoft porcelain factory produced many pieces intended as souvenirs for visitors to the growing seaside resort, many of them showing local scenes of the town as it once was.

From Victorian times, Lowestoft benefited from its miles of golden beaches and quickly became a fashionable destination. Today, people still flock to its beaches – the best ones are near the two piers, the South Pier and the Claremont. The main beaches have lifeguards in summer.

Lowestoft's inner harbour, a scenic area known as Lake Lothing, plugs into Oulton Broad and the River Waveney, the most southeasterly point of the Norfolk Broads, which makes it a popular point of embarkation for holiday trips on the waterways.

If literature and art are your passions, you'll be interested to know that Thomas Nashe, the English poet and dramatist, was born here in 1567, as was composer Benjamin Britten in 1913 (see page 52). Oulton Broad is the place to which Norfolk author George Borrow (1803–81) returned following his travels, and where he wrote many of his books. He died here in 1881. And nearby Blundeston was the birthplace of Dickens' David Copperfield.

VISIT THE MUSEUMS
East Anglia Transport Museum

eatransportmuseum.co.uk
Chapel Road, Carlton Colville,
NR33 8BL | 01502 518459
Open Apr–Oct (days and events vary, see website)

Motor, steam and electrical vehicles are exhibited in this fascinating museum, all of which have seen service around the country over many decades. A highlight is the reconstructed 1930s street scene, which is used as a setting for working vehicles. You can ride by tram, trolley bus and narrow gauge railway within the museum complex. There's a woodland picnic area served by trams.

Maritime Museum

lowestoftmaritimemuseum.co.uk
Sparrows Nest Gardens, Whapload Road, NR32 1XG | 01502 561963
Open mid-Apr–Oct

Housed in a gorgeous flint cottage, which, according to the plaque above the door, was restored in 1828, this museum was founded in 1968 by a group of enthusiasts and has steadily expanded. The cottage, the museum's permanent home, has since been sympathetically extended to make space for all the exhibits. It focuses on maritime history: themed exhibits trace the history of Lowestoft and its connections with the sea, displaying ancient and modern fishing boats, commercial boats, fishing gear, shipwrights' tools, and lifeboats, a wheelhouse, steam drifter cabin and a fish market, with models, charts and other memorabilia. It has a small cinema showing archive film footage on Lowestoft's port.

ENTERTAIN THE FAMILY
Claremont Pier

claremontpier.co.uk
Wellington Esplanade, NR33 0BS
01502 573533

The Claremont Pier was originally built in Victorian times when it was almost obligatory for all seaside resorts to have at least one pier, but a few gales over the years have meant that sections have been replaced. Today, it has a plethora of attractions to suit all tastes, from the Fun Palace amusement arcade and Palace Casino to Rollers, the disco-style rollerskating rink. There are two seafood restaurants with beach and sea views and a music venue.

South Pier

thesouthpier.co.uk
Royal Plain, NR33 0AE
01502 512793

If you fancy a spot of 10-pin bowling followed by a fish and chip supper, then you should visit Lowestoft's South Pier. On this historic pier, where once a reading room and bandstand attracted Victorian visitors, you'll find entertainment for the family, including modern and traditional coin machines and video games.

Pleasurewood Hills

see highlight panel opposite

▶ Pleasurewood Hills   MAP REF 295 F6

pleasurewoodhills.com
Leisure Way, Corton, NR32 5DZ
01502 586000 | Open Apr–late Jul, Sep 10–5 (days vary), late Jul–Aug
daily 10–6

Set in 50 acres of coastal parkland, Pleasurewood Hills has all the ingredients for a great family day out. There are thrills for the bravest adventurers, such as the Wipeout, which hits speeds of 50mph, or the hyperdrive dodgems. There are rides for young children in the Kiddie Zone and shows with sea lions and parrots. When the action gets too much, take a leisurely ride on the alpine chairlift or jump aboard one of two railways that weave their way through the park.

HIT THE BEACH

Lowestoft's beaches are golden and sandy, and those around the Claremont Pier have a Blue Flag accreditation.

PLAY A ROUND

Rookery Park Golf Club

rookeryparkgolfclub.co.uk
Beccles Road, Carlton Colville, NR33 8HJ | 01502 509190
Open daily all year
Mature trees line the parkland courses over gently undulating ground, including two ponds on the signature eighth hole.

EAT AND DRINK

The Crooked Barn Restaurant ⊛⊛

ivyhousecountryhotel.co.uk
Ivy House Country Hotel, Ivy Lane, Oulton Broad, NR33 8HY
01502 501353

On the banks of Oulton Broad, in 20 acres of grounds, the Ivy House Country Hotel has an ace up its sleeve in the form of The Crooked Barn Restaurant, located in a 16th-century barn that has a ceiling exposed to the rafters. There's plenty of room within for the smartly set tables, dressed in white linen and generously spaced around the room, plus views over the pretty garden. The kitchen makes excellent use of the region's produce in dishes that smack of Pan-European eclecticism.

Flying Fifteens

19a The Esplanade, NR33 0QG
01502 581188
All the food at these popular tea rooms is home-cooked using the best ingredients, and chips

▼ South Beach

are banned from the menu. Specialities include locally smoked salmon and ham and, on Saturdays, fresh Cromer crab. There are no set meals, just a choice of sandwiches, soup and omelettes, baguettes and cakes. There are over 40 loose-leaf teas from around the world too. The name Flying Fifteens comes from a 15-foot-long sailing boat designed by Uffa Fox in the 1940s.

▶ **PLACES NEARBY**

Somerleyton Hall in the pretty village of the same name is nearby (see page 241), as is the popular Africa Alive! wildlife park (see page 63). Both Beccles (see page 61) and the lively Great Yarmouth (see page 139) are short journeys away. Heading out towards Great Yarmouth you'll find the Pettitts Animal

Adventure Park in the village of Reedham, a pretty little place on the banks of the River Yare. Trains cross the Yare on the mighty swing bridge.

Pettitts Animal Adventure Park

pettittsadventurepark.co.uk
Reedham, NR13 3UA
01493 700094 | Open Apr–Oct daily 10–5
Aimed at younger children, the lovely Pettitts Animal Adventure Park is three parks in one. Rides include a railway and roller coaster. Its adventure play area has a mini-golf course, ball pond and tea room. Young children will love the entertainment provided by clowns, puppets and live musicians. Among the animals you can see here are miniature horses, tiny tamarind monkeys, meerkats, owls and micro pigs.

▶ **Madingley**
see **Cambridge**, page 99

▶ **Mildenhall** MAP REF 289 D2

Aircraft enthusiasts have long been attracted to Mildenhall, the small Breckland market town that's home to two massive Royal Air Force bases, RAF Mildenhall and RAF Lakenheath, used by the US Air Force. Although the Pentagon announced in 2015 that the USAF would be withdrawing from RAF Mildenhall, it also posted plans to expand RAF Lakenheath to house the first European squadron of US F-35s by 2020. So there should still be sightings of military planes on manoeuvres in the skies.

During World War II, RAF Mildenhall was one of a number of Suffolk airfields used by the Allied forces. Others included Lavenham, Eye and Mendlesham. Wellington bombers from Mildenhall engaged the German Navy within a day of war being declared. Throughout the war they continued to attack German targets as well as providing cover for Allied troops during the D-Day landings in Normandy and the evacuation of Dunkirk. In all, some 200 aircraft from Mildenhall were lost and 1,900 men killed in action during the war. The American presence at Mildenhall began in 1950 and it is the gateway to Britain for more than 100,000 military personnel each year.

Mildenhall revolves around its market place, in the centre of which stands an elaborate hexagonal market cross dating from the 16th century. Here, the community, which is today very much a mix of military and non-military, gathers every Friday for the town's large market, as it has done for around 600 years. From here you can take the short walk to the Mildenhall Museum, which tells the story of the town.

Mildenhall's other claim to fame is the Mildenhall Treasure, the most significant hoard of Roman silverware ever discovered in Britain. The story of its discovery is almost as remarkable as the treasure itself. In January 1943, farmer Gordon Butcher was ploughing at West Row when he found a metal bowl buried in the ground. He showed it to his boss, Sydney Ford, who happened to collect antiques. Curiosity got the better of the pair and between them they dug up 34 pieces of blackened silverware, including plates, goblets and bowls, and a great dish almost 2 feet in diameter, decorated with scenes from Roman mythology. Ford cleaned the objects and kept them on his mantelpiece for three years until eventually someone persuaded him to take them to the police. The hoard was declared a treasure trove and given to the British Museum. Ford and Butcher received a reward.

VISIT THE MUSEUM
Mildenhall Museum
mildenhallmuseum.co.uk
King Street, IP28 7EX
01638 716970 | Open Tue–Thu,
Sat 2–4.30, Fri 10.30–4.30
This bright and fresh museum
housed in two flint cottages
contains a replica set of the
Mildenhall Treasure, including
bowls, ladles and the great dish
(all the originals are in the
British Museum). The museum
also has galleries devoted
to local history, ecology and
RAF Mildenhall.

SEE A LOCAL CHURCH
Church of St Mary
High Street, IP28 7EE
01638 711930
The grandeur of the Grade I
listed Church of St Mary, the
largest in Suffolk, reflects
Mildenhall's prosperous history.
It was rebuilt in the 14th
century on the site of a previous
chapel. Its distinguished
medieval craftsmanship makes
it one of the great churches of
East Anglia.

The tall 15th-century west
tower and the huge decorated
east window are the features
that strike most people first.
The two-storey north porch of
about 1420 makes a fittingly
grand entrance to the church,
with its fine stone vault and roof
bosses. Inside, you'll see even
more remarkable and
extravagant roofs above the
nave and both aisles, which are
embellished with throngs of
carved angels and biblical
figures. The nave roof,
especially, is a remarkable
survival: unable to reach the
immensely high carved angels
to destroy them with their bare
hands, the puritan iconoclasts
tried to shoot them to pieces
instead. Many of the figures are
still peppered with gunshot.

PLAY A ROUND
West Suffolk Golf Centre
westsuffolkgolfcentre.co.uk
New Drove, Beck Row, IP28 8RN
01638 718972 | Open daily all year
This course has been gradually
improved to provide a chance
to play an inland course in all
weather conditions. Situated on
the edge of the Breckland, the
dry nature of the course makes
for easy walking among rare
flora and fauna.

EAT AND DRINK
The Bull Inn ◉
bullinn-bartonmills.com
The Street, Barton Mills,
IP28 6AA | 01638 711001
With its fine roofline, dormer
windows and old coaching
courtyard, this rambling
16th-century building certainly
looks like a traditional roadside
inn. Stepping inside you'll be
wowed by a contemporary
sprucing-up that successfully
blends original oak beams,
wooden floors and big
fireplaces with funky fabrics,
designer wallpapers and bold
colours. Menus evolve with the
seasons, with every effort made
to reduce 'food miles' by
sourcing locally. You can have
sandwiches too, if you prefer.
Accommodation is available.

▶ Newmarket MAP REF 288 C3

Where most English high streets are lined with conventional shops, in Newmarket you'll see saddlers, farriers and bookmakers, cosy little places with the latest jodhpurs and colourful jockey silks on display in their windows and shoe shops selling a nice line in riding and stable boots. Statues of horses stand outside shops. Souvenir shops are crammed with mugs and pictures depicting horses, and secondhand bookshops are full of books telling the story of horseracing. You almost expect the local Waitrose to sell horse feed.

Newmarket has been the capital of British horseracing since James I (1566–1625) built a palace in an acre of land, complete with extensive stables, and moved his summer court here in 1605. The town soon became a fashionable royal resort and the home of the sporting fraternity. Long before that, Queen Boudicca used to race her chariots across Newmarket Heath, but it was James I, followed by Charles I and Charles II, who sealed the town's fate as the top venue for the 'Sport of Kings'.

Don't miss the newly restored Palace House on your visit. Built in the remains of the sporting palace and racing stables that Charles II had constructed in the 1660s, it is now home to the National Heritage Centre for Horseracing and Sporting Art

with a museum and special exhibitions. William Samwell (1628–76), a celebrated English architect, was commissioned to design the palace, said to have been one of the king's favourite homes. Further along Palace Street is a white house with shutters. This is where Nell Gwynne, one of the king's favourite mistresses, lived.

The National Horseracing Museum, which has a fascinating collection of riding clothes, rosettes, photographs and other memorabilia, tells the story of racing, and is one of many things to see on a visit to Newmarket. A 'must' is a visit to Warren Hill to see the famous gallops where the horses train each morning from dawn to around midday. The sight of dozens of horses galloping at speed in the early morning, when there's still dew on the grass and a light mist in the air, furnishes a memory that will last a lifetime.

One of the finest views of the town is from Newmarket Heath. Here you will see the Rowley Mile racecourse and the Millennium Grandstand. Not far from here is Queensberry House, headquarters of the British Bloodstock Agency, the National Stud and Tattersalls, the largest bloodstock auctioneers in Europe and the oldest in the world. See also 'Horseracing at Newmarket', page 33.

▾ Racehorses training at Newmarket

VISIT THE MUSEUM
National Heritage Centre for Horseracing and Sporting Art

palacehousenewmarket.co.uk
Palace House, Palace Street, CB8 8EP
01638 667314 | Open daily 10–5

Set on five acres in the heart of Newmarket, Palace House has been restored and revitalised and now houses the National Horseracing Museum and the Packard Galleries of British Sporting Art, and also offers the opportunity to meet former racehorses learning new skills in the Peter O'Sullevan Arena, the flagship home of Retraining of Racehorses. There are daily demonstrations at 11 and 2.30 that may include, for example, dressage, lunging, pole and gridwork or grooming.

The museum is packed with artefacts that tell the story of the people and horses involved in racing in Britain. See colourful racing silks worn by some of the world's greatest jockeys, including Frankie Dettori when he won every race on a seven-race card in one afternoon. There's a hands-on gallery, too, where you can have a go at riding on the horse simulator – thrilling, but as you'll soon discover, horseracing is not as easy as it looks – and try on racing silks. There's a diverse collection of fine and decorative sporting art to be discovered in the Packard Galleries, from old prints and fine oil paintings to modern art, ceramics and jewellery. Multimedia guides and family trails are available.

TAKE A TOUR
The National Stud

nationalstud.co.uk
discovernewmarket.co.uk
Newmarket, CB8 0XE

Tours daily Mar–Sep Wed–Fri 11.15, Sat–Sun and school holidays 11.15 and 2, Oct Wed–Sun 11.15

▼ National Heritage Centre

▼ Fun in the gallery

Don't miss the chance to go on a tour of the National Stud (pre-booking is essential) – it's the only commercial thoroughbred stud farm in the country that offers an opportunity to see behind the scenes. Tours last about 90 minutes and what you see depends on the weather, the season and the activities happening at the stud at the time. Most tours include visits to the Stallion Unit and in the early spring to the Foaling Unit and nursery paddocks, as well as various yards and paddocks where mares and foals graze. You'll get an overview of the work entailed in producing a future champion.

PLAY A ROUND
Links Golf Club
linksgolfclub.co.uk
Cambridge Road, CB8 0TG
01638 663000 | Open daily all year

With its gently undulating parkland setting surrounded by racecourses, the Links is one of the most attractive golf clubs in the region. Its 18-hole par 72 course is also one of the most challenging for both beginners and experienced players. The club operates a reciprocal arrangement with 12 other clubs around the country, which formed in 1902, the year the Links opened, so if you are a member you can play here too.

EAT AND DRINK
Bedford Lodge Hotel ◉◉
bedfordlodgehotel.co.uk
Bury Road, CB8 7BX
01638 663175
A Georgian hunting lodge built for the Duke of Bedford in the 18th century, this place has been a hotel since the 1940s. Its position near the racing at Newmarket, England's centre

▼ Frankie Dettori's silks

of operations for the sport of kings since medieval times, means that no opportunity is lost in the decorative theming to celebrate the equestrian life, and if you've had a win at the races, there are plenty of ways of celebrating it, from treatments in the award-winning spa to a festive occasion in the fine-dining Squires restaurant. An extensive menu of brasserie dishes spans the range from straightforward classics to more adventurous offerings, all using locally sourced ingredients. The fixed-price menus offer particularly good value.

The Packhorse Inn ⊛⊛

thepackhorseinn.com
Bridge Street, Moulton
CB8 8SP | 01638 751818

The Packhorse reopened in 2013 after a six-month refurbishment. It was formerly the King's Head; its new name reflects the adjacent medieval bridge across the River Kennet. Just two miles from Newmarket Racecourse, it is now a stylish, family-friendly country pub that attracts locals, racegoers and also London professionals looking for somewhere to unwind. The emphasis is on quality food and drink, much of it sourced locally, including beers from Adnams and Woodforde's breweries, and Aspall cider, and the menu is a mix of gently updated pub favourites with more ambitious modern European ideas. The blackboard specials reflect some last-minute inspiration.

The Tack Room: Food by the Pantry

palacehousenewmarket.co.uk
Palace Street, CB8 8EP
01638 666390

A lovely cafe with outdoor seating in summer, it serves traditional British food using the best Suffolk ingredients. Go for breakfast, lunch or afternoon tea, light bites or a hearty meal. By night it becomes an elegant restaurant and wine bar with fresh fish and seafood its speciality. There's also a bakery for takeaway treats.

Wavertree's Coffee Shop

nationalstud.co.uk
Newmarket, CB8 0XE
01638 666789

You don't have to take the tour to visit the National Stud's licensed cafe and equine-focused gift shop. The cakes and pastries are tempting, there are hot daily specials along with the soup, sandwiches, panini and jacket potatoes for lunch, and the traditional cream teas are a popular choice.

▶ **PLACES NEARBY**

Both Wicken Fen National Nature Reserve (see page 279) and Anglesey Abbey and Lode Mill (see page 99) are within a short drive, as is the city of Cambridge (see page 88). For refreshments you could head for Tuddenham Mill, a gorgeous converted watermill in Tuddenham St Mary. Walkers on the Devil's Dyke, ancient earthworks affording panoramic views across the countryside, appreciate the aptly named Dyke's End pub in Reach. In Worlington, you could play golf at the Royal Worlington and Newmarket Golf Club.

Tuddenham Mill ❶❷❸

tuddenhammill.co.uk
High Street, Tuddenham St Mary,
IP28 6SQ | 01638 713552
One of the more striking hotel and dining venues in East Anglia is this converted watermill on the Suffolk-Cambridgeshire border between Newmarket and Bury St Edmunds. Some conversions change the former function of a building, disguising it in the process, whereas at Tuddenham it has become a central feature, the gigantic waterwheel encased in glass in the first-floor restaurant, while inset window panels in the floor allow views of the water rushing by below. There are ducks and swans nesting on the River Kennet, and the view over open countryside from the terrace tables on a summer evening is of a well-nigh perfect English idyll.

The bright, contemporary-style modern British cooking features local and regional produce in creative dishes that utilise lots of skilful and modern culinary techniques.

Dyke's End

dykesend.co.uk
8 Fair Green, Reach, CB25 0JD
01638 743816
Devil's Dyke Anglo-Saxon earthworks is a Site of Special Scientific Interest (SSSI) and a popular walking destination. It separates Newmarket's two racecourses and stretches for over 7 miles from the pretty village of Reach. As its name suggests, the Dyke's End pub is conveniently situated for hikers in need of refreshment, but its reputation for good food and warm atmosphere brings people in from miles around, walkers or not. Menus here change as different produce and game come into season, but always include such pub classics as steak frites and locally made sausages and mash with onion gravy. Sunday lunch is so popular that booking is essential.

Royal Worlington and Newmarket Golf Club

royalworlington.co.uk
Golf Links Road, IP28 8SD
01638 712216 | Open daily all year
The inland links course of the Royal Worlington and Newmarket golf club is renowned as one of the best nine-hole courses in the country. Well drained, it provides excellent winter playing conditions, as well as being a popular summer course. This is also the home of the Cambridge University golf team.

▶ Newton MAP REF 289 F5

Newton in Suffolk has a real community spirit. You can play golf on its huge 40-acre village green – it was turned into a proper nine-hole course around the time the club was formed, over a century ago. Residents gather for special events in the pub, Saracens, which has benches overlooking the green and has acted as an impromptu golfers' club house for years. The Newton Green Golf Club now has a further course, which is more challenging for serious golfers. Newton, which lies near Sudbury (see page 256), is home to the ancient woodlands at Edwardstone Woods, a designated Site of Special Scientific Interest, and Alstrop Wood. Here, many species of trees thrive, some 500 years old, including hornbeam and wild cherry trees.

PLAY A ROUND
Newton Green Golf Club
newtongreengolfclub.co.uk
Newton Green, CO10 0QN
01787 377217 | Open Sun–Fri
all year

The Newton Green Golf Club is one of the oldest in the region, founded in 1907. It has two flat courses that meander around a pond. The first nine holes are open with bunkers and trees, while the second nine holes are tight with ditches and gorse.

▶ PLACES NEARBY
Southeast of Newton is the scenic Constable country of Dedham Vale (see page 110). Stop off in one of the tiny villages on the way for refreshments.

The Case Restaurant with Rooms ◉
thecaserestaurantwithrooms.co.uk
Further Street, Assington,
CO10 5LD | 01787 210483

This charming country inn has bags of character, with low beams and exposed brick in the bar area and a cosy little restaurant with a wood-burning stove, dark wood tables and ceiling beams. Host-led hospitality is the key to its success as well as the quality of the contemporary, brasserie-style cooking. The kitchen displays a great deal of flair in the presentation of its creations and keeps things relatively straightforward.

The Lion
thelioncolchester.com
Honey Tye, CO6 4NX
01206 263434

This traditional country dining pub occupies an enviable spot in an Area of Outstanding Natural Beauty (AONB). The spacious restaurant is decorated in a modern, comfortable style and the bar has low-beamed ceilings and wood-burner. The reasonably priced food here is sourced locally and the menu changes with the seasons. The Lion has a walled beer garden for alfresco eating and drinking in the warmer summer months.

▶ **Norfolk Broads** MAP REF 295 E5

Moving silently between the swaying reedbeds of Barton Broad,
it's hard to imagine that the tranquil landscape through which
you are passing is anything but natural. No visit to Norfolk
would be complete without a trip to the Broads National Park.
This is a patchwork of interlinked streams, lakes and channels
that wind sluggishly over the flat land to the east of Norwich.

▲ Thurne Mill

Today, wildlife-watching is a popular and inspirational experience best enjoyed by visiting one of the many nature reserves. With such a diverse landscape, it is not surprising that other activities are also in demand here – fishing, sailing, windsurfing, rowing, canoeing, boating and walking – so striking the right balance in the provision of amenities, one that is sympathetic to the needs of the Broads rather than to the needs of visitors, is difficult and ongoing.

Natural or manmade?

Three major rivers – the Bure, Waveney and Yare – supply most of the water to the meres, ponds and marshes before entering the great tidal basin at Breydon Water and flowing into the sea at Great Yarmouth. Despite the fact that the Broads comprise one of England's best wilderness areas, most natural historians and archaeologists accept that their origin actually

▼ Hickling Broad

lies in ancient human activity. That is the great paradox of the Norfolk and Suffolk Broads. Like so many British landscapes, even this apparently untouched 'natural' landscape was once the scene of great human industry. Unlike any other national park, it was manmade around 500 years ago in an area of hollows that were the direct result of large-scale medieval peat extraction.

The extent of that extraction was deduced by meticulous examination of the records of St Benet's Abbey, a Benedictine monastery on the banks of the River Bure at Holme, near Ludham. The scanty flint-faced ruin of St Benet's, now dominated by the remains of an 18th-century red-brick tower mill built into the wall of the gatehouse, is one of the most important historic monuments in the Broads, and more than likely dates back to the ninth century. The abbey was rebuilt and endowed with three manors by King Canute in 1020.

▼ St Benet's Abbey

▲ The Broads at Horsey

The abbey's records show that from the 12th century onwards large areas of Hoveton parish were set aside for peat digging, and in one year alone more than a million turves (blocks of peat used for fires) were cut. This industrial-scale extraction went on continuously for more than 200 years and, by the early 14th century, at the height of its importance, the cathedral priory at Norwich was using nearly 400,000 turves annually. The peat diggings were eventually joined to the main river systems when wildfowlers, fishermen and reed cutters dug channels to link them.

Water, water everywhere

But where did all the water come from? From the 13th century onwards there was a slight change in the relative levels of the land and the sea, and coastal and low-lying areas such as the Broads became increasingly at risk from flooding – not unlike the effects of global warming and the predicted rise in sea levels today. There were some cursory attempts to dredge peat from under the steadily rising waters, but by the 15th century peat digging was no longer practical and it was abandoned.

▲ Boathouses, Hickling Broad

Tithe maps from the 1840s show that the Broads once covered nearly 3,000 acres of open water. Since then, the shallow lakes formed from the peat diggings have gradually filled with dead and dying vegetation and sediment. The total area of open water today is less than half that during the 18th century, but there are still 125 miles of lock-free, navigable rivers and broads within the national park. The Broads, which cover 117 sq miles of Norfolk, and parts of Suffolk, became England's 11th national park in 1989. What they lack in crags, mountains and moorlands, the Broads make up for in their ever-changing waterscapes. Today, the Broads are one of the most important wetland landscapes in Europe, and provide a home to many spectacular forms of plants and wildlife.

Mills, often mistakenly called windmills, punctuate the Broads' skyline, but in almost every case these are windpumps, built to drain water from the marshes. Wonderful examples can be seen at Berney Arms, Herringfleet, Turf Fen, How Hill, Boardman's Mill and Thurne Dyke. It makes you wonder if they attracted the same kind of outcry when they were erected as 21st-century wind turbines do today.

Navigating the Broads

There are few major centres of population within the National Park, but just beyond the boundaries lie the city of Norwich (see page 212) and the towns of Great Yarmouth (see page 139) and Lowestoft (see page 189). Here you are on dry land, but the best way to explore the Broads themselves, given that they hug the courses of many rivers, is by boat, for it is then that the illusion of remoteness is heightened and the prospect of seeing something rare and wonderful is enhanced by an approach that is slow and quiet. Indeed, the Broads have been important for leisure sailing and boating since Victorian times, offering a unique navigation system for which special inland sailing craft – wherries – were developed. Wherries have featured on the Broads for centuries and their use in river trade was instrumental in making Norwich England's second city. The earliest wherry-type vessel was square rigged but, by the early 19th century, the wherry had become single-sailed, and better designed for the shallow waters of the Broads.

GO EXPLORING

There are many wonderful places in the Broads. Wroxham (see page 284), the pretty villages of Ludham, Hoveton and Ranworth (see page 234), and the nearby Broads Wildlife Centre (see page 235) shouldn't be missed.

Perhaps the place where its real spirit can best be captured is the thatched and gabled Edwardian house of How Hill. Situated on the highest point of the national park, just 40 feet above the sea, How Hill was built by the Norwich architect Edward Boardman, and now serves as an education centre and nature reserve run by the Broads Authority and the How Hill Trust. The views from the house take in the River Ant and the reedbeds of Reedham, Clayrack and Bisley, all watched over by the red-brick Turf Fen windpump. The How Hill reserve is a microcosm of Broadland, its habitats spanning wet woodland, grazing marshes and wildflower meadows.

▼ Broads Wildlife Centre

▶ **North Walsham**   MAP REF 295 D2

Worsted, a heavy winter-weight fabric produced at nearby Worstead, may be better known, but North Walsham also had its own fabric, lighter in weight and known as 'Walsham'. The town was a thriving weaving centre in the Middle Ages when Protestant settlers from Flanders came to live here to escape religious persecution.

The town's prosperity grew and by the 14th century its people were able to build a magnificent church, complete with one of Norfolk's tallest towers, which became the centre of the community. Even today, North Walsham's church of St Nicholas, with its unique ruined tall tower, remains one of the largest parish churches in England and the town's landmark. You can see it for miles around.

As you wander around the streets of North Walsham, look out for the wayside stone near the water towers that tells how its people were involved in the Peasants' Revolt of 1381, and were defeated in the Battle of North Walsham, one of the last battles in a rebellion that saw peasants throughout England rise up against the authorities.

Nearby is Paston College. Horatio Nelson and his brother William were educated here in the 18th century when it was Paston Grammar School. Horatio was 12 when he left the school to begin his naval career.

EAT AND DRINK
Beechwood Hotel ◉◉
beechwood-hotel.co.uk
20 Cromer Road, NR28 0HD
01692 403231
This handsome creeper-clad Georgian hotel should exert a strong pull for murder and mystery fans, since Agatha Christie came here frequently when it was owned by family friends, and her framed letters are hung in the hallway. It is a lovely personal touch that sums up the exemplary attitude to service and attention to detail that is the hallmark of this charming small hotel. The elegantly traditional dining room is the setting for some well-crafted, contemporary cooking, delivered by a kitchen with a passion for sourcing top-grade Norfolk produce.

▶ PLACES NEARBY
East Ruston Gardens
e-ruston-oldvicaragegardens.co.uk
East Ruston Old Vicarage,
East Ruston, NR12 9HN
01692 650432 | Open Mar–Oct
Wed–Sun 12–5.30
East Ruston Gardens lie a mile and a half from the Norfolk coast and promise an improbable horticultural tour. They are protected from the strong wind by belts of trees and dense hedges, and have all the ambience of the Mediterranean, the luxuriance of the tropics, the aridity of the

Arizona desert and, in a field spattered with cornflowers and poppies, the nostalgia of childhood.

Alan Gray bought the property in 1973 when the former vicarage had a look of desolation and the surrounding two acres were waist-high in weeds. Undeterred, he saw this as a blank canvas on which to create an oasis-like cordon around the Arts and Crafts brick-and-tile house.

Today, the gardens extend over 32 acres. Part of Alan Gray's vision was to maintain a high level of colour and interest, and to give the garden a sense of place by harnessing nearby landmarks; a porthole in a hedge neatly frames the Happisburgh lighthouse.

The extended season of colour is nowhere better exemplified than in a field and woodland garden, which is criss-crossed by meandering paths. Several thousand bulbs are planted each year to reinforce the already glorious display of snowdrops and aconites in February. Special areas include the Fern Garden and the Exotic Garden, which is awash with bedding plants, many no longer available commercially. Bananas and *Tetrapanax papyrifer 'Rex'* add structure with their large imposing foliage, and a tall fountain adds drama.

To protect the tender, rare and unusual plants the owners planted large shelterbelts of Monterey pine, Italian alder, the Mediterranean oak and many eucalypts which, as they have developed, have improved the microclimate. More protection comes from mixed hedgerows, planted for their changing colours and textures and as habitats for birds.

These gardens are a delight. Regular garden events are held here, and Alan Gray gives demonstrations and tours.

▼ Decorated screens, St Nicholas' Church in North Walsham

▶ Norwich MAP REF 294 C4

When William the Conqueror arrived here in 1066 and decided
that this was to be the place for one of the grandest palaces
the country had ever seen, Norwich was already the largest
city in England after London. Both the Romans and the
Anglo-Saxons had developed the city which had its own mint
and a thriving market.

Norwich Castle, which was to become one of William's
favourite royal palaces, was a grand building. In fact,
architecturally, it was one of the most ambitious buildings yet
seen when work commenced in 1067. Its massive 12th-century
stone keep symbolised the king's power and wealth at a time
when buildings tended to be small and made entirely of wood.

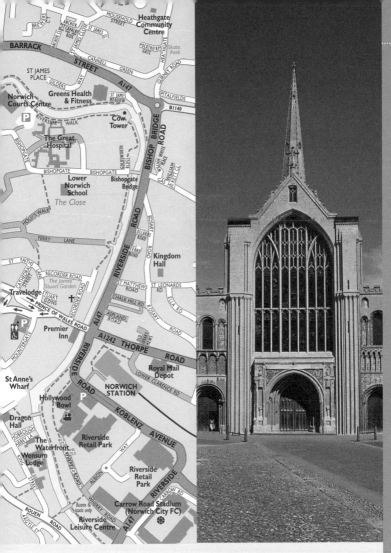

▲ Norwich Cathedral

Today, Norwich Castle is the city's most iconic building and a great museum. Without doubt, it should be the first place on your list to visit while you're in Norwich.

Wealth and the wool trade

Nearly 30 years after work began on the castle, another of Norwich's iconic buildings was conceived. Norwich Cathedral is a magnificent structure which took over 150 years to build. Norwich had become the centre of the Norfolk wool trade and, as such, was supremely wealthy. This is reflected in the grandeur of the cathedral, considered one of the best-preserved, most complete Romanesque buildings in Europe.

▲ Elm Hill, Norwich

Don't miss the opportunity to marvel at the cathedral's wondrous architecture, including its tower, medieval roof boss carvings and the largest monastic cloisters in England. It also has an extraordinary roof and some original wall-paintings. By the 14th century, the main part of the city was enclosed by thick walls, guarded by gates and towers, which meant that access could be restricted – anyone who entered had to pay a toll. By the 15th century, Norwich was the largest walled city in Europe; its 2.5-mile wall enclosed an area greater than that of the City of London. You can still see remains of the city walls dotted around today.

During the Middle Ages, the wealth derived from wool founded no less than 57 churches within the city walls; of these, 31 still remain. This prompted the local saying that Norwich had a church for every week of the year, and a pub for every day.

Norwich's status continued to grow over the next few centuries until, in 1845, the railway brought a direct link with London, bringing with it new opportunities. The city's printing and publishing industry – the *Norwich Post* was the first provincial newspaper published in England in 1701 – flourished, along with its brewing, clothing manufacture and structural engineering industries.

Certainly the overriding impression on visiting Norwich is that of taking a step back in time, in the most agreeable sense. It is a modern city, but the scope for a little self-indulgent time travel is good.

▶ Norwich Castle

museums.norfolk.gov.uk

Castle Meadow, NR1 3JU | 01603 493625 | Open all year Mon–Sat 10–4.30,
Sun 1–4.30, last admission 30 minutes before closing

Norwich Castle was built between 1067 and 1075 as a royal palace
for William the Conqueror, with its magnificent stone keep added
in the 12th century. In the 14th century, the castle was the city gaol,
and remained so for some 500 years. Take a minute to look at the
castle mound; it is the largest in England.

Today the castle houses a fascinating museum with displays
of art, archaeology, natural history, Lowestoft porcelain (see page
189), Norwich silver and a large collection of paintings, with
special emphasis on the Norwich School of painters. A display
of British ceramic teapots is a pleasant diversion.

You can take a guided tour of the dungeons and battlements,
plus there's a programme of exhibitions, children's events, an art
gallery and evening talks throughout the year.

▼ Norwich Castle

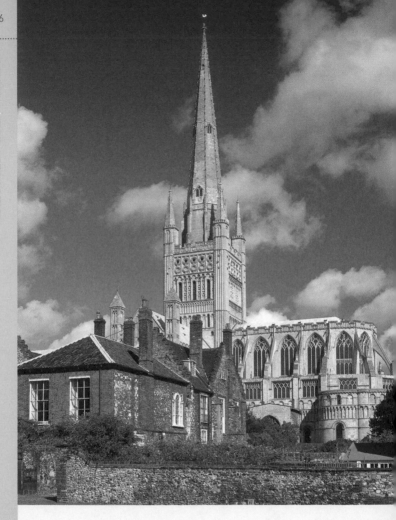

▶ Norwich Cathedral

cathedral.org.uk

12 The Close, NR1 4DH | 01603 218300 | Open daily 7.30–6 (occasionally closed for special services)

The splendid Norman craftsmanship, and the sheer scale and sense of tranquillity of Norwich Cathedral, has attracted visitors and pilgrims here for nearly a millennium. It has the second-highest spire and the largest monastic cloister and Cathedral Close in England. Inside, you'll see the 1,000 or so carved medieval roof bosses and the original wall-paintings in the Jesus Chapel and the presbytery. The soft cream Caen stone building remains a place for quiet reflection as well as for participation in daily services and the rich pageantry of the church's festivals. The website reveals a packed calendar of involving events.

EXPLORE THE CITY

Norwich has so much to offer the visitor, from amazing historic structures to contemporary theatre, fine dining, shopping and leisure activities. Look out for the Great Hospital built in 1249; St Andrew's and Blackfriars' halls dating back to the 14th century and forming the only English friary of that period to survive intact; and the 15th-century Guildhall and Dragon Hall that both host heritage events.

The Georgian Assembly House regularly hosts concerts and exhibitions, while the Forum is pure 21st century and buzzes with activity in its digital galleries and television studios. Regular events take place both in the atrium and outside. Meandering among all these buildings are little lanes and streets lined with designer boutiques and fashionable restaurants.

There are parks, colourful gardens, huge open spaces and riverside walks, while the Norfolk Broads, in the form of the River Wensum on which the city sits, tap a tentative finger at the very gates of Norwich.

TAKE IN SOME HISTORY

Norwich Castle
see highlight panel on page 215

Norwich Cathedral
see highlight panel opposite

▶ Norwich Cathedral cloisters

---

10 country houses

Dragon Hall

writerscentrenorwich.org.uk
King Street, NR1 1QE
01603 877177

This dramatic medieval trading hall was built by a wealthy local merchant, Robert Toppes (1405–67), in 1427, around an earlier brick-and-flint house. He clearly had excellent taste and a seemingless bottomless purse. Here he would have once displayed and stored wool and cloth, probably timber too, and the spices that would have brought him his great wealth. Buyers would come to the hall to trade and this magnificent building was designed to impress them.

On the first floor is an outstanding Great Hall with a crown post roof and superb beams. There's a dragon carved into the wood, which gives the house its name. When Toppes died, the property was sold and partition walls were built inside to divide it into shops and low-cost housing for the poor. The roof was concealed within attic space, and remained hidden for hundreds of years, only to be rediscovered in the 1980s. Today, it is home to the Writers Centre, which offers talks, courses and creative writing workshops.

The Assembly House

assemblyhousenorwich.co.uk
Theatre Street, NR2 1RQ
01603 626402

The Assembly House is an elegant Georgian building designed in 1754 by architect Thomas Ivory and built as a venue for afternoon tea, dancing and assemblies for Norwich's elite. You can see high-ceilinged rooms painted in delicate shades of yellow and cream, still looking as they did in Regency times. Beautiful carvings adorn the ceilings and panelled walls. The gentry would have gathered in the Grand Hall and perhaps moved on to the Noverre Ballroom or the Music Room with its minstrels' gallery. Go for treats in the restaurant or attend one of the many events or concerts.

VISIT THE MUSEUMS AND GALLERIES

Sainsbury Centre for Visual Arts

scva.ac.uk
University of East Anglia, NR4 7TJ
01603 593199 | Open Tue–Fri 10–6,
Sat–Sun 10–5

Housed in a world-class building, designed by Norman Foster, on the edge of the University of East Anglia campus, this is an inspirational public museum exhibiting outstanding art for free. You can see modern and world art in permanent collections, in addition to special exhibitions which change every few months. A library, conservatory display area and gallery cafe can be enjoyed here too. The centre opened in 1978 to house Sir Robert and Lady Sainsbury's collection of art by English artists; this has grown to include works by emerging European artists.

The Forum

theforumnorwich.co.uk
Millennium Plain, NR2 1TF
01603 727950

One of Norwich's most modern-looking buildings, the Forum hosts exhibitions and also has a digital gallery and vast Millennium Library. The complex is home to BBC East, which broadcasts television and radio programmes live, the tourist information office and food outlets.

Museum of Norwich at the Bridewell

museums.norfolk.gov.uk
Bridewell Alley, NR2 1AQ
01603 629127
Open Tue–Sat 10–4.30

Norwich has a long and fascinating history and this museum tells it well. From 1700 when it was England's second city to its rich industrial heritage, trading, shopping, religion and learning, the galleries have engaging displays and audio-visual exhibits. Try out fashionable wigs in the recreated 18th-century coffee house and delve into drawers to discover their secrets. More highlights include the restored Jacquard loom and recreated chemist's shop with its pills and potions. Life in 20th-century Norwich is explored with a host of memorabilia and there's the story of the Bridewell in its days as a gruesome prison. The largest vaulted undercroft in the city lies beneath the museum. It is open for guided tours on the last Saturday of each month.

▼ Museum of Norwich

CATCH A PERFORMANCE

You'll be able to catch a family show, a comedy or pantomime, a musical or operatic performance or some serious drama, even a puppet show, at Norwich's theatres, which include the Norwich Theatre Royal, the Norwich Playhouse and the highly recommended Norwich Puppet Theatre.

Norwich Theatre Royal
theatreroyalnorwich.co.uk
Theatre Street, NR2 1RL
01603 630000

Norwich Playhouse
norwichplayhouse.co.uk
St Georges Street, NR3 1AB
01603 598598

Norwich Puppet Theatre
puppettheatre.co.uk
St James, Whitefriars, NR3 1TN
01603 629921

GO SHOPPING

Head for Norwich Lanes just off Guildhall Hill where you'll find shop after shop of stylish clothes, food and souvenirs. Upmarket goodies can be found in Jarrold department store in Exchange Street, and in the art nouveau 1899 Royal Arcade, off Castle Street. Norwich Market with its 200 or so stalls, opposite City Hall, is the place for bargains. Other shopping streets to make for include quaint Timber Hill, cobbled Elm Hill and the pedestrianised Gentleman's Walk, all in the city centre. Other shopping options include Magdalen Street with its quirky independent shops, the modern Riverside Retail Park and the contemporary Chapelfield Shopping Centre.

PLAY A ROUND

Norwich has a number of excellent golf courses. There's the challenging parkland course with water features at many of the holes at the Dunston Hall club, and the Costessey Park Golf Course where the course lies in the Tud Valley, providing players with a number of holes that bring the river and artificial lakes into play. At Sprowston Manor, the course is set in 100 acres of parkland with an impressive collection of oak trees. The two courses at the Wensum Valley Hotel are set in 350 acres and designed to complement the natural landscape. Eaton Golf Club offers an undulating, tree-lined parkland course. At the Royal Norwich Golf Club, the challenging parkland course has remained largely unchanged since 1924.

Costessey Park Golf Course
costesseypark.com
Old Costessey, NR8 5AL
01603 746333

Dunston Hall
qhotels.co.uk
Ipswich Rd, NR14 8PQ
01508 470444

▶ The Royal Arcade

Eaton Golf Club
eatongc.co.uk
Newmarket Road, NR4 6SF
01603 451686

Royal Norwich Golf Club
royalnorwichgolf.co.uk
Drayton High Road,
Hellesdon, NR6 5AH
01603 429928

Sprowston Manor
marriottsprowstonmanor.co.uk
Wroxham Road, NR7 8RP
01603 410871

**Wensum Valley Hotel,
Golf and Country Club**
wensumvalleyhotel.co.uk
Beech Avenue, Taverham, NR8 6HP
01603 261012

EAT AND DRINK
Adam and Eve
17 Bishopsgate, NR3 1RZ
01603 667423
This enchanting, brick-and-flint inn sits beneath trees at the fringe of the grounds of the cathedral, the builders of which lodged at the pub, and has been licensed since 1249. It's a refreshing step back in time, free of electronic diversions while rich with local beers from Woodforde's and Wolf breweries; spirits here include the ghosts of lingering, long-gone locals. Who can blame them when the food is as rewarding as the ales; visitors resting on a tour of Norwich's finest can expect no-nonsense quality pub classics like filled large Yorkshire pudding, trawlerman's pie, homemade curry or chilli. The hanging basket displays are stunning.

Benedicts 🏵🏵
restaurantbenedicts.com
9 St Benedicts Street, NR2 4PE
01603 926080
This popular city-centre restaurant has been going strong for more than 20 years. A blond-wood floor, pale wooden tables and chairs and pale blue tongue-and-groove panelling all combine to give it a light, airy feel, a convivial place in which to enjoy some consistently accomplished modern British and French cooking based on fresh indigenous produce.

**Best Western Annesley
House Hotel** 🏵🏵
bw-annesleyhouse.co.uk
6 Newmarket Road, NR2 2LA
01603 624553
Annesley began life as a trio of private houses built on the eve of the Victorian age, conjured into one a century later by an enterprising hotelier. Standing just outside the old city walls, its landscaped gardens add a country-house feel, and an old vine supplies sweet red grapes to garnish the cheese plates. In the bright conservatory dining room, with its uncovered tables and floor, an easy-going version of British modernist cuisine is offered, and scores many convincing hits.

Maids Head Hotel 🏵🏵
maidsheadhotel.co.uk

Tombland, NR3 1LB
01603 209955
The brick-built hotel in the city centre lays claim to being the UK's oldest, having been feeding and watering East Anglian travellers for a sterling 800 years. It stands next to the cathedral for company of due venerability, although the Jacobean bar is a relative stripling in the context. Dining goes on in a glassed-in courtyard with a quarry-tiled floor and simple wooden tables, and the menus keep things fairly simple too, albeit in the modern British idiom.

The Red Lion

redlion-eaton.co.uk
50 Eaton Street, Eaton, NR4 7LD
01603 454787
This heavily beamed 17th-century coaching inn has bags of character, thanks to its Dutch gable ends, panelled walls, suit of armour and inglenook fireplaces. The covered terrace enables customers to enjoy one of the real ales or sample a glass from the wine list outside during the summer months. Everyone will find something that appeals on the extensive menus, which include plenty of fish options. There's a light meals and snack menu too.

The Reindeer Pub & Kitchen

thereindeerpub.co.uk
10 Dereham Road, NR2 4AY
01603 612995
At this gastropub real ales share star billing with the food. The chef is passionate about fresh produce and you can expect to find anything from duck hearts, pickled blueberries, fennel and wild rice to Norfolk pheasant, fig, artichoke and mushroom on the menu. Also available all day is a tapas and bar snack menu including homemade Swannington pork crackling, plates of British cured meats and cheeses, and beer-battered whitebait. Wash it all down with your choice of real ale from breweries such as Dark Star and Elgood's. Look out for the summer beer festival.

Ribs of Beef

ribsofbeef.co.uk
24 Wensum Street, NR3 1HY
01603 619517
Originally an alehouse in the 18th century, between the 1960s and 1980s this building was used variously as an antiques shop, electrical store and fashion boutique before it was relicensed in 1985, and to this day continues to welcome locals and holidaymakers cruising the Broads. The pub is valued for its comfy leather seats, range of cask ales, excellent wines and traditional English food using locally sourced produce. Breakfast is available until midday, while hearty choices like beef and ale stew, chilli and wholetail scampi rub shoulders with sandwiches, burgers and jacket potatoes on the varied main menu. Sit outside on the jetty during the warmer months for fabulous river views.

Roger Hickman's Restaurant ❀❀❀

rogerhickmansrestaurant.com
79 Upper St Giles Street, NR2 1AB
01603 633522

The location down a quiet cul-de-sac in the fashionable St Giles district, not far from the cathedral, serves notice that Roger Hickman's place is conceived as something of a haven from urban bustle, as opposed to a noisy brasserie. It looks like a proper restaurant inside, with plain wooden floors, walls adorned with colourful original artworks, and tables dressed in full-length linens, set with high-calibre appointments and stemware. It's a split-level space naturally disposed into sections, run by professional, clued-up staff, who announce each arriving dish with accurate decorum, and are ready with suggestions should they be required. Hickman's style is clearly modern British, with a range of interesting techniques and some evidence of classical French underpinning, offered in the form of fixed-price menus that rise to a seven-course taster with optional wine matches. Dishes look dazzling, and have the impact on the palate to back up the aesthetic appeal. The blowtorched mackerel is something of a signature starter, with its baby beetroots and horseradish, and fish treatments are impressive throughout.

Shiki Japanese Restaurant

shikirestaurant.co.uk
6 Tombland, NR3 1HE
01603 619262

In an historical corner of the city, the decor in this authentic Japanese restaurant is stylishly contemporary. Open for lunch and dinner, it is applauded for its sushi and bento boxes. In the evenings, the concept of Izakaya comes into play – sharing dishes in which everyone can have a bit of everything, from sushi to yakitori. There's a range of vegetarian dishes. Monday evening is Sushi Night, when 'all you can eat in two hours' ordering time' comes at a good value set price. There are three timed sessions between 6 and 10pm and booking is essential (the maximum number for Sushi Night groups is six). The menu spans nigiri and maki, plus hot dishes such as tempura.

St Giles House Hotel ❀❀

stgileshousehotel.com
41–45 St Giles Street, NR2 1JR
01603 275180

You could punctuate your perusal of Norwich city centre's retail opportunities with a pit stop in St Giles House for coffee, a massage, cocktails or something more gastronomically satisfying in the Bistro. This grand Edwardian pile is worth a gander in its own right – beyond its magnificent pillared facade is a palatial interior of marble floors, oak panelling and elaborate plaster ceilings, all sharpened with a slick contemporary makeover. The Bistro's menu is an appealing repertoire of uncomplicated, up-to-date cooking. Clearly defined flavours leap out from every skilfully rendered dish, be it roast pigeon or apple tarte Tatin with cinnamon ice cream. Smartly turned out in black, the front-of-house team are a polished act who keep everything running smoothly.

▶ **PLACES NEARBY**

Less than a 10-minute drive away in the tiny hamlet of Lenwade you'll find the Dinosaur Adventure Park, while on the outskirts of Norwich, the Whitlingham Country Park is the gateway to the watery Broads. Near Norwich Airport, you'll come across the village of Horsham St Faith. Around the late 1930s, the village was home to RAF Horsham St Faith and is today home to the City of Norwich Aviation Museum. At Frettenham, you'll find the Hillside Animal Sanctuary. Refreshments stops are plentiful in the villages that surround Norwich.

Brasteds ◉◉

brasteds.co.uk
Manor Farm Barns, Fox Road, Framingham Pigot, NR14 7PZ
01508 491112
In the village of Framingham Pigot, four miles from the city centre, Brasteds occupies a converted barn, a charming room of raftered ceiling, oak

floor and brick walls. Chris 'Buzz' Busby is a skilful and confident chef, compiling seasonally-changing menus that are all based on impressive Norfolk produce.

City of Norwich Aviation Museum

cnam.org.uk
Old Norwich Road, NR10 3JF
01603 893080 | Open Apr–Oct Tue–Sat 10–5, Sun 12–5, Nov–Mar Wed, Sat 10–4, Sun 11–3
A massive Avro Vulcan bomber, veteran of the Falklands conflict, dominates the collection of military and civilian aircraft at this museum. There are several displays relating to the aeronautical history of Norfolk, including some on the role played by Norfolk-based RAF and USAAF planes during World War II, and a section dedicated to the operations of RAF Bomber Command's 100 Group. A Nimrod shows the development of electronic warfare into the 21st century.

Dinosaur Adventure Park

dinosauradventure.co.uk
Weston Park, NR9 5JW
01603 876310 | Open daily Jan–Mar, Oct–Dec 9.30–4, Apr–late-Jul and mid-Sep 9.30–5, late-Jul–mid-Sep 9.30–6
A short drive from Norwich, Dinosaur Adventure is a must for families visiting the area. There's plenty to see and do for most ages – help the ranger 'Track: T-Rex' on the Dinosaur Trail and meet many

giants from the past as they loom out of the undergrowth – the brachiosaurus and triceratops models are particularly good. Elsewhere, there's a three-level 'Pterodactyl Treehouse' and an indoor 'Dinomite' play area (including a dedicated under-5s section), as well as an outdoor 'Arachnophobia' adventure playground with several climbing frames and an area for smaller budding palaeontologists. More sedate activities include making friends with modern-day creatures, from iguanas to wallabies, in the secret animal garden, or trying your hand at crazy golf in 'Jurassic Putt'. There are several places to eat and a shop packed full with dino-inspired toys and games.

Hillside Animal Sanctuary
hillside.org.uk
Hill Top Farm, Hall Lane, Frettenham, NR12 7LT
01603 736200 | Open Apr–May, Sep–Oct Sun–Thu 10–5, Jun–Aug Sun–Fri 10–5
You can come and see the heavy horses, ponies and donkeys as well as sheep, pigs, rabbits, ducks, hens, goats and many more rescued animals in their home in the beautiful North Norfolk countryside. The Hillside Animal Sanctuary has its own museum where you can relive the farming days of yesteryear surrounded by an extensive collection of carts, wagons and farm machinery.

The Old Rectory ◉◉
oldrectorynorwich.com
103 Yarmouth Road, Thorpe St Andrew, NR7 0HF
01603 700772
Creepers cover the large Georgian house, giving the impression the garden is attempting to reclaim the land – but the red-brick former rectory is here to stay, built to last back in the day and thriving in the 21st century as a country hotel. The dining room has a traditional finish, a room of generous proportions and period details, and is the setting for candlelit dinners (afternoon tea is also available). The daily-changing menu has a good showing of regional produce and keeps to a sensibly manageable choice of three dishes per course.

Park Farm Hotel ◉
parkfarm-hotel.co.uk
Hethersett, NR9 3DL
01603 810264
The family-run hotel has been modified over the past half-century from a rather grand Georgian farmhouse into a modern spa hotel, still surrounded by 200 acres of open countryside not far from Norwich. The restaurant, looking over the gardens, is an open-plan-style room with ceiling spotlights, tall-backed padded chairs at clothed tables and potted plants dotted about. The kitchen has a comprehensive outlook, preparing high-quality ingredients in unfussy style.

Stower Grange ◉

stowergrange.co.uk
40 School Road, Drayton,
NR8 6EF | 01603 860210

The ivy-covered country house in its own wooded grounds a few miles out of Norwich is a charming family-run hotel. Friendly upbeat staff exude a mood of great warmth, and the traditional decorative styling of the place feels fully in keeping. Gathered drapes frame the garden view in the comfortably furnished dining room, where contemporary cooking based on quality ingredients aims to satisfy rather than startle.

Thailand Restaurant ◉

thailandnorwich.co.uk
9 Ring Road, Thorpe St Andrew,
NR7 0XJ | 01603 700444

Plants and colourful hanging baskets add some dash to the exterior of this well-established restaurant. Inside, the decor is as busy on the eye as the bamboo-framed seats are as busy with customers: drapes over the windows, statues in niches, friezes on the ceiling beams and lots of greenery. What marks out the cooking is the sourcing of authentic ingredients, the accurate use of spice and seasoning and spot-on timing to replicate the flavours of Thailand's cuisine in the suburbs of Norwich.

Whitlingham Country Park

Trowse, NR14 8TR
01603 756094

The gateway to the Norfolk

---

10 non-fiction reads

▶ *George Crabbe: Selected Poems*, Penguin Classics

▶ *John Constable: Oil Sketches from the Victoria and Albert Museum* by Mark Evans, Victoria and Albert Museum

▶ *Constable* by Jonathan Clarkson, Phaidon Press

▶ *Henry Blogg of Cromer – The Greatest of the Lifeboatmen* by Cyril Jolly, Poppyland Publishing

▶ *The Anglo-Saxons* by James Campbell, Penguin Books

▶ *Lords and Communities in Early Medieval East Anglia* by Andrew Wareham, Boydell Press

▶ *Hidden Places of East Anglia* by Barbara Vesey, Travel Publishing

▶ *Military Airfields of Britain: East Anglia, Norfolk and Suffolk* by Ken Delve, The Crowood Press

▶ *East Anglia and its North Sea World in the Middle Ages* by David Bates and Robert Liddiard, Boydell Press

▶ *Suffolk Airfields in the Second World War* by Graham Smith, Countryside Books

---

Broads (see page 203), with a visitor centre and an array of adventurous outdoor activities, including sailing, windsurfing, kayaking, rafting and canoeing. Training is available for novices. Do take a guided trip on the solar boat *Ra*.

▲ Orford Castle

▶ **Orford** MAP REF 291 E4

Orford is one of the oldest settlements on the River Alde and has a beautiful 12th-century castle built by Henry II to prove it. The castle is owned by English Heritage and is splendidly preserved, especially its unusual polygonal three-turreted castle keep which has survived almost intact and which has a spiral staircase inside each of the three immense towers. The details of the castle's construction are extensively recorded in royal documents.

The castle has a maze of passageways and small chambers to explore, with the Upper Hall housing the town's local history museum. As the story goes, the king had the castle built in 1165 as a defence against invaders and to control his East Anglian fishing and shipping interests, which included the then thriving medieval port of Orford. Orford was a prosperous place, due to its fishing and shipbuilding industries but, like so many towns up and down this coastline, its waters silted up. Boats also increased in size and access to the river through the silted creeks and the shifting shingle bar at the tip of the spit, which is today known as Orford Ness, became more difficult. By 1673 the fishing trade was struggling and then went into decline. In 1722, Daniel Defoe (1660–1731), described it as 'once a good town, but now decayed'.

Orford today is full of character and has a real sense of community. You'll feel the welcome the moment you arrive. You can admire its pretty brick-and-timber cottages, visit the many traditional craft workshops, and see the small-scale smokehouses and oyster beds. Look out for Butley Creek. It's signposted, but if you have difficulty locating it any local will tell you where it is. Here, the beds yield oysters so fine they have long been a delicacy on the menus of Suffolk restaurants. There's a smokehouse, here, too, founded by Richard Pinney, of Pinney's of Orford, where fishermen smoke trout and mackerel, kippers, eels and salmon over whole oak logs.

Orford village is now separated from the sea by the 10-mile Orford Ness, Europe's largest vegetated shingle spit, which runs parallel to the shore and gets longer every year. Its salt marshes, shingle ridges and lagoons make it an important location for breeding and passage birds and rare plants. Orford Ness and Havergate Island, an RSPB bird reserve in the River Ore and Suffolk's only island (accessible by pre-booked boat trips only), form the Orfordness–Havergate National Nature Reserve. The area is home to many bird and wildlife species. In spring and summer it shelters breeding avocets and terns, while in autumn and winter large numbers of ducks, wigeon, pintail and teal can be seen. Brown hares are also abundant here and can be viewed at close range; they are at their most active in early spring.

The spit has played a significant part in Orford's history. Its isolation made Orford Ness a perfect place for military testing and it became a secret Ministry of Defence site; over 70 years, major advances were made in the fields of radar, military photography, bombs and atomic weapons. Orford Ness's combination of wilderness and strange, derelict structures is oddly compelling and is what makes the spit such a special place, particularly with the knowledge that it was here in the 1930s, along with Bawdsey Manor near Felixstowe, that

Sir Robert Watson-Watt and a small team of scientists took the first steps in the development of the air-defence system that became known as radar. Without the work carried out at Orford Ness, the outcome of the Battle of Britain and the whole course of World War II might have been very different.

You can cross over to Orford Ness by ferry from Orford Quay, and then orient yourself by the former telephone exchange. Take a look inside the building as there's a display that tells the history of Orford Ness and a large aerial photograph of the shingle spit.

Behind the building is an observation platform with views over the Stony Ditch creek and the strange pagoda-type structures of the Atomic Weapons Research Establishment (AWRE), which operated here at the height of the Cold War. A large grey building to the north, known as Cobra Mist, was a top-secret Anglo-American satellite research base alleged to have been involved in tracking UFOs. It now houses transmitters for the BBC World Service, which also uses the tall radio masts beyond.

The pagodas of Orford Ness, which dominate the skyline along with Orford's castle and its red-and-white lighthouse, are a chilling reminder of war. Their distinctive design was to contain any accidental explosions. Today, this is a quiet place. The buildings remain as permanent reminders of another age, and barn owls nest in the abandoned barracks. The National Trust took it over in 1993.

▼ Orford Ness

TAKE IN SOME HISTORY
Orford Castle

english-heritage.org.uk
IP12 2ND | 01394 450472
Open Mar–Nov daily 10–5,
Nov–Dec Sat–Sun 10–4, Jan–Mar
Sat–Sun 10–4 (opening times
can vary)

Dating from the 12th century, and remarkably well preserved, Orford Castle is a must-see attraction when exploring the Suffolk coast. Its rooms offer a real sense of what day-to-day life must have been like in a castle in medieval England.

Inside, there's a maze of passages that lead to the kitchen, a small chapel and bed chambers built within the turrets. You can explore the lower and upper halls with their displays of medieval seals, coins and regalia, and climb right up to the roof where there are fabulous views seaward to Orford Ness.

In the basement of the castle you can see a well, which would have been a vital source of water for its residents, including Henry II who had the castle built in 1165.

As the story goes, when Henry II came to the throne in 1154 he inherited a troubled kingdom from King Stephen. The barons, keen to accrue personal power, had manipulated tensions between Stephen and his rival for the throne, Matilda (Henry's mother). Hugh Bigod, Earl of Norfolk, was one such baron who had immense influence in East Anglia and owned most of its castles. In order to assert his authority, Henry II took castles belonging to Bigod and built Orford Castle to protect Orford's prosperous harbour.

Orford Castle was completed in two years, and comprised an unusual 21-sided keep surrounded by walls and defensive towers. Today, only the keep survives, but it is one of the most remarkable in England due to its design. It rises to some 90 feet in height and has five storeys. If you stand outside and look up at its mighty creamy-grey walls, you can get a sense of how formidable this castle once was to potential invaders.

GET OUTDOORS
Orford Ness National Nature Reserve

nationaltrust.org.uk/orford-ness
IP12 2NU | 01728 648024
Open Apr–Oct, access by National
Trust ferry (sailings subject to
weather, check website for times)

You can take the National Trust ferry across to visit some of the long-abandoned buildings in the Orford Ness National Nature Reserve and learn more about when this remote area was a secret Ministry of Defence site. A flat wilderness of salt marshes, shingle ridges and quiet creeks, Orford Ness is an important breeding ground for birds and other wildlife species, as well as home to a large number of rare plants. If you are lucky you may catch sight of a brown hare. In spring and summer look out for avocets and terns, and in autumn and winter ducks, wigeon, pintail and teal.

EAT AND DRINK
The Crown and Castle ⊛⊛
crownandcastle.co.uk
IP12 2LJ | 01394 450205
There has been a hostelry on this site for 800 years and the tradition of hospitality is in particular good heart in the 21st century. It's co-owned by Ruth Watson (she's also executive chef) who was TV's *Hotel Inspector* once upon a time, and the combination of stylish bedrooms and an easy-going, rustic-chic restaurant is a winning one. There's genuine character to the spaces within, where beams, unclothed wooden tables and comfortable velvet-cushioned chairs and benches create a relaxed vibe. The place is still an inn popular with the locals up for a pint, but it's also something of a foodie destination. The daily-changing menu has an Italian accent, featuring the fashionable Venetian small plates, *cicchetti*, alongside flavour-driven dishes that showcase the region's excellent ingredients.

▶ **Oxborough** MAP REF 293 D5

A wonderful detour when visiting towns such as Swaffham is Oxburgh Hall, the magnificent ancestral home of local barons the Bedingfelds in the village of Oxborough. As you follow the signs for the hall, look out for the remains of Oxborough's church of St John, famous for housing in its surviving chapel two elaborate terracotta tombs of the Bedingfeld family.

Oxborough is also where a massive Bronze Age ceremonial dagger was unearthed in 1988. It is one of only five such oversized daggers, or dirks, known to exist in Europe, and they are so similar that they could well have been made by the same person. It dates from *c*.1300–1400 BC and is so large (nearly 28 inches long) and heavy that there is doubt it was ever used as a dagger. The Oxborough Dirk is now on display in the British Museum in London.

TAKE IN SOME HISTORY
Oxburgh Hall
nationaltrust.org.uk/oxburgh-hall
Oxborough, Swaffham, PE33 9PS
01366 328258 | House open
mid-Feb–Oct daily, Nov–early Feb
Sat–Sun; times vary
Oxburgh Hall is a glorious place to visit. It's a remarkably handsome house with a high gatehouse and surrounded by a wide moat. The outstanding feature of this 15th-century building is its 80-foot-high Tudor gatehouse, which has remained unaltered throughout the centuries. You can visit grand rooms, including the King's Room where Henry VII is said to have stayed in 1487,

before climbing to the top for panoramic views. You can even crawl inside a genuine 16th-century priests' hole.

On display are many priceless treasures; in particular, rare needlework by Mary, Queen of Scots and Bess of Hardwick. Outside, a parterre garden of French design complements the wide moat. Built by Sir Edmund Bedingfeld, a baron of Norfolk, in 1482 as a family home, Oxburgh Hall is now managed by the National Trust. Members of the family still live here today.

10 top delicacies

- ▶ Adnams ales
- ▶ Brancaster mussels
- ▶ Colman's Mustard
- ▶ Cromer crab
- ▶ Nelson slices
- ▶ Norfolk ginger biscuits
- ▶ Orford oysters
- ▶ Samphire
- ▶ 'Stewkey blue' cockles
- ▶ Suffolk Gold cheese

▶ Potter Heigham   MAP REF 295 E3

Potter Heigham is a village standing in one of the most idyllic areas of Norfolk, the gateway to the Upper Thurne and focal point of the northerly Broads. It takes its name from a pottery that once stood here and the Saxon lord, Heacham, who founded the settlement. Potter Heigham is a popular and busy water resort, with a pretty medieval bridge over the River Thurne that runs through the village. The bridge dates from around 1385 and is regarded by experienced boatmen to be the most difficult to negotiate on the Broads. Its opening is so small that hire boats need a pilot to guide them through it.

If you enjoy walking, the long-distance footpath between Cromer and Great Yarmouth, known as Weavers' Way, passes through the village. Nearby is the beautifully preserved church of St Nicholas. Its round tower dates from the 12th century, while part of its main structure dates from the 1300s.

Hickling Broad, the largest and wildest of the Norfolk Broads – used as a seaplane base during World War I – can be found at Potter Heigham. There's an abundance of nature trails and boardwalks around here, plus lots of sailing opportunities.

Birders will find equal pleasure in nearby Horsey Mere, a large triangular-shaped broad, with a nature reserve on the northern bank. The Ludham and Potter Heigham Marshes and the Heigham Holmes nature reserves are here too, though access is limited. You should be able to catch sight of marshland birds such as oystercatchers and snipe, and perhaps even the rare Norfolk hawker dragonfly.

▶ Ranworth MAP REF 295 D4

Ranworth is one of the most picturesque villages in the Broads.
A delightful place, it is located on Malthouse Broad – so called
because of the old malt houses nearby – and divided from the
neighbouring Ranworth Broad nature reserve by a thick bank.
The village itself is dominated by the 14th-century church,
St Helen's, known as the 'Cathedral of the Broads' owing to its
grandeur and height. The view from the tower repays the long
climb up and is one of the finest in the area, extending over the
gardens of the village to the two Broads, towards the dark-
green wet woodlands of Ranworth Marshes, and the silvery,
winding course of the Bure. The church itself – thatched until a
fire in 1963 – contains one of the finest and best-preserved
painted rood screens in the country and an illuminated
songbook, both dating from the 15th century.

With ghostly monks and sightings of the devil carrying
the spirit of a local military man on horseback, Ranworth
lays claim to being the most haunted village on the Broads.
Look out for a cloaked figure
accompanied by a small
dog rowing a boat across
Ranworth Broad in the early
morning – it's said to be the
ghost of a friendly monk.

Another, more traitorous
monk is said to haunt St
Benet's Abbey, a short way
across the marshes and the
River Bure. Following the
Norman Conquest, the monk
betrayed his brethren to the
soldiers of William the
Conqueror in return for being
made abbot. True to their
word, the Normans appointed
him abbot for life – then
promptly nailed him to the
abbey doors and skinned him
alive. The Normans had no
love for traitors, even Saxon
ones. Today, the abbey is
in ruins, but it remains
a distinctive sight, with a
windmill built into the walls of
the gatehouse. See also the
Norfolk Broads, page 205.

GET OUTDOORS
Broads Wildlife Centre
norfolkwildlifetrust.org.uk
Ranworth Broad, NR13 6HY
01603 270479 | Open Apr–Sep daily
10–5, Oct Sat–Sun, half term 10–5
From Ranworth, the Broadlands
Wildlife Centre can be reached
along a nature trail through
woods and marshes. The centre
is housed in an attractive
building with a Norfolk
reed-thatched roof and floats
on pontoons on the edge of
Ranworth Broad, giving superb
views of the boat-free water.
The upper gallery is a good
place from which to observe
the amazing diversity of wildlife
on the Broads.

▶ PLACES NEARBY
Visit the pretty villages of
Hoveton (see page 160) and
Wroxham (see page 284), both
a short drive away.

▶ Reedham
see **Lowestoft**, page 193

▼ Ranworth Broad

▶ Sandringham MAP REF 293 D3

Sandringham is the Norfolk country retreat of Queen Elizabeth II, and stands in glorious countryside between King's Lynn and Hunstanton. The house was built in 1870 for the Prince and Princess of Wales, who later became King Edward VII and Queen Alexandra, and stands in formal grounds full to bursting with shrubs and trees. Edward's son, King George V, wrote that it was the place he loved best in the world. Along with the house and gardens, you can visit the museum, a visitor centre and the parish church attended by the Royal family when they're in Norfolk.

▼ Sandringham House

TAKE IN SOME HISTORY
Sandringham House
sandringhamestate.co.uk
PE35 6EN | 01485 545408
Open Apr to mid-Oct daily 11–4.30

The sumptuous neo-Jacobean house has been handed down through four generations of British monarchy and is now a favourite country retreat for the Queen and her family. The main ground-floor rooms used by the royal family when in residence are open for the public to view. You can see the elaborate decor as it looked in Edwardian times, and personal items collected by members of the family over many decades.

VISIT THE MUSEUM
Sandringham House Museum
Open Apr to mid-Oct daily 11–5

Sandringham's museum is housed in the former coach houses and stables block, and contains fascinating displays of royal memorabilia. A highlight, especially for motor enthusiasts, has to be the royal collection that includes the first car ever owned by a member of the monarchy, a 1900 Daimler Phaeton. There's a mighty fire engine too, a Merryweather from 1939, which was used by the estate's own fire brigade. Elsewhere, there are displays of personal items, such as gifts given to the Queen on state visits abroad, the clock used to time royal racing pigeons and Arts and Crafts tiles and plaques once used in the estate's dairy.

GO ROUND THE GARDENS
Sandringham House Gardens
Open Apr to mid-Oct daily 10.30–5; guided tours Wed and Sat 11 and 2

Sixty acres of glorious grounds surround the house and offer beauty and colour throughout the seasons. In Edwardian times the gardens were laid out in a formal manner as was fashionable then; in more recent times this layout has been complemented with areas of lawns bordered by magnificent trees. In addition to the gardens, a further 600-acre country park surrounds the house. It is dotted with cottages and contains the visitor centre from where you can arrange a tractor tour of the park. There's information, too, on nature trails that criss-cross the park, a sculpture trail and a scenic drive. If shrubs and flowers are your passion, you'll love the plant centre.

SEE A LOCAL CHURCH
Church of St Mary Magdalene
Open Apr–Sep Mon–Sat 11–5, Sun 1–5, Oct Mon–Sat 11–4, Sun 1–4 (open only for services in winter)

St Mary Magdalene is the parish church of Sandringham village attended by the royal family. In its present form, the beautiful carrstone church dates back to the 1500s. You can see the silver altar, silver pulpit and 17th-century Spanish processional cross presented to Queen Alexandra, a ninth-century Greek font and priceless, vivid stained glass windows.

▶ Saxmundham MAP REF 291 E3

Saxmundham conjures up images of pretty Suffolk pink-and-pale-yellow-washed timber-framed cottages lining a bustling market place. In reality, Sax, as it's affectionately known by locals, is exactly that, albeit now surrounded by Victorian and more modern development.

This historic market town was mentioned in the Domesday Book of 1086, and achieved its market charter somewhere around 1272. It was once an important communications link between London and Great Yarmouth, and developed with the coming of the railways in the 19th century. Better communications brought industry and the need for housing. Saxmundham grew at a fast pace in Victorian times. Rows of small cottages and grand 19th-century statements of wealth were built, and can still be seen today.

Not far from Saxmundham, which is at the centre of the unspoiled Suffolk Heritage Coast, is Minsmere, one of the RSPB's most famous nature reserves. Here, you can see thousands of varieties of migrant and wading birds through the course of a year. It has been a reserve for over 50 years and pioneered the use of observation hides.

GET OUTDOORS
RSPB Nature Reserve Minsmere
rspb.org.uk
IP17 3BY | 01728 648281
Open daily dawn–dusk, visitor centre Feb–Oct 9–5, Nov–Jan 9–4
Set on the beautiful Suffolk coast between Southwold and Aldeburgh, the Minsmere reserve offers an enjoyable day out for all. Nature trails take you through a variety of habitats to the excellent hides. Spring is a time for birdsong, including nightingales and booming bitterns. In summer, you can watch breeding avocets and marsh harriers. Autumn is excellent for migrants, and in winter hundreds of wildfowl visit the reserve. Look out for otters and red deer. The visitor centre has a well-stocked shop and licensed tea room, and you can find out more about the reserve. There is a programme of events throughout the year, including several for children and families. Self-guided activity booklets help families make the most of their visit.

EAT AND DRINK
Sibton White Horse Inn ⑥
sibtonwhitehorseinn.co.uk
Halesworth Road, Sibton, IP17 2JJ
01728 660337
In the heart of the Suffolk countryside, but just a couple of miles or so from Saxmundham, this rustic 16th-century inn retains much of its Tudor charm and incorporates stone floors, exposed brickwork and ships' timbers. A genuine free house, the bar with its raised gallery is

the place to enjoy pints of Green Jack Trawlerboys or Woodforde's Once Bittern. There is a choice of dining areas, while the secluded courtyard has a Mediterranean feel when the sun comes out. The owners grow many of their own vegetables behind the pub. At lunch, you can order from the set menu or from the selection of light bites. The à la carte, available at both lunch and dinner, offers old favourites like smoked mackerel pâté and 28-day-hung sirloin steak.

▶ Saxtead Green
see **Framlingham**, page 136

▶ Saxthorpe
see **Holt**, page 156

▶ Sheringham   MAP REF 294 C1

Sheringham is perched on the 'top' of Norfolk, right on the coast, and has the look of a much-loved seaside resort. The Victorian houses, mostly made of flint, lining the esplanade, the manicured gardens and the beach – complemented by the cries of seagulls as the small fleet of fishing boats unload their catch on the quayside – provide a classic scene.

Like many coastal towns in Norfolk, Sheringham grew wealthy because of fish. In its heyday, the town was a bustling place with several hundred boats providing southern England with crabs and lobsters. A good railway link to London meant the seafood could be easily transported to market. There are fewer fishing boats nowadays, but its seafood is still sought after and is a highlight on many a Norfolk restaurant's menu.

Sheringham has all the amenities – including a theatre – that you would expect of a town with a modern community, its numbers bolstered by the visitors who flock here in summer. There's a super museum dedicated to the sea, steam trains on the Poppy Line and, in Upper Sheringham, the National Trust's Sheringham Park. Look out for nearby All Saints' Church. It has many fittings from the 15th century, including a well-preserved rood screen and bench ends, with quirky carvings including a baby in a shroud, a monkey and a mermaid.

Book lovers can delight in the presence of Peters Bookshop, located on St Peters Road (just round the corner from Sheringham Station). This antiquarian and secondhand wonderland is one of the best bookshops in East Anglia and it's very unlikely that you'll come away without a purchase.

VISIT THE MUSEUM
The Mo
sheringhammuseum.co.uk
Lifeboat Plain, NR26 8BG
01263 824482 | Open Mar–May, Oct
Tue–Sat 10–4.30, Jun–Sep and
school holidays daily 10–4.30
The Mo, Sheringham Museum,
has a collection of lifeboats,
fishing boats and seafaring
memorabilia displayed in
the Boat Hall in the ground
floor galleries. Peek into a
fisherman's cottage and learn
of the crafts and traditions of
fisherfolk. Diverse displays
upstairs include the colourful
shops of Shannock Street. A
viewing tower provides fabulous
views over the sea and town.

GO ROUND THE GARDENS
Sheringham Park
nationaltrust.org.uk/sheringham
Wood Farm, Upper Sheringham,
NR26 8TL | 01263 820550
Open dawn–dusk, visitor centre
and cafe open Jan to mid-Mar,
Nov–Dec Sat 9.30–4, Sun 11–4,
mid-Mar to Sep daily 10–5, Sep–Oct
Thu–Mon 10–5
Sheringham Park is best known
for its outstanding displays of
rhododendrons and azaleas
from mid-May to June. There
are more than 80 species of
them. The park is one of the
finest examples of landscape
design in the country and
surrounds Sheringham Hall,
which is privately owned and
occupied. Look out for the
gazebo and viewing towers in
the gardens, from which you
can get stunning views of the
Norfolk coast.

TAKE A TRAIN RIDE
North Norfolk Railway
(The Poppy Line)
nnrailway.co.uk
Sheringham Station, NR26 8RA
01263 820800 | Open Apr–Oct daily,
Feb–Mar, Nov weekends, plus Santa
Specials in Dec
North Norfolk Railway is a
full-sized heritage steam
railway network running
between Sheringham and Holt,
with an intermediate station at
Weybourne. The route,
affectionately known as The
Poppy Line, runs for over
5 miles along the coast, and
up through the heathland.
En route are three genuine
Victorian stations. Sheringham
station features the Railway
Shop and children's activity
coach. At Holt Station, the
William Marriott Railway
Museum (open Mar to Oct) is
housed in a replica goods shed
and tells the story of the
Midland and Great Northern
Joint Railway from its birth.

GO TO THE THEATRE
Sheringham Little Theatre
sheringhamlittletheatre.com
Station Road, NR26 8RE
01263 822347
The Sheringham Little Theatre
has a programme of drama,
film, music and comedies
throughout the year, including
its summer repertory season
(one of the last surviving
examples in the country) and
Christmas panto. The work of
local artists is a feature in the
foyer and the theatre runs
regular stage skills courses.

PLAY A ROUND
Sheringham Golf Club
sheringhamgolfclub.co.uk
Weybourne Road, NR26 8HG
01263 823488 | Open daily all year
The course is laid out along a gorse-clad clifftop from where the sea is visible on every hole. The par 4 holes are superb, with a fine view along the cliffs from the fifth tee.

EAT AND DRINK
Dales Country House Hotel ◉◉
mackenziehotels.com
Lodge Hill, NR26 8TJ
01263 824555
Handy for a stopover if you've been ogling the spectacular rhododendrons and azaleas in Sheringham Park gardens, you'll find that these grounds are no slouch either. Just a mile or so inland from Sheringham and the coast, the stepped-gabled Victorian house has heaps of period charm, although the cooking in Upchers restaurant takes a rather more contemporary European view of things. With the briny so near, fish and seafood are always going to be a good idea.

▶ **PLACES NEARBY**
Barely a 10-minute drive away in Weybourne is the fabulous Muckleburgh Military Collection centre, where you can see working tanks and all manner of military vehicles.

The Muckleburgh Military Collection
muckleburgh.co.uk
Weybourne, NR25 7EH
01263 588210 | Open Apr–Oct daily 10–5
The Muckleburgh Military Collection is the largest privately owned military centre of its kind in Norfolk. Exhibits include restored and working tanks, armoured cars, trucks and artillery of World War II, and equipment and weapons from the Falklands and the Gulf War. There are live tank demonstrations most days during the school holidays, and even the chance to hop aboard for a ride in military vehicles and visit the restored shore defence gun pits. The centre incorporates the Museum of the Suffolk and Norfolk Yeomanry. A cafe, children's play area and picnic area are further attractions.

▶ **Somerleyton** MAP REF 295 E5
The village of Somerleyton is famous for being the home of English engineer Christopher Cockerell (1910–99) when he invented the hovercraft – a commemorative column stands in the village centre – and for supplying bricks from its small brickworks for the construction of Liverpool Street Station in London. But today it may be even more famous for the lavish pile that is Somerleyton Hall. The village was once part of the Somerleyton Hall estate and there are gorgeous red-brick,

thatched cottages all grouped together around the green. The scene is pure chocolate-box pretty, which, indeed, was the original idea: the cottages and their layout were designed to resemble a traditional idyllic village street scene, but in reality they were the homes of people who worked at the hall.

The village is named after a Viking, Sumarlithi, a non-aggressive invader who arrived in the 10th century and found the Norfolk countryside much to his liking. There's a real sense of calm and tranquillity in the village, which lies close to the River Waveney, a few miles northwest of Lowestoft in Suffolk.

TAKE IN SOME HISTORY
Somerleyton Hall
somerleyton.co.uk
NR32 5QQ | 0871 222 4244
Open mid-Apr–Sep Tue–Thu, Sun 10–5 (Wed gardens only). Hall tours (45 minutes) 11.30–3

Somerleyton Hall is one of the most lavish country houses in East Anglia, indeed in England. Beautiful architecture and antique furniture, trademark Crossley carpets, a distinct and pleasing 'lived-in' feel, and a yew maze of mind-boggling ingenuity provides huge appeal.

You can enjoy 12 acres of gardens and parkland, which feature a walled garden full of ornate greenhouses, old species of flowers and trees and a small museum of gardening memorabilia. For the youngsters there's an adventure playground, a mini-farmyard and a Viking fort, as well as pony treks. Within the grounds Fritton Lake offers boat trips and fishing.

Highlights of the hall include the lavishly wood-panelled entrance hall, a beautiful ballroom with sculpted marble features, a dining room and the library.

The hall dates back to 1240 when nobleman Peter Fitzosbert had a manor house built on the site, and over the course of the next few centuries it grew in size. In 1604, the house was bought by entrepreneur John Wentworth who turned it into a beautiful Tudor-Jacobean mansion.

Over the years it has had many owners, including Sir Thomas Allin (1612–85), an admiral who fought in the English Civil War, and Sir Samuel Morton Peto, an MP and wealthy businessman. Peto adored Italian architecture and gardens, and over the course of the next few years had extensive work done at Somerleyton Hall to transform it into the Anglo-Italian masterpiece standing in immaculately sculpted gardens you can see today.

The estate was later owned by Sir Francis Crossley (1817–72), an MP and famous carpet manufacturer, who was created a baronet for services to industry. Today, the estate is owned and lived in by the fourth Baron Somerleyton, Hugh Crossley.

EAT AND DRINK
The Duke's Head
dukesheadsomerleyton.co.uk
Slug's Lane, NR32 5QR
01502 730281

Owned by and overlooking the Somerleyton Estate, this spruced-up red-brick pub stands tucked away down Slug's Lane on the edge of the village. Renowned locally for its imaginative seasonal menus, which champion game and meats reared on the estate farms, it thrives as a gastro-pub and the rambling and very relaxed bar and dining areas fill early with diners in the know. Savour the views over a pint of Woodforde's Wherry in the lovely garden in summer.

Four miles away in the village of Fritton, the Fritton Arms is also part of the Somerleyton Estate. Like the Duke's Head, the atmosphere is relaxed, a number of Suffolk ales are on tap and the food is excellent.

10 top rainy day attractions

▶ **Anglesey Abbey**, Lode, page 99

▶ **The Caister Castle Car Collection**, Caister, page 84

▶ **The Forum**, Norwich, page 219

▶ **Houghton Hall**, Houghton, page 182

▶ **Hunstanton Sea Life Sanctuary**, Hunstanton, page 162

▶ **The Muckleburgh Military Collection**, Weybourne, page 241

▶ **North Norfolk Railway (The Poppy Line)**, Sheringham Station, page 240

▶ **Norwich Castle**, Norwich, page 215

▶ **Oliver Cromwell's House**, Ely, page 127

▶ **The Thursford Collection**, Thursford, page 131

▶ South Walsham
see **Wroxham**, page 284

▶ Southwold MAP REF 291 F2

One of the most picturesque towns on the Suffolk coast, Southwold has an ancient pedigree dating to before the Domesday Book of 1086. Packed with interest for both historians and visitors, it is a genteel sort of place, not unlike a typical seaside resort of the 1920s and 1930s, and a great place to stay when exploring the Suffolk coastline.

There's none of the boisterousness of Suffolk's Felixstowe (see page 131) or neighbouring Norfolk's Great Yarmouth (see page 139). If you visualise rows of brightly coloured beach huts sitting in line next to the sandy beach, a pier devoid of gambling machines that for decades received paddle steamers, and beer from the Adnams brewery, the town's largest employer, delivered to pubs on horse-drawn drays, then you have the character of Southwold.

Southwold, which was granted a market charter in 1489, sits on a virtual island surrounded by marshes, creeks and reedbeds between the River Blyth and the sea. Today, it's a seaside resort with centuries-old cottages, elegant Georgian houses, small quiet streets and peaceful greenswards, but this hasn't always been the case. In Saxon times it was one of East Anglia's busiest ports, later becoming an important medieval fishing harbour and in Victorian times it was a popular, if understated, place for weekend excursions.

Like so many towns on the east coast, Southwold faced the problem of silting, which brought about a decline in the importance of the harbour and the town's prosperity. And like Great Yarmouth, Southwold had to reinvent itself. Its revival took the form of a flourishing yet refined resort when, in Victorian times, it became fashionable to enjoy the seaside.

Today, the pier dominates Southwold's seafront. It was originally built between 1899 and 1900 and, at over an eighth of a mile long, could easily accommodate the sea-going paddle steamers that plied along the coast in late Victorian times. The lovely old restored 1947 paddle steamer *Waverley* was a welcome visitor to Southwold in more recent times. The town itself is dominated by a 100-foot-tall lighthouse that was built in 1890 and electrified in 1938. Also worth a visit is the small but impressive museum, and the 500-year-old Grade I listed church of St Edmund, King and Martyr, one of four churches in the town. Elsewhere, pink-and blue-washed cottages and Georgian town houses, including Buckenham House, one of East Anglia's finest modern art galleries, sit around greens that have been left undeveloped to serve as firebreaks – a disastrous fire in 1659 destroyed much of the town.

VISIT THE MUSEUMS AND GALLERIES
Southwold Museum
southwoldmuseum.org
9–11 Victoria Street, IP18 6HZ
07708 781317 | Open Easter–Oct
daily 2–4
You'll love this superb little museum housed in a Dutch-style cottage complete with beams and nooks. It tells the story of Southwold's maritime past, its archaeology, geology and natural history. Old paintings and photographs, models and wildlife exhibits, sit very comfortably with 21st-century interactive displays.

▶ Southwold beach

▶ Southwold Pier

southwoldpier.co.uk

North Parade, IP18 6BN | 01502 722105 | Open May–Sep daily from 9, Sep–May from 10 (closing times vary)

This historic pier has a small pavilion which houses a quirky collection of modern penny arcade-style machines by English inventor and cartoonist Tim Hunkin. Known as the Under the Pier Show, it will make you roar with laughter. Don't miss the Water Clock Tower and the Quantum Tunnelling Telescope. The tower's message is about water recycling and the telescope about what could occur in the North Sea – both are hilarious fun.

The pier has a small interactive family amusement arcade too, which the pier owners are proud to say has no gambling machines, along with a handful of shops selling upmarket souvenirs and organic produce. The Seaweed and Salt has a great collection of textiles and ceramics, prints, jewellery and fashion accessories, while the Treasure Chest has beautifully made gifts, quality toys and eye-catching trinkets. From magnets to mugs and postcards to puzzles, there are all sorts of mementoes to be found here. All ages love the sweets and locally made ice cream at the Treat Parlour. The pier has three eateries. The Beach Cafe serves the freshest fish and chips and is famed throughout East Anglia; the Clockhouse offers light meals; and the à la carte Boardwalk Restaurant (booking recommended) has a menu that offers a fusion of tastes accompanied by great sea views.

Buckenham House

buckenhamgalleries.co.uk
81 High Street, IP18 6DS
01502 725418 | Open Mon,
Thu–Sat 10–5

Buckenham House is one of the most elegant Georgian houses in Southwold – and you'll find it's one of its most intriguing. Externally it looks every inch a Georgian town house, but step inside and you'll see it's pure 16th century. It was built by a wealthy Tudor merchant. Today, it houses the Buckenham Galleries, one of the finest contemporary art galleries in the region with an eclectic mix of paintings, ceramics, glass work, jewellery, wood-turning, furniture and sculptures. Its permanent exhibition features the work of artists engaged by the gallery, with the emphasis on displaying different styles and mediums. You'll be sure to find something that catches your eye. It also hosts further exhibitions by invited artists throughout the year. The gallery occupies the ground and first floor, and the cellar has been transformed into a cosy coffee house serving cream cakes.

ENTERTAIN THE FAMILY
Southwold Pier
see highlight panel opposite

SEE A LOCAL CHURCH
St Edmund, King and Martyr Church
Bartholomew Green,
IP18 6JA | 01502 725424

Cathedral-like St Edmund's, which dates from the 15th century, is one of Suffolk's finest Perpendicular churches. It is one of a chain of such churches that once stretched the entire length of Suffolk's coastline from Southwold to Felixstowe when the county was one of the richest in England.

Made of flint that gives it a subtle grey hue and standing in richly-planted gardens, St Edmund's would have been at the heart of medieval village life. Markets and village fairs would have taken place on the green next to the church, and festivals held inside under its high vaulted ceiling. Indeed, festivals are still held here. The church's 100-foot-high tower can be seen for miles.

When you approach the church, take a minute to study its exterior walls. It has superb examples of flushwork (flat planes of flint and ashlar), which are particularly fine at the west end of the tower. Here, panels of flint framed in stone rise above the window to a Latin inscription that translates as 'St Edmund Pray for Us'. Above that is chequerwork panelling of flint and stone. The two-storey south porch is just as good, with 'M' for St Mary picked out on the lower panels. Above the door, framed by two windows, is a modern statue of St Edmund, shown bound in the ropes that tied him to a tree when he was killed by Danish archers. St Edmund died in November 869 at the hands of Danish invaders set on conquering swathes of East

Anglian soil. The interior of the church is packed with interest. Some of its artefacts date back to the 15th century. The medieval rood screen, separating the nave and aisles from the chancel and chapels, is magnificent. It retains its original colour – a riot of reds and yellows – with paintings depicting the 12 apostles.

The painted and gilded pulpit and font cover are successful 20th-century restorations and re-creations of medieval decorative woodwork. The font itself is original, but has clearly seen better times. It is said that during Henry VIII's reign when he was breaking away from the Catholic Church the font was attacked by his followers, and still bears axe marks.

Near the tower, there's a figure dressed in armour with a sword in one hand and an axe in the other. Next to him is a bell. He is affectionately known as Southwold Jack. The figure is incredibly rare and is believed to date from when the church was built. He has worn well. Today, as in medieval times, he is made to raise his axe, which rings the bell to tell the congregation the service is about to start.

TAKE TO THE WATER
Coastal Voyager
coastalvoyager.co.uk
Stage S35, Blackshore, 8 Southwold Harbour, IP18 6TA | 07887 525 082
Open daily 8–4 (times vary)
If you fancy taking to the water around Southwold, then head for the harbour and the *Coastal Voyager*. A rigid inflatable boat with a deep V hull, *Coastal Voyager* can accommodate 12 in wraparound-style seats. Its 'Sea Blast' trip is not for the faint-hearted, though. The journey is high speed and fast; you should expect to get splashed. It follows a course around Sole Bay. For a calmer trip, you can try the *Coastal Voyager*'s 'River Blyth' cruise, which follows a steady course along the river and heads past Walberswick to Blythburgh. It lasts three hours, including a pub lunch stop. If you are lucky, you may catch sight of seals that can often be seen playing in these quiet river creeks.

VISIT A LANDMARK
Southwold Lighthouse
trinityhouse.co.uk
Stradbrook Road, IP18 6LQ
01255 245000 | Visitor Centre open Apr–Oct; days and times vary
Unusually for a lighthouse, this one stands in the middle of town, a Grade II listed, 100-foot-tall white tower soaring above the red-brick row houses at its feet. Giving one flash every 10 seconds, it provides a coastal waymark for passing shipping and guides vessels into Southwold harbour. Construction began in 1887 and the lighthouse came into operation in 1890, replacing three local lighthouses under threat from coastal erosion at nearby Orford Ness. It was electrified and automated in 1938, converted to battery

▲ Adnams sign on brewery, Southwold

operation in 2001, and its range increased from 17 to 24 nautical miles in 2012. You can visit and take a guided tour of this Southwold landmark in summer months – the lantern is reached via two winding staircases and 113 steps.

WATCH A FILM
Electric Picture Palace
exploresouthwold.co.uk
Blackmill Road, IP18 6AQ
07815 769565 | Box office open
Tue 10.30–12; tours some Sats at 12;
film times vary
See a film or take a tour of this super 68-seat cinema that has been designed to resemble an early 1900s picture house. The Electric Picture Palace was opened in 2002 by the actor Michael Palin. New and old classic films are shown in seasons – spring through to winter. If you are in Southwold for only a short time, you can take out a membership for just one season. Take a minute to look at the decor, the beautiful organ in front of the screen and the seating in the stalls and circle; all are designed to be authentic to the period.

EAT AND DRINK
The Crown Hotel
adnams.co.uk
90 High Street, IP18 6DP
01502 722275
Right in the centre of town, this Adnams' brewery-managed pub, restaurant and wine bar within a hotel has something for everyone. It's informal and lively throughout, whether you're in the pub-brasserie or the restaurant with its scrubbed pine tables. The Adnams wine list is as good as you'd expect,

with a great selection by the glass. The young and enthusiastic kitchen team turn out some appealing modern, rustic British dishes, with plenty of Mediterranean sunshine along the way, and good quality ingredients at the heart of everything.

Sutherland House ®®

sutherlandhouse.co.uk
56 High Street, IP18 6DN
01502 724544

The original parts of the building date from the 15th century, with the Georgians and Victorians chipping in along the way, to create a period house of genuine charm. There are wooden beams from ships that fought in the battle of

▼ Southwold lighthouse

Sole Bay (and that was in 1672!) and ornate ceilings, coving and real fireplaces throughout. The fixtures and fittings cut a more contemporary dash, giving a decidedly chic finish. Likewise, the cooking impresses with its modern ambitions, passion for seafood, and loyalty to local ingredients (fruit and veg come from their own allotment, and there's a local flavour all round).

Swan Hotel

adnams.co.uk
High Street, Market Place,
IP18 6EG | 01502 722186

The Adnams empire has things pretty tied up in Southwold, where it is the seaside town's brewer, main publican, wine merchant and hotelier. Just in front of the brewery, the Swan – its handsome bay-fronted Victorian facade occupying pole position among the boutiques – is the centre of operations. Inside, its 17th-century origins are revealed: there are wall panels, genuine 18th-century oil paintings and gilt chandeliers, but time has not stood still, so it is all leavened with smart contemporary styling. Afternoon tea in the drawing room is something of a local institution, but try not to spoil your appetite for dinner in the smart dining room. As one would hope from a set-up with its roots deep in the local area, the provenance of the raw materials is emphatically regional, and the cooking is confident, full-flavoured stuff.

▶ **PLACES NEARBY**

Picturesque Aldeburgh, famous as the home of composer Benjamin Britten and for its world-class music festival, lies along the coast (see page 52), while the ancient market town of Saxmundham is a 10-minute drive away (see page 238). You can learn all about Dunwich, the town lost to the sea and take walks on Dunwich Heath (see page 120) or play golf at nearby Halesworth Golf Club. Walberswick is a compact village and harbour lying just across the River Blyth from Southwold. It is a popular lunch spot, with a handful of eateries, including the Anchor and the Bell Inn, and you'll pass the Harbour Inn on the way, sitting on the river. Your children will love the chance to see camels and other pets at the Oasis Camel Park in Linstead, near Halesworth. For refreshment stops, head for the Randolph in Reydon or the Westleton Crown in Westleton.

Halesworth Golf Club

halesworthgolf.co.uk
Bramfield Road, IP19 9XA
01986 875567 | Open daily all year
There is an 18-hole championship course and nine-hole 'play and pay' course here, set in 190 acres of undulating Suffolk countryside and close to the coast. Both courses offer golfers of all levels a challenge, but the shorter Valley course is particularly suitable for the less experienced golfer.

The Anchor

anchoratwalberswick.com
Main Street, Walberswick,
IP18 6UA | 01502 722112
This striking Arts and Crafts pub on the Suffolk coast is more than just a village local. The adjoining wildflower meadow is perfect for a picnic, especially during the mid-August beer festival.

The Bell Inn

bellinnwalberswick.co.uk
Ferry Road, Walberswick,
IP18 6TN | 01502 723109
Six centuries old and going stronger than ever, The Bell stands close to the Southwold ferry, the Suffolk Coastal Path and the marshes. Character is certainly not in short supply, with oak-beamed ceilings, hidden alcoves, worn flagstone floors and open fires. At the back is a family-friendly garden overlooking a creek and the beach; here too is the Barn Cafe, offering everything you need for a picnic.

The Harbour Inn

harbourinnsouthwold.co.uk
Blackshore Quay, IP18 6TA
01502 722381
In contrast to those pubs that don't tolerate wellies indoors, during the winter this one actually recommends them because it stands right by the water, sometimes in it, as the sobering flood-level markers testify. Inside the old fisherman's pub are two snug, photograph-plastered bars, the upper, nautically themed one

with a wood-burner, while in the lower one staff must stoop to serve pints through a hatch.

Oasis Camel Park

oasiscamelpark.co.uk
Orchard Farm, Linstead, IP19 0DT
07836 734748 | Open Apr–Oct daily
10.30–5

Along with the camels, which you can ride, there are donkeys, llamas and deer and small pets such as rabbits and guinea pigs which are cared for at this popular centre. Children can enjoy cuddle sessions with some of the animals, plus there are paddock walks, crazy golf, a mini-maze and a play area.

The Randolph

therandolph.co.uk
41 Wangford Road, Reydon,
IP18 6PZ | 01502 723603

Easily walkable from Southwold, this majestic pub was built in 1899 by the town's well-known Adnams Brewery, whose directors were pally with Lord Randolph Churchill, Sir Winston's father. Showing no real sign today of its late-Victorian origins, the light and airy bar is furnished with contemporary high-backed chairs and comfortable sofas; the well-protected garden is lovely in the sun. The bar and restaurant serve up modern British food with a twist; children can opt to select from their own menu. The pub even owns its own beach hut.

The Westleton Crown ◉◉

westletoncrown.co.uk
The Street, Westleton, IP17 3AD
01728 648777

In a peaceful village close to the RSPB's Minsmere, this traditional coaching inn dates back to the 12th century and provides a comfortable base for exploring Suffolk's glorious Heritage Coast. The pub retains plenty of rustic charm, complemented by all the comforts of contemporary living, including crackling log fires on winter days. Local real ales include Brandon Rusty Bucket and Adnams Southwold Bitter, and there's an extensive menu that includes innovative daily specials and classic dishes with a twist, freshly prepared from the best local produce. Eat in the cosy bar, the elegant dining room, or in the garden room. Sandwiches are made with a choice of The Crown's own breads, and served with sea-salted crisps and a dressed salad. The large terraced gardens are floodlit in the evening.

▶ **Stalham** MAP REF 295 D3

If you want to know more about the history of the Norfolk Broads then Stalham is an ideal place to head for. Situated in the heart of the Broadlands, this lovely market town can trace its history back before the Domesday Book, and still has its original name, derived from 'stal', a pool of water, and 'ham', a settlement or village. Here, the Museum of the Broads tells how people lived and worked in the region, and how weather and fashions have left their legacy.

Evidence suggests that Stalham has been a prosperous place over the centuries. It lies on the old Roman road that connected the main north Norfolk towns and would have been a popular staging post for traders heading to Caister, Great Yarmouth and Lowestoft. Much building has taken place over the years, with the church of St Mary in the 15th century and the Jacobean manor house, Stalham Hall, in the 17th century. Progress was steady rather than rapid, and by the 1880s the town, largely self-sufficient, still had a population of only 852. Its economy was mainly based on agriculture and was a base from which to export grain and livestock by road and river, and eventually by rail. The town is connected to the River Ant by a dyke, with its own staithe, where wherries and other trading vessels could moor while the town grew more prosperous when the railway came to Norfolk.

Today, with its narrow high street, Stalham remains a gentle and agreeable place with an air of times gone by. It is home to one of the principal holiday boat hirers in Norfolk, and is perfectly placed for exploring the Broads, especially Hickling and Barton Broads (see page 203). Look out for Sutton Mill, near Stalham. It is the tallest surviving tower mill in the country with nine floors and a fascinating collection of old farm machinery and tools. It was in operation until 1940, when its sails were destroyed after being struck (for a second time) by lightning.

VISIT THE MUSEUM
Museum of the Broads
museumofthebroads.org.uk
The Staithe, NR12 9DA
01692 581681 | Open late-Mar–Oct,
Sun–Fri 10–4
Located right on the waterside in Stalham Staithe, one of the prettiest areas of the Broadlands, the museum is housed in four buildings,

▶ Sutton Mill, near Stalham

including a former wherry shed and a boat store. Moored up alongside is the museum's own boat, on which you can take a short trip. Inside, you'll see varied displays of memorabilia that tell of how thatching, eel-catching and boat-building have played a major role in local people's lives, from Roman times right through to the present day. An audio tour explains what you're seeing.

▶ Stowmarket   MAP REF 290 B4

A small but rapidly growing Suffolk market town, Stowmarket lies on the River Gipping just a few miles west of Ipswich. Its historic market square – it was granted a market charter by Edward III in 1347 – is surrounded by elegant Georgian and Victorian red-brick houses, most now used as shops and offices, while shiny new homes have been built around the town in recent years.

Stowmarket, or simply Stow as some locals refer to it, was one of England's major producers of malt which, when the river was developed as a canal, could be easily transported to Ipswich and onwards to London. The railway brought further prosperity. It still has the air of a prosperous place today.

When you first arrive in Stowmarket you'll notice its green spaces and many trees. The English poet John Milton (1608–74), who spent a great deal of time in the town, is said to have planted many of the trees. In front of the town council offices, housed in a former vicarage dating from the 1500s, is a huge tree, dubbed Milton's Tree.

Your visit to Stowmarket could include the Museum of East Anglian Life, one of the largest such attractions in Suffolk, and a visit to the fascinating John Peel Centre for Creative Arts. The townspeople have a liking for festivals; look out for its programme of events that includes the StowFest music festival.

VISIT THE MUSEUM
Museum of East Anglian Life
eastanglianlife.org.uk
IP14 1DL | 01449 612229
Open Mar–Nov Tue–Sat 10–4.30, Sun 11–4.30

The Abbot's Hall estate goes back to medieval times and part of the key to its years of efficiency was having its own farm, Home Farm. In the 1960s, the then owners of the estate, Misses Vera and Ena Longe, donated 70 acres of farmland, Home Farm, the hall itself, and gardens to be used as a museum after local collectors had amassed a huge array of historic local memorabilia. The result is the Museum of East Anglian Life, which features farming as well as day-to-day living. This all-weather museum, which opened its doors in 1967, is set in an attractive river valley site. It has seemingly endless woodland and riverside nature trails for you to follow. There are reconstructed buildings, including a working watermill, a smithy, a windpump, and the Boby Building that houses craft workshops.

The refurbished Abbot's Hall is open as part of the museum, and houses exhibitions across eight rooms. There are displays on Victorian domestic life, gypsies, farming and industry. There's still a working farm, and vegetables, as well as flowers from the colourful walled garden, are often sold outside the Osier Cafe.

CATCH A PERFORMANCE
John Peel Centre for Creative Arts
johnpeelcentre.com
Church Walk, IP14 1ET
01449 774678

You can see drama, poetry, film, comedy, acoustic artists and concerts by local and national bands at this arts centre in a converted corn exchange in the middle of town. Run by volunteers, it is named after the popular radio presenter and DJ who died in 2004. John Peel lived near here and his family helped to develop the arts centre as a lasting memorial to him.

▼ Museum of East Anglian Life

PLAY A ROUND
Stowmarket Golf Club
stowmarketgolfclub.co.uk
Lower Road, Onehouse, IP14 3DA
01449 736473 | Open daily
all year

The parkland course of the
Stowmarket Golf Club is set
in rolling countryside with river
in play on three holes. There
are many mature trees and
fine views of the Suffolk
countryside. There is a bar and
catering facilities offering tea,
coffee and sandwiches.

EAT AND DRINK
The Buxhall Crown
thebuxhallcrown.co.uk
Mill Road, Buxhall, IP14 3DW
01449 736521

A fetching mix of cosy 17th-
century cottage and Georgian
artisan's house, this gastropub
retains the atmosphere of a
traditional old village inn,
complete with log fire and
timeworn quarry tiles. There's a
pergola-lined patio with restful
views across the rich farmland,
and Adnams beers are on tap.

▶ Sudbury   MAP REF 289 E5

Sudbury is an attractive town that has its roots in Saxon
England. At that time it was a small hamlet, but grew in
status when its market was founded in around 1009. Further
prosperity came when its weaving and silk industries
expanded. If you wander around Sudbury today, you'll notice
period cottages and merchants' houses that date back 600
years or more, built when the town was flourishing. It still has
the feel of a thriving place.

The town is best known as the birthplace of two great men:
Simon Sudbury (c.1316–81) and Thomas Gainsborough

▼ Gainsborough's House

(1727–88). Simon Sudbury was the Archbishop of Canterbury from 1375 until his death, and the Lord Chancellor of England in 1381. He invented the poll tax, which made him an unpopular man. During the Peasants' Revolt, Sudbury was in the Tower of London when a band of locals, enraged by the tax, gained entry, dragged him to Tower Hill and beheaded him. His skull is in the church of St Gregory and can be viewed, should you wish to do so.

In 1727 Thomas Gainsborough was born in a beautiful Georgian-fronted brick house near Market Hill, in the centre of the town, and he lived here till his early teens. Known as Gainsborough's House, the building has been restored and houses a museum dedicated to the 18th-century landscape and portrait painter. You can see a statue of the painter outside the landmark church of St Peter on Market Hill.

VISIT THE MUSEUM AND GALLERY

Gainsborough's House

gainsborough.org
46 Gainsborough Street, CO10 2EU
01787 372958 | Open Mon–Sat 10–5, Sun 11–5

Birthplace of painter Thomas Gainsborough, the house is open as a museum. Here you can see the most complete collection of his work on display anywhere in the world, including his first known portraits of a boy and a girl, a miniature of his wife, and some 20 portraits of rich clergymen, politicians and landowners. A small cabinet holds Gainsborough's personal items, such as his pocket watch, snuff box, pipe stopper and paint scraper. The walled garden has a 400-year-old mulberry tree and plants that were available in Gainsborough's time. A varied programme of temporary exhibitions on British art takes place throughout the year.

Sudbury Heritage Museum

sudburysuffolk.co.uk
Town Hall, Gaol Lane, CO10 1TL
01787 371880 | Open Mon–Fri 10–4

The Sudbury Heritage Museum contains a fascinating exhibition of photographs and memorabilia that tells the history of the town from prehistoric and Saxon times to the present day.

GO TO THE THEATRE

The Quay Theatre

quaysudbury.com
Quay Lane, CO10 2AN
01787 374745

Housed in a converted granary, the Quay Theatre hosts a variety of drama, music shows, films and comedies.

▶ PLACES NEARBY

The gorgeous village of Long Melford with its grand country mansions, Kentwell Hall and Melford Hall, is barely a five-minute drive away (see page 187).

▶ Suffolk Heritage Coast MAP REF 291 E4

An area dotted with impossibly pretty towns and villages and craggy coastlines, reed-fringed creeks bursting with wildlife, brilliant sunsets and sweeping skies, the Suffolk Heritage Coast is one of the finest stretches of land in England. Here, some of the last wild lowland heaths in England sweep down to salt marshes. Harbours filled with life in Suffolk's herring and fishing heyday, several of them the scene of battles, are now some of East Anglia's most select holiday resorts.

A total of 35 miles of the Suffolk Heritage Coast has been designated an Area of Outstanding Natural Beauty (AONB). Sand marsh and mudflats, along with acres of heathland, reedbeds and hay meadows, dykes, creeks and pools, grazing marshes and a variety of woodlands, provide the perfect habitat for many species of plants, birds and wildlife. Habitats such as these are severely threatened in lowland Britain.

The coast in Suffolk is deeply indented by the slow-flowing estuaries of the rivers Blyth, Alde, Deben and Orwell, and the

▼ The Dunwich coast

River Stour on the Suffolk–Essex border. They may look picturesque, but they present issues such as silting. The coast is bounded by crumbling low sea cliffs and tidal shingle spits, which fight a constant losing battle against the ever-encroaching North Sea. The AONB's protection is vital along this stretch of coastline. It was bestowed on the area in 1969 and covers 156 sq miles from Lowestoft in the north to Felixstowe in the south; it includes three National Nature Reserves and the Minsmere RSPB Reserve, along with the Suffolk Heritage Coast coastline itself.

Dingle Marshes, near Dunwich (see page 120), is one of the coastal reserves. Jointly owned and managed by the RSPB and the Suffolk Wildlife Trust, the reserve attracts breeding and wintering wildfowl and waders, including avocets, white-fronted geese, lapwings and redshanks. Nearby, the Orfordness–Havergate National Nature Reserve (page 231) has one of the country's largest vegetated shingle spits, formed when the River Alde was at one time diverted, which supports a number of rare invertebrates, particularly spiders and beetles.

Inland, ancient heathlands of heather and bracken, known as sandlings, were plentiful in medieval times when they provided grazing for huge flocks of sheep. Today, they are rare.

▲ Dunwich Heath

At Dunwich Heath (see page 120), one of a just a few such heaths in the country, rare species of heather, gorse and broom can be seen. From July to September, the heath is a patchwork of colour with pink and purple heather vying for attention with the coconut-scented golden gorse.

Picturesque towns and villages, many with towering church spires, punctuate the rolling countryside of the Suffolk Heritage Coast. Southwold, one of the prettiest towns today and still a genteel holiday resort, has seen industry and battles, and has contributed much to the coastline's formidable heritage (see page 243). A port since Saxon times, it enjoyed prosperity thanks to the herring industry. However, it was the herring trade that was partly instrumental in starting three vicious naval battles here: the first in 1653 off Orford Ness, the second in 1664 near Lowestoft, and the Battle of Sole Bay in 1672, which was to be the first battle of the Third Anglo-Dutch War. Southwold, like other towns along the Suffolk coast, and that of its neighbouring county Norfolk, suffered from silting. Its herring industry collapsed as a result, and its fortunes waned, but all that changed in Victorian times when the town reinvented itself as a seaside resort at a time when it became fashionable to take coastal jaunts.

Today, when you visit Southwold, you'll see the pier dominates its seafront. It was originally built between 1899 and 1900 when the town was flourishing and, at over an eighth of a mile long, could easily accommodate the sea-going

▲ Woodbridge

paddle steamers that plied along the coast in late Victorian times. During World War II it was split into two as a precaution against German invasion, and a mighty gale in 1955 destroyed chunks of its structure. It remained in a sorry state until 2001, when it was rebuilt and restored. In fact, Southwold's pier has earned a place in recent history as the first to be built in England since the 1950s.

Aldeburgh, like Southwold, is a delightful town of pink- and blue-washed cottages and Georgian town houses that enjoyed a buoyant fishing and shipbuilding industry (see page 52). It, too, brought tremendous prosperity to the town, until its decline due to silting. Aldeburgh managed to turn its own fortunes around, not so much by becoming a seaside resort, but more because it was the home of 20th-century composer Benjamin Britten (1913–76) who, through his music, and the foundation of the highly respected Aldeburgh Festival, gave the town an international musical reputation. Snape Maltings concert hall, housed in a converted maltings building amid reeds and marshes on the outskirts of Aldeburgh, hosts a regular programme of concerts as well as the Aldeburgh Festival, which features some of the world's finest musicians (see page 52). Further south is the village of Orford (see page 228), which is famous for its beautifully preserved castle built by Henry II when it, too, was a thriving port, and Orford Ness, which is Europe's largest vegetated shingle spit and home to many birds and other wildlife (see page 231).

▸ Sutton Hoo MAP REF 291 D4

nationaltrust.org.uk/suttonhoo
IP12 3DJ | 01394 389700
See website for details of opening times

A short distance from the town of Woodbridge, at Sutton Hoo, is the Anglo-Saxon royal burial site of King Raedwald, where a vast treasure was discovered in a huge ship grave. Sutton Hoo is arguably one of the most vital archaeological sites in Britain. Lying on a low spur of land above the River Deben, several large mounds were excavated in 1939 and one revealed a warrior's helmet and shield and a collection of gold ornaments in the remains of an 89-foot ship. The 7th-century burial site of an Anglo-Saxon king, which had been missed by grave-robbers, and lay undisturbed for 1,300 years. The significance of this important discovery is incalculable, and has been described as 'page one of English history'.

When, in the early 5th century, the Romans withdrew from Britain, the way was left open for people from Denmark, Germany and the lower Rhine to settle here, displacing and enslaving the remnant Celtic and Roman people. These early settlers were the Anglo-Saxons, and their language formed the basis of the English spoken today. Two hundred years later, new kingdoms were formed: Suffolk and Norfolk becoming the Kingdom of the East Angles, and thereby setting the foundations of England as a country.

Anglo-Saxon custom decreed that important people were buried beneath mounds, often along with precious goods as a sign of their wealth and importance. The burial of an entire ship is

▾ Sutton Hoo burial mounds ▸ Sutton Hoo helmet

something else again, unique to East Anglia and Scandinavia, and the burial mound at Sutton Hoo was a prominent and fitting memorial to a powerful leader.

The National Trust exhibition hall at Sutton Hoo relates the history of how its treasures lay undisturbed. The burial mounds form part of a much larger estate. You can only stand on the mounds with a guide, but the lovely walks here across heathland with estuary views or along woodland trails are open to all.

You can see displays that tell how Anglo-Saxon nobles lived, and how they went to war and founded a new kingdom in East Anglia. The centrepiece is a full-sized replica of an Anglo-Saxon warrior king's burial chamber. The discoveries at Sutton Hoo changed forever our perceptions of the 'Dark' Ages by revealing a culture rich in craftsmanship, trade and legend (see also Land of Anglo-Saxon Kings, page 36). The King's River Cafe has views of the estate from its balcony.

▶ Swaffham MAP REF 293 E4

Swaffham is an elegant sort of place, largely thanks to it having been a fashionable centre for well-connected people to attend balls, soirées and concerts in Regency and late Victorian times. One of the places they met was at the handsome Assembly Rooms, now a school, built between 1776 and 1778, which you can see as you stroll around the lively town centre. Lord Nelson himself is said to have favoured Swaffham as a weekend retreat.

People gathered in Swaffham for 'the season', and so many clergymen ranked among their numbers that the Bishop of Norwich was reported as being concerned that they were neglecting their parishioners. One of the most prestigious events in the days of the Regency was the annual hare coursing hosted by the Swaffham Club. This was established by Lord Orford, a nephew of the writer Horace Walpole, in 1776. By this time, though, Swaffham was already a prosperous town. It had buoyant wool and sheep industries, and a large market place where traders would come from all over Suffolk. The market is still going, albeit with no livestock. Today, you can see the large and ornate buttercross that marks its heart.

While you're out and about around Swaffham, take a minute to look at its village sign. It shows the legendary Pedlar of Swaffham. As the story goes, a local man called John Chapman went to London and met a stranger on London Bridge. The stranger told him about a dream in which he had discovered treasure in a garden, and the garden he described was the peddlar's. The peddlar set off home with great haste, discovered the treasure and donated his money to the town's church. Legend has it that the fabulous Tudor windows of the north aisle of the church of St Peter and St Paul were paid for by Chapman.

◀ Swaffham village sign

Another famous local was Howard Carter (1874–1939), the eminent Egyptologist who discovered Tutankhamun's tomb in the Valley of the Kings and who is rumoured to have died prematurely as the result of the boy-king's curse. An exhibition of Carter's work in Egypt can be seen in the town museum.

VISIT THE MUSEUM
Swaffham Museum
swaffhammuseum.co.uk
4 London Street, PE37 7DQ
01760 721230 | Open Feb–Dec
Mon–Fri 10–4, Sat 10–1
This small, social history museum reveals Swaffham from prehistory to the present, with an excellent gallery dedicated to Howard Carter and his discoveries in Egypt, plus changing exhibitions.

PLAY A ROUND
Swaffham Golf Club
club-noticeboard.co.uk
Cley Road, PE37 8AE
01760 721621 | Open daily all year
This heathland course and designated wildlife site lies in the heart of Breckland country. It has excellent drainage and good all-year golfing.

▶ PLACES NEARBY
Castle Acre is a picturesque, once fortified village that is best known for its small castle and the rather dramatic remains of Castle Acre Priory. You could also visit the gorgeous 15th-century moated Oxburgh Hall in nearby Oxborough (see page 232). South of Swaffham you'll find the gorgeous parkland Richmond Park Golf Club, and a little further away, the Chequers Inn at Thompson on the road to Thetford.

Castle Acre Priory and Castle
english-heritage.org.uk
South Acre Road, PE32 2XD
01760 755394 | Priory open Apr–Sep daily 10–6, Oct daily 10–5, Nov–Mar Sat–Sun 10–4; castle Jul–Mar during daylight hours
A castle mound was raised here by the Earls of Surrey in about AD 1080, and the first stone castle was added a little later. Enormous earthworks were dug to protect it – great grassy ditches and ramparts swing around the castle, enclosing a sizeable portion of land. The Priory, one of the country's largest and best-preserved monastic sites, was home to the first Cluniac order of monks to come to England.

Chequers Inn
thompsonchequers.co.uk
Griston Road, Thompson
IP24 1PX | 01953 483360
Breckland is a region of gorse-covered sandy heath straddling south Norfolk and north Suffolk. Within its boundaries you'll find this splendid, long and low, thatched 17th-century inn, where manorial courts were held in the 18th century. It's more fun here today. Beneath its steeply raked thatch lies a series of low-ceilinged, interconnecting rooms served by a long bar. The

overall impression of the interior is of skew-whiff wall timbers, squat doorways, open log fires, rustic old furniture and farming implements. Although not long, the main menu more than adequately covers most bases, and it's supplemented by specials. You'll find picnic tables in the large rear garden, where dogs are welcome.

Richmond Park Golf Club
richmondpark.co.uk
Saham Road, Watton, IP25 6EA
01953 881803 | Open daily all year
The compact parkland course has mature and young trees set around the Little Wissey River, and is spread over 100 acres of countryside. Facilities include a practice area and putting green and a club house with two restaurants.

▶ Thetford   MAP REF 289 E1

The market town of Thetford has gone down in history as being the place where Boudicca, the Queen of the Iceni tribe who lived in Norfolk around 2,000 years ago, spent most of her time. In later years, the town was the home of many East Anglian monarchs. It was also a bishopric and had a thriving wool industry. In short, Thetford was a prosperous hub and one of the most important in south Norfolk. Today, the town is a pleasing place surrounded by the great expanse of the Thetford Forest, the largest lowland pine forest in the country. If you call into the High Lodge Visitor Centre, you'll find out all you need to know about the forest, plus there's a playground for the children, cycle hire, walking trails leaflets and the Go Ape! high wire adventure course.

TAKE IN SOME HISTORY
Thetford Priory
english-heritage.org.uk
0370 333 1181 | Open daily 8–4
The Priory of Our Lady of Thetford belonged to the Order of Cluny, and was founded in 1103 by Roger Bigod, an old soldier and friend of William the Conqueror. Here the dukes and earls of Norfolk would have been buried. The priory remains are dramatic. You can see the walls of the church and cloister, and an almost complete gatehouse. This site gives you a glimpse of medieval religious life before the Dissolution of the Monasteries.

VISIT A MUSEUM
Ancient House Museum
museums.norfolk.gov.uk
21–23 White Hart Street,
IP24 1AA | 01842 752599
Open Apr–Sep Tue–Sat 10–5,
Oct–Mar Tue–Sat 10–4
This excellent Museum of Thetford Life, housed in an early Tudor timber-framed

▶ Thetford Forest

house with beautifully carved beamed ceilings, tells of the town's long history in interesting displays, audio guides and films, together with changing exhibitions. There's a small period garden in the rear courtyard and regular events.

Dad's Army Museum
dadsarmythetford.org.uk
The Old Fire Station, Cage Lane, IP24 2DS | 07562 688641
Open Apr–Jun, Oct–Nov Sat 10–3, Jul–Sep Tue, Sat 10–3
This little museum appeals to fans of the iconic television series, filmed in Thetford between 1968 and 1977.

WALK THE HIGH ROPES
Go Ape! Thetford
goape.co.uk
High Lodge Forest Centre, Santon Downham, Brandon, IP27 0AF
0845 643 9215 | Open Apr–Oct daily, Mar, Nov Sat–Sun
You can burn some energy at Go Ape! Thetford. Set in the heart of the forest, this area has around 30 miles of bike and walking trails from which to explore 50,000 acres of woodland. As well as the famed wind-in-your-face zip wires and high ropes obstacles, the Tree Top Adventure features a Tarzan Swing, back-to-back black crossings and an Alpine Zip that goes from tree to tree. There's a Tree Top Junior Adventure for younger participants, too, and the opportunity to go for adventure off the beaten track with Forest Segway.

PLAY A ROUND
Thetford Golf Club
thetfordgolfclub.co.uk
Brandon Road, IP24 3NE
01842 752169 | Open Mon, Wed–Fri after 10, Tue, Sat–Sun after 2
Thetford Golf Club's course has a good pedigree. It was laid out by the fine golfer C H Mayo, later altered by James Braid and then altered again by another famous course designer, Mackenzie Ross. It is a testing heathland course with a particularly stiff finish.

EAT AND DRINK
Angel Inn
angel-larling.co.uk
Larling, NR16 2QU
01953 717963
This 17th-century former coaching inn on the edge of Breckland and Thetford Forest Park has a good local feel and offers visitors a warm welcome. In the heavily beamed public bar, a jukebox, dartboard and fruit machine add to the entertainment, while the oak-panelled lounge bar has dining tables with cushioned wheel-back chairs, a wood burner and a huge collection of water jugs. Five guest ales, including Crouch Vale Brewers Gold, are served, as well as more than a hundred whiskies. Menus make good use of local ingredients, with lighter snacks including sandwiches, jacket potatoes, burgers and salads. Each August, the Angel hosts Norfolk's largest outdoor beer festival, with over 100 real ales.

Crown Hotel

the-crown-hotel.co.uk
Crown Road, Mundford,
IP26 5HQ | 01842 878233

Roofed with traditional Norfolk pantiles, this historic inn on the edge of Thetford Forest dates from 1652. Originally a hunting lodge, it has also served as a magistrate's court. Today it's a popular pub with two restaurants, the Old Court and the Club Room, whose menus use as many local ingredients as possible. In addition to Woodforde's Wherry, guest ales and wines by the glass, the bars stock over 50 malt whiskies. The pub being on a slight rise, the garden is at first-floor level.

▶ PLACES NEARBY

Just a couple miles away is the village of Euston, where you could spend a good day at Euston Hall, or visit Grime's Graves, the site of Neolithic mines, in nearby Lynford. In the village of Weeting, a short drive from Thetford, is the remains of Weeting Castle. For local produce, and much more, try the Elveden Estate.

Euston Hall

eustonhall.co.uk
IP24 2QP | 01842 766366
Open Jul–Aug on selected days
only 2.30–5

You can see a magnificent collection of 17th-century courtly paintings on a visit to Euston Hall. One-time owner Henry FitzRoy's origins were indisputably Stuart, and Stuart portraits fill every corner. There is a portrait of Charles I painted by Van Dyck, and another of Charles II by Lely.

The house was originally built between 1670 and 1676 for the Duke of Arlington, Charles II's Secretary of State. He made a splendid match for his daughter Isabella when she was only five years old, betrothing her to Henry FitzRoy, the illegitimate son of the king and his mistress Barbara Villiers. Henry FitzRoy was made the Duke of Grafton, and Euston Hall, which he inherited from Arlington, has been the family home of the Graftons ever since.

Euston Hall was probably one of the first English country houses to have the luxury of a mechanically pumped water supply. The diarist John Evelyn visited Euston in 1671 and commented on the 'pretty engine' that pumped water from a nearby canal for all the house's needs, with enough left over to run the fountains and a corn mill.

Henry FitzRoy enjoyed his inheritance for only five years before he died. His son, the second Duke, then commissioned Matthew Brettingham to remodel the house. William Kent designed the park and a Palladian-style folly, and Lancelot 'Capability' Brown added some fashionable landscaping featuring weirs, pools and rivers.

In 1902 a great fire raged at Euston Hall. The south and west wings were gutted, destroying, among other priceless treasures, the 18th-century ceilings painted by Verrio. Only the north wing remained. The burned wings were quickly rebuilt, but were demolished in 1952 so that the hall that can be seen today dates mainly from the 1740s. The completion of a lengthy restoration of the grounds was timed to coincide with Brown's tercentenary in 2016.

Grime's Graves
english-heritage.org.uk
Lynford, IP26 5DE | Open Mar–Sep daily 10–5, Oct Wed–Sun 10–5
These unique and remarkable neolithic flint mines are the earliest remaining major industrial site in Europe. Using antlers as picks, prehistoric miners sank shafts and tunnels deep into the ground following seams of flint. Visitors can descend 30 feet by ladder into one excavated shaft to see the flint. A small exhibition area gives the site's history. Rare plants flourish here.

Weeting Castle
english-heritage.org.uk
Weeting, IP27 0RQ | 0370 333 1181
Open at any reasonable time
Weeting Castle is the ruin of an 11th-century fortified manor house in a moated enclosure. You can see the remains of a three-storey cross-wing and a brick ice house.

Elveden Courtyard Restaurant ❀
elveden.com
London Road, Elveden, IP24 3TQ | 01842 898068

▼ Grime's Graves, near Weeting

The 10,000 acres of the Guinness estate in Norfolk are the base for a modern agricultural enterprise, supplying a formidable annual tonnage of fresh produce to East Anglia and beyond, with a raftered farm shop at its heart. The all-day cafe it incorporates is a bright, open space with granite tables and a wall of deep windows. At lunchtimes, it hosts quite a press of enthusiastic regular business, but service remains attentive and focused, and the weekend pre-Christmas party nights are a blast. The weekly changing menu offers sensitively cooked seasonal dishes, precisely seasoned and always neatly presented.

▶ Thorpeness MAP REF 291 E4

The village of Thorpeness, near Aldeburgh in Suffolk, is largely the creation of one man, the Scottish barrister, architect and playwright Glencairn Stuart Ogilvie. He inherited the Ogilvie estate of c.6,000 acres on the death of his mother in 1908. The land had been amassed by his father Alexander who made his fortune designing railways across the world.

Glencairn Stuart Ogilvie aimed to transform the tiny fishing hamlet of Thorpeness and the countryside that surrounded it into an upmarket holiday village for the middle classes to enjoy wholesome family holidays. Along with a colonial-style country club, complete with verandah, golf course, swimming pool and tennis courts, Ogilvie constructed a slice of England – mock Tudor and Jacobean cottages, almshouses, a working windmill and many architectural follies, including the House in the Clouds. This cleverly designed water tower was disguised as a weatherboarded and tile-hung house, and has become the dominant feature of the Thorpeness skyline. From a distance it appears to be lodged in the trees.

The town's focal point is the Meare, a shallow artificial lake with islands and play houses themed around the story of *Peter Pan*. Ogilvie clearly drew his inspiration from his friendship with the author J M Barrie. Until the 1970s most of Thorpeness remained owned by the Ogilvie family. Today many of the buildings have been sympathetically refurbished and in August the Meare is the location for a regatta and firework display.

EAT AND DRINK
The Dolphin Inn
thorpenessdolphin.com
Peace Place, IP16 4NA
01728 454994

A stone's throw from Suffolk's Heritage Coast and in a conservation area, this community-focused free house replaced a 1910 predecessor, destroyed by fire in 1995. At the bar are real ales from Adnams and Earl Soham, nearly 20 wines by the glass, and whiskies in abundance. After a bracing walk on the beach, sit beside the fire and tuck into one of their homemade pies; in summer barbecues are held in the huge garden.

Thorpeness Hotel ◉
thorpeness.co.uk
Lakeside Avenue, IP16 4NH
01728 452176

The heathland golf course adjacent to the sea was opened in 1922 and has brought golfers to the region ever since, although there's plenty else to do hereabouts. The restaurant serves up views over the third tee in a traditional and roomy setting (there's also a wood-panelled bar and a terrace with a watery vista). The daily-changing menu keeps things relatively simple, and the traditional Sunday lunch roast is an institution.

▼ The House in the Clouds

▶ **Walsingham** MAP REF 293 F2

Walsingham is a village of two halves, divided by the River Stiffkey. Little Walsingham is the newer area of the two, and it tends to get all the attention because of shrines dedicated to Our Lady of Walsingham, while Great Walsingham, the original village, is the smaller. Both have a long history of pilgrimage, said to date back to the 11th century, or even before, and both have a wealth of fabulous period buildings.

The original shrine to Our Lady of Walsingham was, according to legend, built in 1061 after a devout local noblewomen, Richeldis de Faverches, had a vision in which the Virgin Mary led her to Nazareth. Richeldis was shown the house where the Virgin Mary learned that she would become the mother of Jesus, and was told to build a replica of the holy house in Walsingham. The house became a place of pilgrimage; indeed, it was one of the most famous shrines in medieval Christendom. Walsingham grew in significance. The Augustinian Canons built a priory here in 1153 in recognition of its importance. This was all but destroyed during the reign of Henry VIII, but you can still see the hugely dramatic remains standing in peaceful gardens. The original shrine was also destroyed during the Reformation, but some years later a 700-year-old chapel, known as the Slipper Chapel, was restored, pilgrims returned and in 1934 it was named the Roman Catholic National Shrine of Our Lady. An Anglican Marian shrine was established in 1931, a place of pilgrimage also dedicated to Our Lady of Walsingham. The former Little Walsingham railway station has been converted into the Orthodox church of St Seraphim.

Walsingham is served by the Wells and Walsingham Light Railway in summer (see page 277).

TAKE IN SOME HISTORY

Walsingham Abbey Grounds and Shirehall Museum

walsinghamabbey.com
Common Place, NR22 6BP
01328 820510 | Open Apr–Oct daily 11–4; grounds also Nov–Mar Mon–Fri 11–1, 2–4

In the grounds of Walsingham Abbey are the spectacular ruins of the original Augustinian priory built here in the 1100s. At the entrance to the grounds is the Shirehall Museum housed in what was once a pilgrims' hostel and then for 200 years a Georgian courthouse. Here, you can see displays on the history of Walsingham together with many local artefacts. The priory ruins and museum stand in 20 acres of tranquil and picturesque gardens, which are famous for their dramatic display of snowdrops in February, with access to woodland and river walks across the ancient parkland.

SEE SOME LOCAL CHURCHES

National Shrine of Our Lady of Walsingham

walsingham.org.uk

Slipper Chapel, NR22 6AL

01328 820495

The delightful Slipper Chapel was built in the mid-14th century and had fallen into disrepair until its restoration in 1896. You can see a statue of Our Lady of Walsingham, to whom the chapel is dedicated, along with modern windows depicting the Annunciation. See the Cloister Garden with its holy water fountain, the Chapel of the Holy Spirit and the Chapel of Reconciliation. The shrine remains a place of pilgrimage for Roman Catholics from around the world, welcoming over 100,000 people during the pilgrimage season from May to the end of September.

The Shrine of Our Lady of Walsingham

walsinghamanglican.org.uk

2 Common Place, NR22 6EE

01328 820255

In the centre of Little Walsingham is the Shrine to Our Lady of Walsingham for the Anglican Church. It is a modern building believed to stand on the site of the original 11th-century priory and represents the house in Nazareth which was the scene of the annunciation. You can see a beautiful image of Our Lady of Walsingham carved in 1922 from a seal of the priory, and a Holy Well.

St Peter, Great Walsingham

Great Walsingham is much smaller than its neighbour Little Walsingham, and is dominated by the church of St Peter. It is a fine 14th-century building with a 15th-century porch. It has no chancel, giving it a somewhat curtailed appearance, but this does not detract from the beauty of the windows, among the best of their kind.

The church's special treasure is its 40 benches dating from the 15th century. These still stand on their original wooden sills, a most unusual survival. The carving on many of the benches is exceptional, especially those with latticework backs. Some have linenfold panelled backs, a further refinement of medieval seating. There are carvings of saints on some of the benches, and others have animals and imaginary creatures on them.

▶ **Weeting**
see **Thetford**, page 270

▶ **Wells-next-the-Sea** MAP REF 293 F1
If you want to blend in with the locals, refer to this pretty
town simply as Wells. This is a working harbour town with a
quayside full to bursting with colourful fishing boats and dock
equipment, even though it is no longer actually beside the sea.
In fact, Wells is a mile or so inland on a muddy creek created by
silting over the centuries.

The quay is dominated by the six-storey 1903 granary
building, now converted into luxury flats with grand views. Its
roofed overhead gantry spans the road. Behind the quay are
narrow streets of flint houses, while inland a little are elegant
Georgian and Victorian buildings.

On the seafront is a memorial that commemorates the
11 lifeboat men who were lost at sea in 1880. Close by is Ware
Hall House, a 15th-century timber-framed building that
originally stood in Ware, Hertfordshire, but when the council
wanted to demolish it, it was taken apart and moved to Wells
by lorries and rebuilt, timber by timber and brick by brick,
almost singlehandedly over 23 years, by its elderly owner
Miss May Savidge. After her death in 1993, the house was
completed by her niece.

A high embankment, known as 'The Bank', was constructed
by Lord Leicester of nearby Holkham Hall (see page 154) in

▼ Wells-next-the-Sea

1859, to reclaim an area of salt marsh and to help preserve the harbour. It now provides a pleasant walk to the beaches, woods and caravan and camping site north of the town, with the seasonal option of a ride on the narrow-gauge railway running alongside. The vast sands stretch west to one of Britain's largest coastal nature reserves at Holkham Gap and are backed by dense coastal pinewoods, dunes and a fine array of lovingly preserved beach huts.

Locals collect samphire from the mudflats and salt marshes between the tides in summer. This coastal delicacy, a fleshy green plant, can be pickled or served freshly boiled with butter or malt vinegar.

▼ Wells-next-the-Sea beach huts

TAKE A TRAIN RIDE
Wells and Walsingham Light Railway
wwlr.co.uk
NR23 1QB | 01328 711630
Open Easter–Oct daily

The railway covers the four miles between Wells and the neighbouring village of Walsingham (see page 273), and is the longest ten-and-a-quarter inch gauge track in the world. The line passes through some very attractive countryside, particularly noted for its wild flowers and butterflies. This is the home of the unique Garratt steam locomotive specially built for this line; two Garratt locos are now in service. A former Great Eastern Railways signal box is used as a tearoom at Wells.

EAT AND DRINK
The Crown Hotel
crownhotelnorfolk.co.uk
The Buttlands, NR23 1EX
01328 710209

This 17th-century former coaching inn overlooks the tree-lined green known as the Buttlands. The Crown's striking contemporary decor blends effortlessly with its old-world charm, and beneath the bar's ancient beams East Anglian ales and Aspall Cyder are on tap. Whether you eat in the bar, more formally in the restaurant, in the cheerful Orangery, or outside with great views, the menus offer traditional favourites, modern British cuisine, and internationally influenced dishes.

Bang! In Wells
banginwells.co.uk
2 Staithe Street, NR23 1AF
01328 712149

The fun name reflects the light-hearted, relaxed atmosphere of this friendly little cafe and bar in one of the town's oldest buildings. The decor is simple, bright and colourful and the all-day menu spans traditional breakfast favourites, soup, salads, memorable sandwiches and tempting cakes, with all ingredients sourced locally. Eat out in the courtyard in summer.

Three Horseshoes
Warham All Saints, NR23 1NL
01328 710547

In a row of brick-and-flint stands this timeless village pub, its rambling period-piece rooms recalling long-gone taverns. The bar is lit by gas mantles and beers from the likes of Wolf and Woodforde's breweries are often gravity-served from barrels stillaged behind the servery. A curious green and red dial in the ceiling turns out to be a rare example of Norfolk Twister, an ancient drinking game. As befits such a rural pub, robust artisan food is the order of the day and generous homemade pies the undoubted stalwarts of the chalkboard menu, along with fish dishes. Alfresco enjoyment can be taken in a rose-bedecked courtyard or grassy garden, whilst dog-lovers can treat their pooch to the doggy-biscuit menu.

> **PLACES NEARBY**

The old harbour and quay at Stiffkey (pronounced 'stewkey') has long since silted up and now the Norfolk Coast Path runs between the village and the sea. It is famous for the cockles, stained blue by the mud they live in, known as 'stewkey blues'. Vast expanses of salt marshes, their twisting creeks and muddy basins subjected to unpredictable tidal flooding, attract large numbers of waders and wintering wildfowl. In summer the marshes are swathed in purple sea lavender. Thousands of winter-roosting northern lapwings inhabit the reed beds, freshwater lagoon and islands of Stiffkey Fen, a nature reserve created from farmland. The village has narrow streets, flint houses and a good pub, the Stiffkey Red Lion.

The Stiffkey Red Lion
stiffkey.com
44 Wells Road, NR23 1AJ
01328 830552

Dating from the 17th century, this comfortable inn has been a house and even a doctor's surgery in the course of its long life. Located on the North Norfolk coast, it is now a

popular bolt-hole for walkers and birders stepping off the nearby salt marshes. Grab an old pew by one of the four log fires and warm up over a glass of Nelson's Revenge and locally sourced seasonal dishes such as fresh lobster and crab, Norfolk ale-battered fish of the day with hand cut chips or Sunday roasts. There's a great daily specials board, too.

> **Welney**
see **Ely**, page 128

> **West Stow**
see **Bury St Edmunds**, page 80

▲ Windmill at Wicken Fen

▶ **Weybourne**
see **Sheringham**, page 241

▶ **Wicken Fen National Nature Reserve**
MAP REF 288 B3

nationaltrust.org.uk/wicken-fen

Lode Lane, Wicken, Ely, CB7 5XP | 01353 720274 | Open daily dawn–dusk

You will be amazed by the sheer size of the fabulous Wicken Fen National Nature Reserve, Britain's oldest wetlands park and home to more than 8,500 species of plants and wildlife. A network of raised boardwalks and grass droves take you through reedbeds and flowering meadows ablaze with colour so you can easily see all areas of the reserve and witness nature at its most natural. Wicken is a top site nationally for molluscs, aquatic beetles, rove beetles and caddis flies.

Wicken Fen is one of only four 'wild' fens which still survive in the Great Fen Basin. Its importance is demonstrated by the fact that it is not just a National Nature Reserve, but also a Site of Special Scientific Interest, a Special Area of Conservation and a Ramsar site (an international wetland designation).

The nature of the wetland has played an important role in the social and economic life of the area, providing materials for bedding and animal feed, fish and fowl for food, and peat for fuel. Reeds were used for thatching roofs and the sedge went into the making of the ridge along the top of the roofs.

As well as a source of building materials, the marshes also provided people with water and food – waterfowl, fish and eels. Then, as the necessity to keep cattle grew, the fens were drained to provide grazing marshes, a series of open fields laced by a network of dykes, and dotted with windpumps that provided the power to push the water along the dykes. In time, this became a unique landscape, threatened for a while in the 1970s, as a move to develop arable land gained sway, but finally brought within the embrace of a National Park, which now manages and protects this priceless landscape heritage.

▼ Wicken Fen

In the words of the Norfolk naturalist, the late Ted Ellis, the Fens, and in particular the Broads, are 'a breathing space for the cure of souls'. But they are more than that: these sometimes intimate nooks and crannies of reed-fringed pools, sometimes sky-laden expanses of open appeal, are a corner of heaven set aside for lovers of enchantment and the English countryside.

Today, Wicken Fen is a surviving fragment of the wilderness that once covered East Anglia, and can be explored along traditional wide droves and lush green paths, giving access to hides, two of which are equipped for wheelchairs. There's a boardwalk nature trail or you can hire a cycle or take a boat along fenland waterways. Wicken Fen has its own cafe for a light meal – and a welcome break from exploring – and a shop where you can buy bird food.

▶ **PLACES NEARBY**

A short drive away is lovely Anglesey Abbey, Garden and Lode Mill (see page 99), the exhilarating university town Cambridge (see page 88) with charming Grantchester on its outskirts (see page 137).

▶ **Woodbridge** MAP REF 291 D4

The riverside town of Woodbridge is full of character and is one of Suffolk's most engaging places. It rises from the banks of the hugely picturesque River Deben and is a mix of enchanting Tudor timber-framed cottages, elegant Georgian houses and grand Regency mansions. At the heart of the historic town, you'll see the parish church of St Mary. In fact, you can hardly miss the church since its noble 108-foot-high tower of flint and stone dominates the skyline. It stands in a churchyard of fantastically tall trees and table tombs.

Close by you'll find the 16th-century Shire Hall, resplendent in red brick with a curly Dutch gable. Built by Thomas Seckford of the Court of Requests to Queen Elizabeth I and used for judicial purposes, it now houses the Town Council Chamber and is a popular location for weddings. In front is the Victorian Gothic parish pump, erected in 1876 and with separate troughs for horses and dogs.

Woodbridge is often full of yachting types who have taken on the challenge of the River Deben and its many sandbanks, and won. Its quayside bustles with sailing and fishing boats as it has for centuries. The scene is dominated by the elegant white weatherboarded facade of the Tide Mill. A mill has stood here since the 12th century; this one dates from 1793, worked until 1957 and is now a museum. It is operated by tidal water, artfully trapped in a pool behind the mill and used to drive the wheel when the tide has fallen. You can see it working naturally when the tide is right.

East of the town is the Sutton Hoo, an evocative Edwardian house and estate with grassy burial mounds overlooking the estuary, where a celebrated Saxon ship burial and its treasures were discovered in 1939 (see page 262).

GET INDUSTRIAL
Woodbridge Tide Mill
woodbridgetidemill.org.uk
Tide Mill Way, IP12 1BY
01394 385295 | Open Easter–Sep
daily 11–5, Oct Sat–Sun 11–5
The machinery of this fabulous 18th-century mill has been completely restored in recent years and you can see how it works. It is operated using tidal power whenever the tide permits, but even at low water you can see it working by alternative power. If you time your visit right, you can catch one of its special milling days when the traditional process of making flour is demonstrated.

There are photographs and working models on display. Situated on a busy quayside, the unique building looks over towards the historic site of the Sutton Hoo Ship Burial.

PLAY A ROUND
Woodbridge has some superb golf courses. Three of the best are listed here.

Seckford Golf Club
seckfordgolf.co.uk
Seckford Hall Road, Great Bealings, IP13 6NT | 01394 388000
Open daily all year
At the Seckford Golf Club the course is interspersed with maturing tree plantations, many bunkers, water hazards and undulating fairways, providing a challenge for all levels of golfer.

Ufford Park Hotel Golf and Spa
uffordpark.co.uk
Yarmouth Road, Melton, IP12 1QW
01394 383555 | Open daily all year
The Ufford Park Hotel course is set in 120 acres of ancient parkland with 12 water features and has been voted one of the best British winter courses. It enjoys excellent natural drainage and has a floodlit driving range and golf academy.

Woodbridge Golf Club
woodbridge.intelligentgolf.co.uk
Bromeswell Heath, IP12 2PF
01394 382038 | Open Mon–Fri all year
The Woodbridge Golf Club's 18-hole heathland course requires strategic golfing skills to manoeuvre around.

EAT AND DRINK
The Crown at Woodbridge ◉◉
thecrownatwoodbridge.co.uk
2 Thoroughfare, IP12 1AD
01394 384242
The Crown has a decidedly boutique look, combining 16th-century features with a

fresh, contemporary design ethos in four dining areas. One has glowing paprika red walls, another is done out in cool shades of grey and features an etched glass mural screen, while a Windermere skiff hangs above the glass-roofed bar. The kitchen raids the Suffolk larder for its unfussy, big-hearted modern cooking. Local fish and seafood make a good showing on a wide-ranging menu.

Seckford Hall Hotel ◉◉
seckford.co.uk
IP13 6NU | 01394 385678
Approached by a sweeping drive, the imposing Tudor pile of Seckford – with its brick facade, soaring chimneys, carved-oak entrance door and well-preened grounds – is as impressive as when Elizabeth I held court here. Its interior successfully blends its regal past with modern-day comforts. The main dining room embodies that classical look, with oak panelling, rich tapestries, white linen and rich drapes, while the accomplished kitchen deals in country-house cooking with a modern spin.

Cherry Tree Inn
thecherrytreepub.co.uk
73 Cumberland Street, IP12 4AG
01394 384627
The Cherry Tree has a large central counter, and several distinct seating areas amidst the twisting oak beams. The year sees around eight guest

▶ River Tide Mill in Woodbridge

10 famous people from Suffolk

▶ **Benjamin Britten**, composer
▶ **John Constable**, painter
▶ **George Crabbe**, poet
▶ **Thomas Gainsborough**, painter
▶ **Ralph Fiennes**, actor
▶ **Matthew Hopkins**, witchfinder general
▶ **Bob Hoskins**, actor
▶ **Sir Alfred Munnings**, painter
▶ **Simon Sudbury**, Bishop of London
▶ **Thomas Wolsey**, cardinal

ales rotate, with Adnams and Aspall cider in permanent residence, and a beer festival in early July. The focus on customer care manifests in many ways: the availability of board games, play equipment for children in the large enclosed garden, free WiFi, and many gluten-free options among the locally sourced and home-cooked menu dishes.

▶ **Wroxham** MAP REF 295 D4

Among the villages located on the Broads, Wroxham has long been regarded as the capital, although it's an accolade often challenged by adjacent Hoveton. The Norfolk village lies some eight miles northeast of Norwich. Attractively set on the River Bure, which runs right through the heart of the village, Wroxham is a centre for boat hire and holidays, and today, with Hoveton, has become a major tourist centre for the Broads.

Wroxham is where boating holidays really took off in the late 1800s. It has developed commercially over the years, with many hotels, tea rooms and gift shops springing up near the river.

One of the features of the village is Wroxham Bridge, built in 1619, a picturesque semicircular road bridge that has very low headroom at high water. It's considered to be the second most difficult bridge to navigate after the one in the village of Potter Heigham (see page 233). Many boats have hit the bridge and it's a key concern for anyone wanting to continue sailing upriver to the limit of navigation at Coltishall. See also the Norfolk Broads (page 203).

TAKE A TRAIN RIDE
Bure Valley Railway
bvrw.co.uk
Aylesham Station, Norwich Road,
Aylsham, NR11 6BW
01263 733858

The 15-inch-gauge railway trains of the Bure Valley Railway run for nine miles between Wroxham and Aylsham. You can ride on any one of the five steam locomotives and one diesel that operate on the line.

▶ PLACES NEARBY

A short drive from Wroxham is South Walsham, a quiet village in the heart of the Norfolk Broads. Here, you can spend some time enjoying boat trips and nature trails at the Fairhaven Woodland and Water Garden. Nearby, you will also find Hoveton (see page 160) and Ranworth (see page 234).

Fairhaven Woodland and Water Garden
fairhavengarden.co.uk
School Road, South Walsham
NR13 6DZ | 01603 270449
Open daily Mar–Sep 10–5,
Oct–Feb 10–4

Set in around 130 acres of ancient woodland, this gorgeous nature garden lies right next to the South Walsham Broad. If your family enjoys trips out on the water, birding from a boat or setting off to explore nature on foot, then this is the place to come.

In spring there are masses of primroses and bluebells, with huge colourful displays of rhododendrons and pink azaleas dotted around the gardens. You can see the sunny colours of the candelabra primulas and some unusual plants growing near the waterways. Summer flowers include day lilies, ligularia, hostas, hydrangeas and flowering shrubs. In summer the wild flowers provide ample food for visiting butterflies, bees and dragonflies.

The garden has its own tearoom and plant sales, plus a whole host of special events throughout the year.

Norfolk Mead Hotel ◉◉
norfolkmead.co.uk
Church Loke, Coltishall,
NR12 7DN | 01603 737531
The handsome old house in the heart of the beautiful Norfolk Broads has never looked so dapper. Refurbishment by new owners has given the Norfolk Mead a contemporary, country-chic look, never more so than in the restaurant, where period features are combined with white walls broken up with abstract artwork, wooden floors and tables decorated with simple flower arrangements. Windows look out over the pretty gardens – a must for a pre- or post-prandial stroll down to the river – while the charming small bar offers a range of whiskies and real ales, with the bonus of a delightful sun-trap terrace. Chef Anna Duttson sources the finest, freshest local ingredients for her attractively presented modern British cooking with a local flavour.

▶ Wymondham MAP REF 294 B5

It is difficult to believe that peaceful Wymondham was once the site of a bitter dispute between its parishioners and the abbey's Benedictine monks. The two parties could not agree. They did not like the times when each other rang their bells and they did not like sharing the church. Matters came to a head in the 15th century when the monks began to build a church tower, making it clear that this was going to be for their use only. In retaliation, in 1447, the townsfolk began to build their own tower – and then installed a peal of bells. The result is a church with two towers. The dispute dragged on for many years and was only laid to rest during the Dissolution, when the abbey buildings were destroyed and the monks expelled by Henry VIII.

TAKE IN SOME HISTORY
Wymondham Abbey
wymondhamabbey.org.uk
Wymondham, NR18 0PH
01953 607062 | Open Mon–Sat 10–4
Founded in 1107 by William d'Albini the abbey church of St Mary and St Thomas of Canterbury is well worth a visit. The first thing you notice is that the grand central tower is nothing more than a shell, with the great arch that once led up to the abbey buildings open to the elements. This was the monks' tower, completed in 1409. It effectively divided the

church in half, and left the parishioners staring at a blank wall, while the monks enjoyed the chancel. The east wall remained blank until the screen was erected in the early 20th century. Inside, the church is a delight. There are Norman arches in the nave and an angel roof, all drawing the eye forward to the gold extravaganza of the altar screen on the east wall.

VISIT THE MUSEUM
Wymondham Heritage Museum
wymondhamheritagemuseum.co.uk
10 The Bridewell, Norwich Road, NR18 0NS | 01953 600205
Open Mar–Oct Mon–Sat 10–4
Featuring permanent exhibitions on the Wymondham Bridewell model prison (including a re-creation of a dungeon) and brushmaking, (once a major employer in the town), the Heritage Museum also hosts special displays and events throughout the year.

TAKE A TRAIN RIDE
Mid-Norfolk Railway
mnr.org.uk
Dereham Station, NR19 1DF
01362 851723 | Open Apr–Oct, Santa Specials in Dec
Operating on the old Wymondham to Wells-next-the-Sea branch line this heritage railway is a delight. It runs between Wymondham Abbey and Dereham (see page 116) and charter and excursion trains also use the line via the link with the national rail network at Wymondham.

EAT AND DRINK
Number Twenty Four Restaurant ◉
number24.co.uk
24 Middleton Street, NR18 0AD | 01953 607750
A row of Grade II listed 18th-century cottages in the heart of Wymondham is the setting for this smart, family-run restaurant. The dining room is a period gem done out with linen-clothed, widely-spaced tables set against warm, soothing colours, and the vibe is good humoured and unstuffy. There is dedication to good old-fashioned hard work in the kitchen – everything is cooked from scratch and in tune with the seasons and local larder.

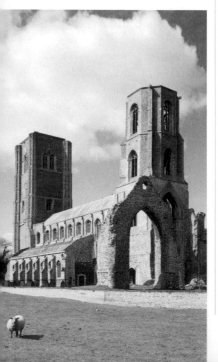

◀ Wymondham Abbey

0 | 10 miles
0 | 10 | 20 kilometres

Mablethorpe

A16

A158

A52

Skegness

Sheringham
Cromer

The Wash

Hunstanton

North Walsham

A148

Fakenham

A140

King's Lynn

A1065

294–5

Caister-on-Sea

A17

A47

A1101

A10

292–3

Dereham

THE BROADS

NORWICH

A47

GREAT YARMOUTH

March

Downham Market

Swaffham

A47

NORFOLK

A11

LOWESTOFT

A161

A134

A1065

Attleborough

Bungay

Beccles

A140

A1066

Diss

A143

Ely

Mildenhall

A11

Thetford

SUFFOLK

Southwold

A142

A143

A12

CAMBRIDGESHIRE

Newmarket

Bury St Edmunds

A140

A14

CAMBRIDGE

288–9

Stowmarket

290–1

Aldeburgh

A10

A11

M11

A134

A14

Woodbridge

Haverhill

IPSWICH

Sudbury

A14

Felixstowe

A12

Halstead

A120

Harwich

Braintree

COLCHESTER

A133

Bishop's Stortford

ESSEX

A12

CLACTON-ON-SEA

CHELMSFORD

A414

M25

M11

BRENTWOOD

A127

BASILDON

A13

SOUTHEND-ON-SEA

Dartford

GRAVESEND

MARGATE

CHATHAM

M2

DOVER

FOLKESTONE

EAST SUSSEX

A259

ATLAS

★ A-Z places listed

• Places Nearby

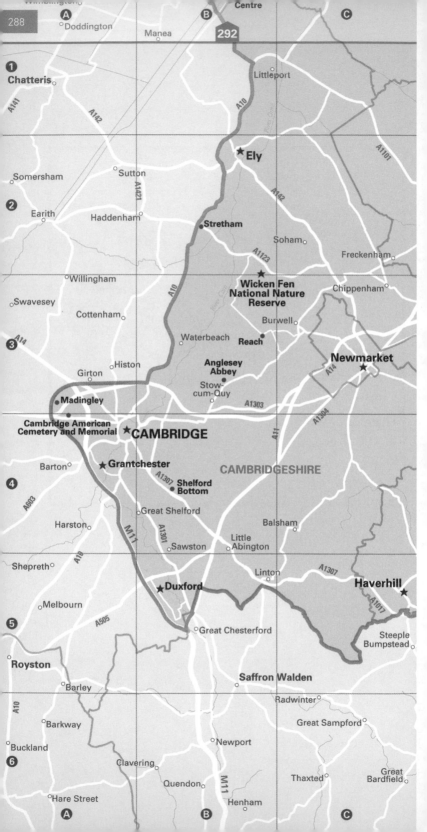

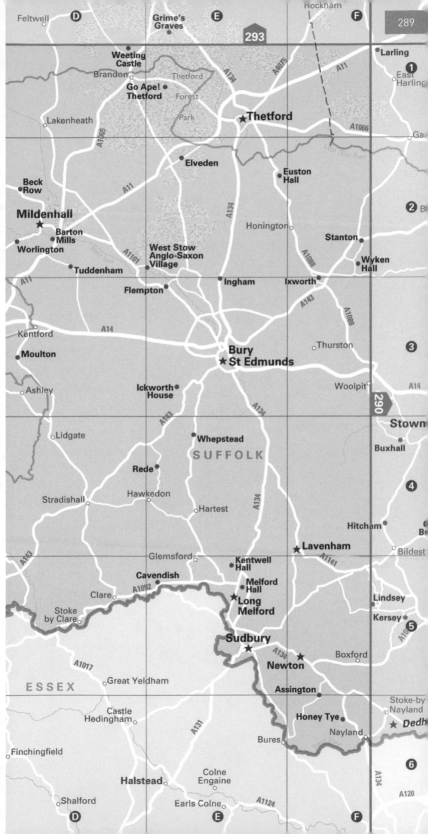

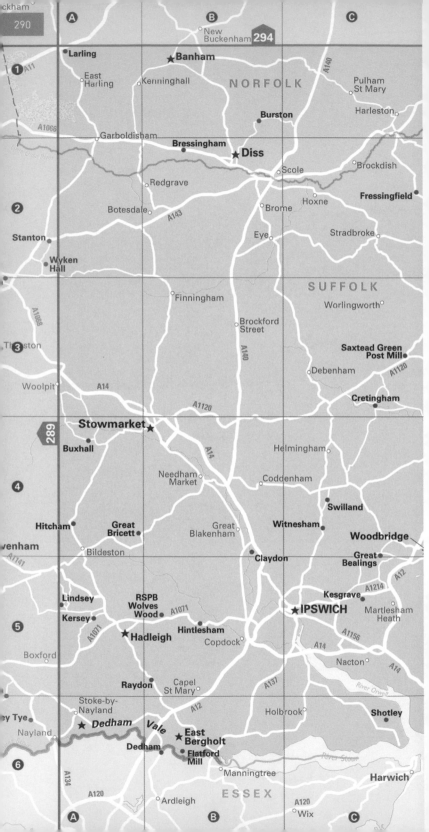

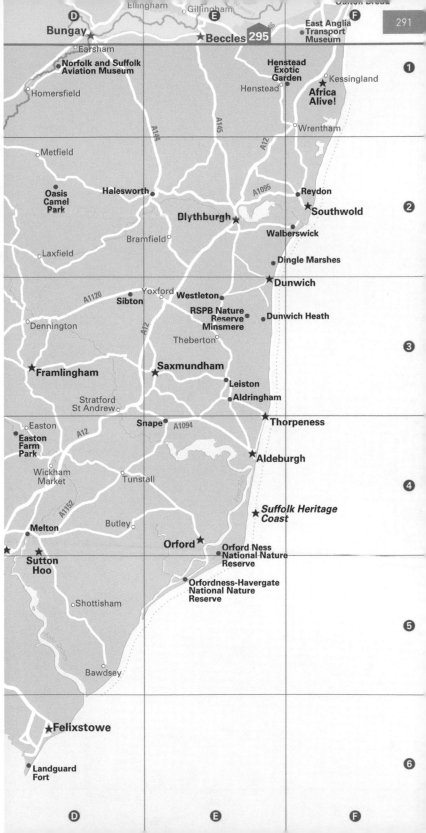

D
Bungay ★
○ Earsham

Norfolk and Suffolk
Aviation Museum ●

○ Homersfield

○ Metfield

Oasis
Camel
Park ●

Halesworth ●

○ Bramfield

○ Laxfield

Dennington ○

Framlingham ★

Stratford
St Andrew ○

○ Easton
Easton Farm
Park ●

Wickham ○
Market

Melton ●

★
Sutton
Hoo

○ Shottisham

○ Bawdsey

★**Felixstowe**

Landguard
Fort ●

D

○ Ellingham   ○ Gillingham   **E**

★**Beccles** **295**

Henstead
Exotic
Garden ●

Henstead ○

A1145

○ Wrentham

A1095

Blythburgh ★

○ Bramfield

A1120

Yoxford ○
Sibton ●

Westleton ●
RSPB Nature
Reserve ●
Minsmere

Theberton ○

Saxmundham ★

Leiston ●
Aldringham ●

Snape ● **A1094**

★**Aldeburgh**

Tunstall ○

Butley ○

Orford ★
●**Orford Ness**
National Nature
Reserve

● **Orfordness-Havergate**
National Nature
Reserve

E

F

East Anglia
Transport
Museum ●

1

★ Kessingland

Africa
Alive!

Reydon ●

★**Southwold**

2

Walberswick ●

Dingle Marshes ●

★**Dunwich**

Dunwich Heath ●

3

★**Thorpeness**

4

★ *Suffolk Heritage*
Coast

5

6

F

A O Leake
Wrangle
B
C

1
Butterwick O

T H E   W A S H

Hunstanton ★

Heacham ★

2

Gedney
Drove End O

LINCOLNSHIRE

A17
Holbeach O

Long
Sutton O

Sutton
Bridge O

Terrington
St Clement O

West
Lynn O

**King's
Lynn** ★

3

A149
**Castle
Rising** O

**Castle Rising
Castle** O

A1101

River Nene

A17
**Tilney
All Saints** O

Middleton O

A47

Wiggenhall
St Germans O

Setchey O

River Nar

4
Wisbech O

Middle Level Drain

R Great Ouse

A10

A134

Guyhirn O

A47

A1101
Outwell O

Downham
Market O

**Stow
Bardolph** O
Stradsett O

5

A605

A1122

Denver ★

A141

A1101

Old & New Bedford Rivers

A10

March O

Southery O

CAMBRIDGESHIRE

Welney O
**Welney
Wetland
Centre** O

Wimblington O

6
Doddington O

Manea O

288

A
Chatteris O

B
Littleport O

C

D **E** **F**

1

Blakeney Nat
Nature Rese

Scolt Head
Island

*Peddars Way &
Norfolk Coast Path*

Blak

RSPB
Nature Reserve
Titchwell Marsh

Brancaster
Staithe

Burnham
Overy-
Staithe

Holkham

Wells-next-
the-sea

Morston

Brancaster

Thornham

Titchwell

Burnham
Deepdale

Holkham
Hall

Stiffkey

Burnham
Market

Burnham
Thorpe

Warham
All Saints

Norfolk
Lavender

Creake
Abbey

*Wells &
Walsingham
Light Railway*

Le

Docking

North
Creake

2

Sedgeford

Walsingham

Thursford

Snettisham

Snettisham
Park

Bircham
Windmill

Syderstone

Dersingham

Great
Bircham

Fakenham

Pensthorpe
Natural Park

Sandringham

Houghton
Hall

East
Rudham

Fakenham
Racecourse

3

West
Newton

Peddars Way & Norfolk Coast Path

A148

Guist

Grimston

Great
Massingham

South
Raynham

North
Elmham

Gayton

Weasenham
All Saints

A1065

A1607

294

A47

Litcham

Gressenhall
Farm and
Workhouse

Beetley

West
Bilney

Castle Acre
Priory & Castle

Dereham

4

Narborough

NORFOLK

A47

Necton

Mid

Swaffham

A1122

Shipdham

Fincham

A1075

Hin

Vereham

Oxborough

Watton

5

Stoke
Ferry

A1065

Scoulton

Northwold

Methwold

Thompson

Attlebo

Mundford

Great
Hockham

Feltwell

6

Grime's
Graves

Weeting
Castle

289

Larling

Brandon

Thetford

A134

A40

A11

East
Harling

Go Apel

D **E** **F**

Trimingham

Mundesley

Bacton

Happisburgh

North Walsham

East Ruston Gardens

N O R F O L K

Sea Palling

Stalham

Sutton Mill

Horsey

Horsey Windpump

Coltishall

Wroxham Barns

Catfield

RAF Air Defence Radar Museum

Potter Heigham

Winterton-on-Sea

Hoveton

BeWILDerwood

Wroxham

Ludham

Hemsby

Rackheath

Rollesby

Ormesby St Margaret

Ranworth

Fairhaven Woodland and Water Garden

South Walsham

Filby

Thorpe End

Thorpe St Andrew

Thrigby Wildlife Gardens

★ Caister-on-Sea

Great Yarmouth Racecourse

Brundall

Acle

NORFOLK

★

BROADS

★ **GREAT YARMOUTH**

Burgh Castle

Yelverton

Pettitt's Animal Adventure Park

Reedham

Burgh Castle

Belton

Gorleston-on-Sea

Brooke

St Olave's Priory

Fritton

Hopton on Sea

Loddon

Somerleyton

Corton

Hales

Haddiscoe

Pleasurewood Hills

LOWESTOFT

Ellingham

Gillingham

East Anglia Transport Museum

Oulton Broad

Bungay

★**Beccles**

Earsham

Norfolk and Suffolk Aviation Museum

Henstead Exotic Garden

Kessingland

291

Index, themed

Page numbers in **bold** refer to main text entries

Index, places

Page numbers in **bold** refer to main entries; page numbers in *italics* refer to town plans

The Automobile Association wishes to thank the following photographers and organisations for their assistance in the preparation of this book.

Abbreviations for the picture credits are as follows – (t) top; (m) middle; (b) bottom; (l) left; (r) right; (c) centre; (AA) AA World Travel Library.

4b AA/T Mackie; 4tl AA/T Mackie; 4tr AA/T Mackie; 5r AA/C Coe; 5bl AA/T Mackie; 8–9 AA/T Mackie; 11 AA/L Noble; 12t Richard Bowden/Alamy; 12b AA/L Noble; 13t AA/T Mackie; 13m Kumar Sriskandan/Alamy; 13b Courtesy of BeWILDerwood; 14t Courtesy of Pleasurewood Hills; 14m PhotoDisc; 14b David Lyons/Alamy; 15t AA/L Noble; 15m Skyscan Photolibrary/Alamy; 15b AA/T Mackie; 16–7 Jon Gibbs/Alamy; 18 Chris Dorney/Alamy; 19 Clearview/Alamy; 20–1 AA/L Noble; 22 AA/A J Hopkins; 23tr PhotoDisc; 24 AA/S&O Mathews; 25 AA/T Mackie; 26 T.M.O.Landscapes/Alamy; 27 Heritage Image Partnership Ltd/Alamy; 30-1 International Photobank/Alamy; 32 AA/T Mackie; 33 Rod Edwards/Alamy; 34–5 AA/M Birkitt; 36 QEDimages/Alamy; 38 AA/T Mackie; 39 AA/T Mackie; 40 AA/J Tims; 42 AA/A Baker; 43 The National Trust Photolibrary/Alamy; 44 AA/C Coe, 45r AA/M Birkitt; 47 67 photo/Alamy; 48 AA/A Burton; 50–1 AA/T Mackie; 53 AA/T Mackie; 55 AA/T Mackie; 62–3 PhotoDisc; 64-5 AA/T Mackie; 67 AA/T Mackie; 70–1 AA/S&O Mathews; 76 Loop Images Ltd/Alamy; 77 Terence Waeland/Alamy Stock Photo; 81 AA/M Birkitt; 83 Courtesy of Caister Castle Car Collection; 84 AA/B Bachman; 88l AA/L Noble; 88–9 AA/L Noble; 89r AA/L Noble; 90 AA/M Moody; 92 AA/C Coe; 93 travelbild.com/Alamy; 95 Geoffrey Robinson/Alamy; 100 AA/M Birkitt; 101 AA/T Souter; 104–5 AA/T Mackie; 110 AA/S&O Mathews; 111 AA/T Mackie; 112–3 AA/T Mackie; 115 AA/S&O Mathews; 118–9 AA/T Mackie; 120-1 AA/T Mackie; 124b Steve Vidler/Alamy; 124t AA/M Birkitt; 126 AA/T Mackie; 127 David Lyons/Alamy; 132 AA/A Baker; 134 AA/D Forss; 140–1 Kathy Wright/Alamy; 142 AA/J Miller; 146–7 AA/A Baker; 153 AA/T Mackie; 154 Skyscan Photolibrary/Alamy; 156 Stuart Sneddon/Alamy; 158–9 AA/M Birkitt; 161 Courtesy of BeWILDerwood; 163 AA/T Mackie; 165 AA/L Whitman; 168–9 Peter Smith/Alamy; 171 AA/A Baker; 176 Howard Taylor/Alamy; 179 AA/A Baker; 181 AA/R J Edwards; 184 AA/T Mackie; 186 AA/T Mackie; 187 Robert Wyatt/Alamy; 191 Courtesy of Pleasurewood Hills; 192–3 Mark Dyball/Alamy; 196–7 AA/M Birkitt; 198bl LH Images/Alamy; 198–9 Courtesy of National Horse Racing Museum; 199r Courtesy of National Horse Racing Museum; 203 AA/T Souter; 204–5 AA/T Mackie; 205r Jon Gibbs/Alamy; 206 AA/C Coe; 207 AA/T Mackie; 208-9 AA/T Mackie; 211 AA/S&O Mathews; 213 AA/A Baker; 214 AA/R Ireland; 215 Chris Dorney/Alamy; 216 AA/T Mackie; 217 AA/L Whitman; 219 Colin Palmer Photography/Alamy; 221 AA/T Mackie; 228 AA/T Mackie; 230 Terry Mathews/Alamy; 234-5 AA/T Mackie; 237 AA/T Mackie; 240 AA/S&O Mathews; 245 AA/T Mackie; 246 eye35/Alamy; 249 AA/T Mackie; 250 AA/T Mackie; 253 AA/A Baker; 255 AA/M Birkitt; 256 AA/S&O Mathews; 258–9 AA/T Mackie; 260–1 AA/T Mackie; 261r AA/T Mackie; 262 The National Trust Photolibrary/Alamy; 263 David Lyons/Alamy; 264 Simon Pocklington/Alamy; 267 AA/A Baker; 270 AA/M Birkitt; 272 Loop Images Ltd/Alamy; 274-5; AA/T Mackie; 276 nobleIMAGES/Alamy; 278–9 AA/T Mackie; 280 The National Trust Photolibrary/Alamy; 283 AA/S&O Mathews; 284 AA/A Perkins; 286 Robert Estall photo agency/Alamy

Every effort has been made to trace the copyright holders, and we apologise in advance for any unintentional omissions or errors. We would be pleased to apply any corrections in any following edition of this publication.

Series editor: Rebecca Needes
Author: Carole French
Updater: Sue Dobson
Project editor: Cambridge Publishing Management

Designer: Tom Whitlock
Proofreader: Jackie Bates
Digital imaging & repro: Ian Little
Art director: James Tims

Additional writing by other AA contributors. *Lore of the Land* feature by Ruth Binney. Some content may appear in other AA books and publications.

Has something changed? Email us at travelguides@theaa.com.

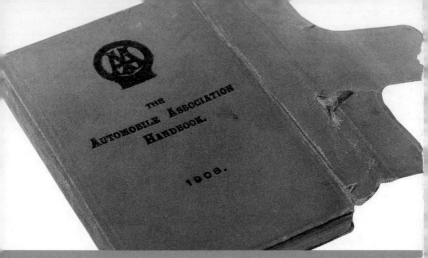

YOUR TRUSTED GUIDE

The AA was founded in 1905 as a body initially intended
to help motorists avoid police speed traps. As motoring
became more popular, so did we, and our activities have
continued to expand into a great variety of areas.

The first edition of the *AA Members' Handbook* appeared in
1908. Due to the difficulty many motorists were having finding
reasonable meals and accommodation while on the road, the
AA introduced a new scheme to include listings for 'about one
thousand of the leading hotels' in the second edition in 1909.
As a result the AA has been recommending and assessing
establishments for over a century, and each year our professional
inspectors anonymously visit and rate thousands of hotels,
restaurants, guest accommodations and campsites. We are relied
upon for our trustworthy and objective Star, Rosette and Pennant
ratings systems, which you will see used in this guide to denote
AA-inspected restaurants and campsites.

In 1912 we published our first handwritten routes and our atlas
of town plans, and in 1925 our classic touring guide, *The AA Road
Book of England and Wales,* appeared. Together, our accurate
mapping and in-depth knowledge of places to visit were to set
the benchmark for British travel publishing.

Since the 1990s we have dramatically expanded our publishing
activities, producing high quality atlases, maps, walking and travel
guides for the UK and the rest of the world. In this new series of
regional travel guides we are drawing on more than a hundred
years of experience to bring you the very best of Britain.